# The
# Conference
# Book

**Gulf Publishing Company**
**Book Division**
**Houston, Texas**

# The Conference Book

76576

## Dr. Leonard Nadler
## Zeace Nadler

**THE CONFERENCE BOOK**

Library of Congress
Catalog Card Number
76-52238
ISBN 0-87201-140-2


First Edition

*First Printing,* June 1977
*Second Printing,* March 1980

**Building Blocks of Human Potential Series**
Leonard Nadler, Series Editor

Other titles include
*The Adult Educator—A Handbook for Staff Development,* by Harry G. Miller and
John R. Verduin
*The Adult Learner: A Neglected Species/2nd edition,* by Malcolm Knowles
*Managing Cultural Differences,* by Philip R. Harris and Robert T. Moran
*Creative Worklife,* by Donald Scobel
*The Client-Consultant Handbook,* by Chip R. Bell and Leonard Nadler
*People, Evaluation, & Achievement,* by George Nixon
*Handbook of Creative Learning Exercises,* by Herbert M. Engel
*Leadership Development for Public Service,* by Barry A. Passett
*HRD: The European Approach,* by H. Eric Frank
*The Small Meeting Planner,* by Leslie E. This
*The NOW Employee,* by David Nadler

Dedicated with love
to earlier results of our
collaboration,
David, Mark, and Scott

# Preface

This book was written as a result of requests from clients, friends, students—people who have gone to a conference where we have been the Coordinators and were satisfied with the results. They often asked us, "How did you do it?" Particularly in the past ten years, we have been doing a significant amount of conference work not only in the United States but in other parts of the world. This involvement has included writing articles for magazines or for internal consumption in a Sponsor's organization, consulting with Sponsors and suppliers, and helping other Coordinators to improve the conferences they were working on.

We reached the point where it became difficult to respond to some of the requests for help and consultation without having some primary written source to which people could refer. This book is organized so that the various people concerned with conferences (i.e. Sponsors, Coordinators, participants, suppliers, etc.) would have some common reference points. It can enable them to recognize each other's responsibilities, though the focus of the book is on the role in which we have had most of our experience—the Coordinator. In helping others learn how to meet their conference responsibilities, we have been urged to share our experiences with them. This proved to be an effective tool, so we have continued the practice in this book. Interposed throughout the text are our experiences with various aspects of conferences. This is more than merely telling stories or satisfying our own egos. The incidents are chosen to give specific examples which relate to general points being made. All of the anecdotes are from real situations—situations in which we have been resource people, Coordinators (Chapter 2 will discuss these terms), or participants who had no influence over or responsibility for conference proceedings.

When "we" or "us" is used in this book, it is not editorial or imperial. It refers to two authors who have worked together for more than thirty years in the field of adult learning. This book is the joint product of the experiences and insights of both authors.

With regard to sex, always an important issue, we have tried to avoid being male oriented. Yet, we found that "he/she" was ponderous and not particularly helpful. We hope that no one is annoyed by the use of "he, fellow, him" and other words with a male connotation. In the absence of a suitable common word, the male pronoun is used unless there is a specific reason to differentiate.

This book does not have footnotes. This does not mean that we have ignored what others have done and written. Rather, it seems to us that the reader of this book is concerned not so much with research as with practice and experience. In the last chapter we share some other published sources which the reader may find helpful.

The variety of meetings, conferences, conventions, institutes, and hallmark events is so broad that no one book could ever cover all the possibilities. Constant advances in technology, shifts in the economy, and development of alternative energy resources are calling for new, more efficient forms of conferences. To keep this book from being outdated too rapidly, we have avoided some of the more experimental and esoteric practices. We do not intend to demean them in any way, but we do suggest that the "hot item" of this year can become rapidly obsolete. In this book we have examined those practices that are most likely to continue as basic to the functioning of any successful conference.

Suppliers may feel that we have not given adequate space to their involvement and concerns. We would agree. Our reasoning is that there are many organizations of suppliers (e.g. American Society of Travel Agents, American Hotel and Motel Association, Air Travel Association, International Association of Visitors and Convention Bureaus) and too few organizations of those that coordinate conferences. We are not concerned with redressing the imbalance but with providing a basis for communication among the various parties concerned with producing a successful conference.

How do we include acknowledgments? It is not possible to list all the individuals and organizations who have contributed to our understanding of how to produce successful conferences. Various people in the field of conference work have read different sections of the manuscript and have been extremely helpful with their feedback. We want to express our appreciation to all those unnamed but very helpful people who took the time to react to the contents of this book.

Leonard Nadler
Zeace Nadler
College Park, Maryland
May, 1977

# Contents

# The
# Conference
# Book

# 1.
# What is a
# Conference?

The immediate problem of writing about conferences is the woeful lack of agreement on just what the term describes. To help the reader understand what this book contains, this first chapter will be concerned with

- Physical Aspects
- Purposes of Conferences
- Related Terms

## Physical Aspects

Responses from colleagues indicate the impossibility of defining "conference" to everyone's satisfaction. However, if this book is to communicate, we and the reader must have some similar images. Therefore, we will establish a reference point by describing conferences in the following terms.

### Size

There is no fixed rule on size. Generally, the lower limit would be about ten persons. It is possible to have a conference for fewer than that number, but it is highly unlikely. There is no upper limit; a conference can have thousands of participants. Most conferences, including those described in this book, involve from 25 to 2,000 people.

The size of the conference group has many implications, and where needed, we will examine how it affects various aspects of a conference. No attempt can be made to describe the best size, although we have been asked for this kind of recommendation very often. There are many variables to be explored, and we will do just that in the chapters which follow.

## Face-to-Face Happenings

When the term "conference" is used, the assumption is that all the participants are meeting at one site. This includes groups of participants in several places using a technological umbilical cord, such as closed-circuit TV or telephone hook-up. This is still face to face, although there is a technological intervention.

The conferences we are concerned with involve people in meetings and activities that require interaction and interpersonal relations. Various kinds of communication involve an individual with a mediating device (computer), or self-learning situations (reading). These are excellent activities, but they are not conferences.

Futurists paint wonderful pictures of the massive changes which are just over the horizon. It is quite likely that the forms of some of our conferences will change in the decades to come, as technology advances. For the foreseeable future, most of the world will rely on conferences as described in this book, with emphasis on groups meeting at a single place, and sharing the common experience. This is a conference.

## Duration

As with size, lower and upper limits of duration can be established for conferences. The lower limit is generally half a day. That is, a solid block of at least three hours. Less than that, it could be a meeting of some kind, but not necessarily a conference. The upper limit is almost endless, but no one is expected to spend his entire life in a conference. The conferences with which we are usually concerned are no longer than two weeks in duration. Most conferences are only one week long, although travel and related activities might extend this period.

## Purposes of Conferences

There is no end to the list of purposes for conferences because there will always be somebody who will add, "But I also use a conference for _____."

The following are the most frequent reasons for holding conferences. These should not be confused with objectives, which are much more specific.

## The Annual Affair

It is almost humorous at times to see a conference billed as the "First Annual Conference." How do the Sponsors know that there will ever be a second annual conference if this is only the first one? Possibly, it is mere optimism, or just good advertising. People often prefer to be part of something with a longer life. Note the companies that boast of being in existence since the last century. In some parts of the world older things are scoffed at. Yet, as countries and people grow older, they tend to move toward veneration of age and perpetuity.

There are sound reasons, other than the psychological, for holding annual conferences. It enables people to plan their schedules, vacations, and other activities. Usually, the annual conference is held as close to the same time each year as possible. The dates may change, but the time of year is held fairly constant.

For some membership organizations in the U.S. the laws of the state in which they are incorporated require an annual meeting of the membership, and this is arranged so that it will coincide with the annual conference. These two are by no means identical meetings. Conference participants may not necessarily hold membership in the sponsoring organization. Conversely, there are probably members who will not attend the conference.

When the Sponsor is a membership organization that has been in existence for any period of time, an expectation has probably developed among the members. They look forward to the annual meeting for the opportunity to see old friends and renew acquaintances. Frequently, they prefer that this annual conference be subject to as little change as possible. They come back each year to repeat a number of accepted rituals, and they eagerly look forward to the repetitive aspects.

—— • ——

Representatives from each state in the country came to Washington for their annual conference. The records of earlier meetings were reviewed carefully, and a design committee was formed. (The design committee will be discussed in more detail in Chapter 3.) The consensus of the design committee was that the regular members were dissatisfied with the annual ritual of the meeting in Washington, D.C. They preferred to meet in that city, but wanted more than the usual speeches and handouts. So, a new design was developed by the Coordinator, approved by the design committee, and the conference was conducted accordingly. The evaluations were devastating. Overwhelmingly, the participants responded negatively to the new design and apparently longed for what they had done in the past. The design committee had been trapped by its own enthusiasm, which was not shared by the membership. The participants at the conference wanted change, or so they had said, but were not prepared for what was actually offered.

—— • ——

In retrospect the Coordinator should have brought the changes about much more slowly. The plan should have been to make changes over a period of years, during the course of several conferences, rather than make drastic changes in one year. The new design had conflicted with the participants' expectations. Despite the information gathered from the preconference questionnaires, the participants were not amenable to rapid change.

Annual conferences of membership/professional organizations serve another function. Hardly one of these is conducted without provision for some kind of job exchange. Job seekers and prospective employers gear their seeking and hiring practices to the annual conference.

The annual conference can be a trap for repeating previous behavior *ad nauseum*, but if it meets the expectations of the members and participants, then perhaps it is fulfilling its function in organizational life.

## Learning

Conferences designed to produce learning will have more specific objectives than almost any other type of conference. Although it is true that almost any conference provides some learning experiences, that may not be the essential purpose.

Learning conferences go by a variety of names, and towards the end of this chapter we will explore some of them. Any experienced conferee knows that the name, title, and even description of the activity may not fully communicate what the participant will experience. When learning is the purpose, the experience may be called a workshop rather than a conference. In a more formal sense, others will be labeled as "a course using conference methods." Once again, we are trapped by the lack of agreement in using these terms.

When learning is the main purpose for a conference, much attention will be paid to evaluation as well as to objectives. Specific behavioral changes will be indicated and possibly measured.

## Sharing Information and Experiences

In this very busy world it is virtually impossible for any individual to keep up-to-date without a commitment of time and energy. One can hope to keep abreast of activities in the field by reading appropriate professional journals and trade magazines. Yet, some of the busy people with ideas and unique experiences do not contribute to these written media. They are either too busy "doing," or perhaps writing is not their "thing." So, they utilize the conference of their associates to share their experiences and receive information from others.

Most professional organizations use their annual conferences for this specific purpose. Sessions and activities are purposely arranged so that people can share. Speakers are chosen because they have something to share in the way of information, ideas, and experiences.

**Generating New Ideas and Proposals**

It may seem self-defeating to gather a large number of people together to generate ideas. However, there are many people who function more effectively when they are stimulated by others. There are ideas and proposals that are best generated by a group, either homogeneous or heterogenous.

A conference is used when an organization has a new product and is seeking ways to gain market acceptance. The participants will include sales people as well as potential customers. Out of such a conference can come exciting proposals and ideas for the marketing and use of the new product. Our concern with the future has given rise to conferences in this area.

—— • ——

An organization offered a conference with the title "Probable Futures—Possible Responses." The purpose was to have the participants understand some of what we know about what the future could look like. From this, they were encouraged to generate proposals and possible responses for what they could do in the present to prepare for the future.

—— • ——

Conferences using brainstorming, synectics, and other creative thinking experiences are specifically geared to provide participants with new ways of looking at old concerns.

**Coordination**

Coordination among different units or groups is frequently thought of as a management function, and so it is. However, when different groups need to coordinate their activities, a meeting can be helpful. One such activity has been labelled the "management retreat." The participants come together in a conference situation, away from their regular work site. The purpose is for them to share their goals and plans, and to explore how they can coordinate.

A multi-site organization found that face-to-face meetings of people who are usually separated are necessary to facilitate coordination. These may be held as frequently as once a month, or as infrequently as once a year.

When several different organizations appear to be having difficulty coordinating their efforts, a conference can be utilized.

—— • ——

In 1972, there were more than twenty different organizations in the Philippines concerned with aspects of family planning and adult literacy. One of these, the Family Planning Organization of the Philippines, took the initiative, and arranged to have a conference of representatives from all these organizations to ascertain how they could coordinate their efforts.

This conference was very successful in bringing about coordination, and making more effective use of the various resources of all the organizations, with each one retaining its own identity.

——— ● ———

## Decision Making

A large conference may not be the best place to make decisions, but sometimes it's appropriate. The most obvious occasions are the political conventions/conferences held every four years to nominate persons for President and Vice-President of the United States. Since the Democratic Convention of 1968, there have been some questions as to the effectiveness of this approach to nominate individuals for such crucial positions. However, in the absence of any alternatives it would appear that we can anticipate these decision-making conferences every four years.

A related conference is one where recommendations are offered. Although decisions may be made at another time and place (perhaps even at another conference) a recommending conference is quite similar to a decision-making one. To arrive at recommendations, a vote or at least consensus must be possible. Many of the UN agencies use conferences for making recommendations to be passed on to higher levels of the UN organization.

Decision-making conferences can be conducted by any of the various Sponsors discussed in Chapter 2.

## Inspirational

A questionable use of the conference method is to inspire participants. The reason for the doubt rests not in the inspiration aspect, but the method. Frequently, the inspirational activity is concerned with areas of emotion which are best developed and utilized by a particular kind of Sponsor and Coordinator.

The inspirational conference would be similar to the activities of the Nazis in pre-WWII Germany. They utilized meetings of various sizes, but they were all one-way communication to inspire and arouse. The material in this book is not addressed to such meetings.

Conferences to inspire can be economic as well as religious or political. A Sponsor may organize a conference to inspire salespersons to sell more. A membership organization might have a conference to arouse its members to become more active in the organization. Various religious denominations utilize conferences (in addition to religious services) to inspire their membership.

## Combinations of the Above

It would be much simpler if a conference could be confined to a single purpose. Actually, this is highly unlikely. A small conference (in terms of numbers of participants) is more likely to be called for a single purpose. As the size of the group increases, many more agendas are involved, and the need to meet that variety results in the multi-purpose conference.

Conferences can be called for more than one reason. Within any large conference, lasting for several days, one is able to find many of the purposes discussed above. There is certainly nothing wrong with this, as long as the Sponsors and the participants are able to identify the various purposes. Without such distinctions being made, Sponsors and participants alike are in a quandry as to appropriate behavior, the utilization of resources, and the expected outcomes.

The more purposes for having a conference, the more difficult it is to design. A multi-purpose conference may appeal to more participants and therefore may be more appealing to a Sponsor than a series of small, single-purpose conferences.

## Related Terms

Now we have to confront semantics. Some readers will undoubtedly say that what we have been discussing is a

workshop
seminar
symposium
convention
small group meeting
large group meeting

Each writer uses the term or terms he is most familiar and comfortable with. There is nothing wrong with this, but it does present some limitations. Throughout this book we will use the term "conference" consistently. It refers to the kinds of group experiences we have described in this chapter.

# 2.
# Conference
# Personnel

In Chapter 1 the elements of a conference were established. This chapter will identify, define, and discuss the labels used for conference personnel. There is much more agreement on these terms than on those discussed in the previous chapter. Problems still exist because conference personnel come from so many different backgrounds and geographical locations that the same terms may not be in general use.

The strict grammarian may have some difficulty with one form of capitalizing that we have found useful. Sponsor and Coordinator will be spelled with a capital first letter because feedback from readers on some of our earlier writings on this subject indicated that this clarified the content. All other personnel will be included in lower case.

The personnel to be discussed are

- Sponsor
- Coordinator
- Participant
- Resource people
- Secretariat
- Exhibitors
- Suppliers

## Sponsor

The Sponsor is the person or organization offering the conference. Usually, the Sponsor will be an organization, and the word will be used to refer to that organization. The Sponsor designates one or more individuals to be responsible for the conference.

There are three main kinds of Sponsors, and sometimes the needs of one are not the needs of others. Specific attention will be given to each kind, as well as to matters generally related to all Sponsors.

## Employer Sponsors

The Employer Sponsor (ES) usually offers conferences for its employees in the form of "training" conferences. However, the ES also offers conferences for nonemployees. These include independent salespersons, distributors, commission merchants, and jobbers. In general, they are those who handle the merchandise of the "employer" but not as employees. They are independent of the employer, but have a financial relationship.

In a similar vein are franchisees such as fast food or ice cream shops. The owner is not an employee of the franchisor, but the financial relationship qualifies their conferences to be included in the ES category.

## Public Seminar Sponsors

Public Seminar Sponsors (PS) offer conferences on a wide variety of topics to people who are not financially associated with them. Usually, this is the general public, but in some cases participation may be limited to certain prescribed groups and individuals.

There are two general types of PS: profit and nonprofit. The *profit* PS is an individual or company that offers a conference on a specific topic to all who are willing to pay to attend. Many of these conferences are directly related to improving the participant's economic status, or to improving his job effectiveness. There are also conferences designed to help participants who wish to improve their understanding of themselves, to improve their reading skills, or for general self-improvement (often called liberal learning).

The *nonprofit* PS is usually an organization, very seldom an individual. The profit/nonprofit distinction made here is not similar to that made by tax authorities. Rather, the distinction is between those (profit) that are in business to make money and those (nonprofit) that use the profits for other purposes, not principally as a source of income for the Sponsor. Actually, it is an interesting group which includes government, voluntary and welfare associations, membership associations, and private business, and all conduct nonprofit PS conferences.

Government agencies conduct many conferences for participants who are not government employees. Examples are the Internal Revenue Service conferences for accountants, Department of Defense conferences for potential contractors, and Office of Education conferences for local school personnel. The list could fill many pages. Almost each piece of legislation, which directly affects the general public, has some component that lends itself to the PS conference. In most cases, the participants do not pay any fees, and sometimes they even receive reimbursement for expenses.

Voluntary and welfare agencies and associations conduct many conferences for those who can use their services. Some conferences are open to the general public while others are limited to an invited list of participants.

The purpose of the conference would be to inform people of the programs of the agencies and associations.

Membership associations also offer a PS type of conference. For example, an accounting association may offer a conference on changes in tax law to its members or an engineering society may offer a conference on new research in nondestructive testing for its members. Both of these examples might be a profit PS, depending upon the decision of the membership association. Some associations have discovered that the PS can be a good source of income, and therefore they conduct these conferences for profit. Generally, they are designed as nonprofit conferences.

The private sector has been discussed under ES, but a profit-making organization can also conduct a nonprofit conference as a PS. An obvious example is a consumer product company which offers a conference for the public who might become users of its products. The private company wants to make a profit, but not from the conference. Attendance may be open to any who wish to attend.

## Membership Sponsors

It is almost impossible to name a Membership Sponsor (MS) that does not conduct at least one conference per year. Most MS offer many conferences per year. These are not under the previously discussed PS category, where anybody who pays the fee can attend.

For some conferences, the MS may limit participation to members only. For others, the MS may allow any who wish to take part to do so, but there will usually be a higher fee for nonmembers. The focus is different from the membership organization functioning as a PS. In the PS, membership in the organization is a minimal factor. The organization may sponsor, but do little else.

The focus of an MS is on the membership aspect with full attention to the officers, bylaws, and all the other organizational trappings. Organizational business is a legitimate and necessary part of the MS conference.

There are various kinds of membership organizations. The most general and obvious are the national fraternal or social organizations, such as Lions, Elks, and Masons.

As our work life becomes more specialized, we become members of organizations related to our occupational identification. Some organizations are professional, while others are occupational. Some have strict requirements, including certification and license, while others merely require the payment of dues.

Almost all of the religious organizations in the U.S. hold conferences for their members. On the local level, there are civic organizations that offer conferences for their members. We have been called a nation of joiners, and the list of associations and organizations justifies this label.

There are also trade associations. These organizations appeal to those who are in the same kinds of business, and they also offer conferences as part of their membership activities.

## Coordinator

In any conference there must be a single person with specified responsibilities for putting it all together. This is the Coordinator. Other names might be meeting planner, conference director, training director, convention convener, conference leader, etc. The term Coordinator is the generic name for all of these, and the many others which are sometimes used.

The duties of the Coordinator are the essence of this book, so we will not summarize them here. Much more on the Coordinator will appear early in the next chapter.

The Coordinator can be either *internal* or *external*. The distinction is the Coordinator's relationship to the Sponsor and the organization.

### Internal

An internal Coordinator will come from the sponsoring organization. This can be a person whose major function is to work with conferences, or who is given the job of Coordinator for a single conference.

There are no definite criteria for selecting a Coordinator. A Sponsor may choose an employee as Coordinator who is competent in the subject matter area of the conference. This employee may then read books like this one, attend meetings of associations whose members serve as Coordinators, or rely upon his own experience as a participant at previous conferences.

Organizations that conduct many conferences will have an internal Coordinator, and perhaps even a whole unit from which the internal Coordinator can be selected.

### External

An external Coordinator comes from outside the sponsoring organization. This person is frequently called a *consultant*, but this is not the correct term, despite its common usage.

A Sponsor who seeks an external Coordinator can find one in any of the several professional organizations and societies, such as the American Society for Training and Development, Adult Education Association, and Society of Meeting Planners.

This list is far from complete, and it should not be considered as an endorsement of those which appear nor a rejection of those omitted. There are also excellent Coordinators who do not belong to any association.

## Participants

The term "participant" refers to those persons who attend a conference. Without some form of registration, it is doubtful if the activity qualifies as a conference. Therefore, we can go further and state that a participant is a person who registers for a conference. Note, we cannot guarantee that every participant will actually take part in conference activities. Individuals register for a variety of reasons. When we use the term participant, we are assuming registration and participation in at least some of the conference activities.

It is possible for a participant to play other roles, such as resource person or supplier. This is a problem for the participant and the Coordinator. The participant may have to respond on two levels, but the Coordinator can assist in clarifying which role the person is filling at a particular time. A participant will never be the Coordinator—or put it another way, the Coordinator should not be considered a participant.

There is a special kind of participant, the *spouse*. A spouse may be either the husband or wife of the participant, or merely a companion of the participant.

A conference may have *observers* whose status, because of its variablity, should be clearly specified. A conference that relies heavily on process (*how* things are happening as opposed to *what* is being communicated, which is content) may have some people who are there, but are not expected to be active as participants. Most Coordinators discourage observers at this kind of conference, but may modify their stance when the Sponsor can give legitimate reasons for such observers.

International and formal conferences tend to have people with observer status. They cannot be considered as participants, as this category is reserved for those who are officially selected by their organizations or governments. The observers are in a lesser status and come to the conference with this understanding.

For an ES conference, observers may be from some other part of the organization and may be attending just to get a feel for what is going on, but they do not want the responsibility of being a participant.

Sometimes observers will be present because they are shopping around for a Coordinator. One way to make a good selection is to attend a conference where the person being considered is the Coordinator. The observers do not want a participant role, but they do want to move in and out of things, observing the Coordinator in action.

There is another kind of observer, one who is more prevalent outside the U.S. However, with foreign companies operating in the U.S. more and more, the following could easily happen here.

—— ● ——

The conference was held in. Europe and involved top-level government officials. It was to help the participants coordinate their relationships and activities in regard to a new program, which involved them all. The group consisted of twenty-five people and the Coordinator was from the U.S. After the design had been completed, the Coordinator and several members of the design committee visited the site, to double check the facility. They found that they had been placed in a large room with four huge tables forming a very large rectangle on the floor below a dais. First, the Coordinator and the design committee discussed the effect of the chairs on the platform and how it would isolate the chairperson from the rest of the participants. As the chairperson was one of the participants, such an arrangement might communicate an attempt at control rather than coordination. The design committee readily accepted this, and removed the chairs from the dais and brought them down to the level of the tables.

Then, the Coordinator suggested that the rectangle be rearranged to form a diamond shape, so that the participants could more readily see each other. This would facilitate communication by providing eye contact. The design committee agreed, and everybody cooperated in moving the heavy tables and chairs.

The room now appeared to be set up in relation to the purpose and design of the conference. Then, one of the design committee members asked, "What about the observers?" This was the first time the Coordinator had heard about observers for this particular conference. He asked who the observers might be. The response was, "In our country, when you have persons of this high level at a conference, you have to expect two things. First, they will not stay for all the sessions, a gesture that their offices can run without them. And second, each person at this level will bring along two or three others of lesser rank who will take notes for them, read papers they have prepared, and sit at the table in their place, when they are not present." The Coordinator tried to explain what this would do to the carefully developed design, but was met with, "But we have always done it this way." After much discussion, with the Coordinator relying on the skills of diplomacy and small group behavior, agreement was reached on several points. Seats would be provided for the observers in the back of the room. It then turned out that the official government and press and radio must also be accommodated, though publicity could be counterproductive to the purposes of the conference. But it could not be expected that officials of this rank could meet without such coverage. Another agreement reached was that subordinates would not take the seats of their superiors when they were not in attendance, but would remain in the observer seat.

——— ● ———

One result of the compromises was that participants attended more sessions! Evaluation after the conference indicated that few of the participants wanted to signify their lack of interest by leaving their seats vacant, so they showed up for almost every session. At the suggestion of the steering committee (see Chapter 11), the design was changed so that the participants could spend part of each day in their offices. This resulted is almost 100% conference attendance!

## Resource People

Resource people are individuals who present a session related to the conference objectives. They are not exhibitors or suppliers. The selection of resource people is discussed in Chapter 4.

A small conference may not use any resource people. They are not required unless there is a specific reason. For some small conferences, the Coordinator may also be the resource person, or one of the small group of resource people. This is possible, but it is important that the Coordinator, Sponsor, and the participants are aware of which role the individual is filling at a particular time.

Resource people can be internal or external, similar to a Coordinator. This is a decision of the design committee, which is discussed in Chapter 3.

## Secretariat

This term is probably not too familiar to many readers. It is borrowed from international conferences, and is helpful in describing the individual or group which provides the logistic support for the conference. Reference will be made to the secretariat throughout the book.

Other terms applied to this function are administrative group, conference office, and support group. The term secretariat says this and much more. As the reader will clearly see, there are many functions to be performed and the broader term secretariat is very appropriate.

## Exhibitors

Exhibitors are those individuals and organizations that purchase space at a conference to exhibit their products and/or services. They may all be gathered in one place, an exhibit area, or they may take separate rooms in the same hotel/motel where the conference is being conducted.

Not every conference has exhibitors, but they are becoming more and more prevalent, particularly in large MS conferences and in some PS conferences. Chapter 7 contains a detailed discussion of exhibits and exhibitors.

## Suppliers

Suppliers are essential to a successful conference. There are many kinds of suppliers and they will be referred to at the proper times. However, the three major kinds of suppliers—site personnel, travel personnel, and entertainment personnel—will receive the most attention.

The *site* refers to the physical facility where the conference is being conducted. In some situations, the site will include the bedrooms (sometimes called guest rooms) as well as the meeting rooms. Large conferences in major cities may identify (most conference centers do not provide bedrooms) housing for the participants in regular hotels and motels. The sessions may be conducted in another facility often called a *convention center* or a *conference center*. The latter term causes some confusion, as there are other facilities, usually outside major cities, which are also called conference centers. Those provide both bedrooms and meeting rooms at the same site. Throughout the book, we will identify which kind of site is being discussed. Where just site is used, it will refer to a facility which provides both the sleeping and meeting facility.

Most conferences require *travel*. This can range from international travel, to taking a taxi, or just driving to a different part of town. Most of the conferences covered in this book require at least some kind of domestic travel. Therefore, travel is important. Reference will also be made to ground transportation from the airport or train to the site, as well as provision for transportation related to field trips and recreation.

More and more conferences include various forms of *recreation* and *entertainment*. Some Coordinators prefer to leave this to the option of the participants. In larger conferences recreation and entertainment are built into the design and are a significant part of the conference. Much more will be said about this in Chapter 5.

Beginning with Chapter 3, the concluding part of most chapters will be entitled "From the Suppliers' Viewpoint." This book is written essentially for the Coordinator and the Sponsor. Yet, obviously, without the suppliers, most conferences would not function. This book can help the suppliers learn more about what Coordinators do and what Sponsors expect. It could also improve conferences if Coordinators and Sponsors try to see some of the conference aspects from the viewpoint of the suppliers.

# 3.
# The Design
# Committee
# and the
# Coordinator

In recent years there have been many jokes about committee activities. Readers probably heard the definition that a camel is a horse put together by a committee! Or, that the best committee is composed of three persons—one of whom is out of town and another who is sick. These jibes do not deprecate the value of committees, but indicate that time spent in committees could be used more effectively.

In this chapter we will be exploring the relationship and work of the Coordinator and the design committee (DC), but not the design itself. That will be the subject of Chapters 4 and 5.

Although we will be focusing on the Coordinator and the DC, there are other people and fuctions to be discussed including:

- The Coordinator
- Responsibilities of the design committee
- Membership of the design committee
- Conference objectives
- Site selection
- Coordinating resources
- Identifying the participant
- Duration of the conference
- Setting dates for the conference
- Reviewing actions of the design committee
- Reports of the design committee.

## The Coordinator

Whenever possible, the Sponsor should select one person to be conference Coordinator. This Coordinator may be either internal or external to the sponsoring organization, but the person is usually external. This is because the work of the Coordinator is highly specialized and requires certain skills that are not usually found within an organization. An ES which does not sponsor many conferences would find it costly to employ an individual internally for such a purpose. Where the ES does have many significant conferences, as in some sales organizations, it is likely that the Coordinator is internally employed. When the sponsor uses an internal person who lacks the requisite skills, the organization may at first appear to be saving money. In the end it will prove much more costly. Inevitably, the sponsoring organization pays for this in some way, such as poor design, an unsuccessful conference, or excessive costs.

Generally, the Coordinator should have prior experience in this function, as well as have skills in working with others in small group situations (particularly useful for working with the design committee) and some understanding of the dynamics of a conference. Throughout this book there will be many references to the actions of the Coordinator that will provide additional clues to the kind of person the Sponsor should seek in identifying the appropriate Coordinator for the particular conference being planned. A caution at this point—there are organizations and individuals who advertise that they will handle all the elements of a conference for a Sponsor. Most of these organizations are primarily concerned with the logistics of conference operations. Such organizations do have an important role in various types of conferences, which are discussed later. However, the Coordinator we are concerned with is different from one who handles the logistics, and the reader is cautioned to be sensitive to this difference as the role of the Coordinator unrolls in the following pages.

The Sponsor is supposed to either provide the necessary budget or in some way indicate how the economic resources are to be obtained. If it is a conference open to the public, the Sponsor may recover the costs by charging a fee. The Sponsor may also be seeking to make a profit from the experience, which is a legitimate objective of some conferences. For an ES conference it is expected that somebody within the organization will provide the necessary budget to cover travel, meals, and other related costs, such as those for outside resource people. The Coordinator will probably report to the Sponsor, but in some situations, the Sponsor may delegate this responsibility to the design committee, so that the Coordinator works both with and for the design committee. The Sponsor will want feedback and evaluation from the conference, as well as recommendations for future action from the Coordinator.

### Responsibilities of the Design Committee

The functions of any committee can be diverse, and unless there are some clearly identified parameters, the committee is doomed to conflict. When the design committee is activated, there should be a clear understanding of the areas in which it is to function. This becomes even more necessary if conflict with the Coordinator and the Sponsor is to be avoided. From among the various possibilities let us examine three areas in which a DC can function:

- Recommend
- React
- Decide

The area of confusion, which must be reconciled as early as possible in the life of the DC, is which factors fall under which heading. Very seldom does a DC act completely in one of these three modes. Realistically, for each situation they must know whether they will recommend, react, or decide. It is not always easy to make this distinction in the early life of the DC, but every effort should be made to draw the lines as soon as possible. The worksheet in Figure 3-1 can be helpful for this purpose.

### Recommend

In many of the DC areas of concern there are alternative courses of action. The DC can explore possibilities, each of which has advantages and limitations for the particular conference being planned. The DC could visit various sites, have discussions with site personnel, and then recommend the particular site which they think most closely meets the needs of the conference.

When recommending, the DC should be generating alternatives—and avoid getting locked into any of them. They should recognize that their recommendation does not bind the Sponsor or the Coordinator. One of the most difficult tasks is to have the DC recognize this limitation. When the area of responsibility is to recommend, the decision rests somewhere else.

### React

In this mode the DC is being asked to react to work done by others. This can be design proposals by participants or resource people. At some point decisions will have to be made, but at this time the DC may only be asked to react.

During this stage all members of the DC need to be most considerate of the opinions and reactions of their fellow DC members. If the DC is to fully benefit from each of its members, the climate should be established that, when reacting, members do not have to engage in a full-fledged defense of their opinions. The reaction of each member is to be encouraged and valued.

| | Recommend | React | Decide |
|---|---|---|---|
| Develop conference objectives | | | |
| Site selection | | | |
| Coordinating resources | | | |
| Identify the participants | | | |
| Duration | | | |
| Dates | | | |

**Figure 3-1.** This worksheet clearly indicates the responsibilities of the design committee.

## Decide

Decision making is one of the major responsibilities of the DC. There should be as clear an understanding as possible, as early as possible, of those items about which the DC can and must make decisions. Equally as important is identifying the kinds of decisions which will be made by others.

For example, if the dates of the conference have been previously decided upon by the Sponsor, this decision should be made clear to the DC. It is useless to ask them to recommend dates, in view of the decision. They might be asked to react to the dates, but only if there is a possibility of change. With set dates, the DC can only mark their worksheet (Figure 3-1) with an "X" for all three areas next to "Dates," for there is absolutely nothing they can do about them.

## Membership of the Design Committee

Should the Sponsor first select the DC and then have them assist in selecting the Coordinator, or should the Sponsor select a Coordinator and then have that person assist in selecting the DC? This is difficult to answer, for the question may not come in quite that form. The DC may be selected in the closing phases of a first conference to function in that capacity for a second conference. The Coordinator may not be chosen until later. Whatever the order, the Sponsor must eventually approve the DC membership.

Frequently, the Sponsor selects the Coordinator, and the DC does not begin to come into existence until the Coordinator has convinced the Sponsor that one is desirable. When the Coordinator makes such a suggestion, the Sponsor might respond, "What do you need others for? You are getting a nice fee to design and conduct this conference for us. If you are going to need other people from this organization to help you design, perhaps we don't need you."

The Coordinator can react to this challenge by doing the whole job himself, or by convincing the Sponsor that a DC, which includes prospective participants, can assure a higher level of success for the conference.

Once there is agreement on having a DC, the selection should be a careful process. It should not be the "fishing" approach. That is, there are a lot of people swimming around out there and we'll just throw out a net and see what falls into it.

For an MS conference the effort should be made to identify those individuals who represent some of the various subgroups within the organization, and the potential participants. This may be based upon geographical location, length of time with the organization, ethnic group, sex, etc. When the conference concerns a work theme, even though sponsored by an MS, the DC should include some persons who are actually doing that kind of work. This is not to suggest a quota system, as such an approach has not met with much success. It is, however, important to try to represent as many of the diverse groups within the organization as possible.

For an ES conference the members of the DC should likewise represent some of the different subgroups within the organization. This may be based upon level, from executive down to the lowest echelons of the organization, or it may include different kinds of work, such as production, sales, and clerical. The possible configurations are numerous, and suffice it to say that the DC should represent those groups that are expected to participate, as well as those that might be affected in any way by the outcomes of the conference.

A profit PS will usually rely on its own internal resources for both the Coordinator and the DC. A nonprofit PS is more likely to use an internal Coordinator but an external DC.

An early decision, which must be made by the Sponsor, relates to the size of the DC. The DC should not be so large as to be unmanageable. The desirable size will vary between 5 and 15 persons. Fewer than 5 persons may not provide adequate opportunity for a variety of opinions and groups to be represented, and more than 15 creates almost insurmountable logistical and administrative tasks. In a larger group there is a tendency for some good people to be lost, and their ideas never surface. Also, in a larger group the attendance is likely to vary, which complicates the work of the committee.

It is the responsibility of the Sponsor to identify the theme or the general purpose of the conference. This is not to be confused with the objectives, which will be developed by the DC. At this point, there is the need for only a general theme. For an MS conference this might be an annual theme that the organization's executive board (who are the Sponsors) have decided on. For an ES conference the theme will come from the situation which created the need for the conference. It may be the annual sales conference, and therefore there are certain kinds of products that need to be emphasized. Or, there may be a special conference being called because of a particular situation within the organization which has created the need. The theme should be stated clearly enough so that the members of the DC and the Coordinator can identify how they relate to it.

After there is an identified theme, it is possible to approach the proposed members of the DC through a simple questionnaire, such as the one in Figure 3-2. It may appear that this procedure is not necessary, and all that needs to be done is that the ES direct people to be on the DC. However, when the individual directed to such an assignment has little or no choice in the decision, his behavior may be less than contributory to the work of the DC. Such a person may go through the motions, as he does not want to jeopardize his job. But the DC needs more than passive participation. Within an employing organization, there should be some latitude for an individual to signify a negative response to any of the three questions posed in Figure 3-2 without fear of reprisal either covert or overt.

For people being asked to join an MS design committee, question 2 of Figure 3-2 may be the crucial one. Meetings of the DC will require that they be away from their job or business. They may be required to bear all or part of the cost of attending the meetings. Where the MS can provide budget, at least part of this situation can be alleviated. Obviously, if the MS asks prospective members of the DC to provide their own funds, the range of possibilities becomes limited. This can also produce a DC which is less sensitive to the needs of the members who are not affluent.

Possible members for the DC should be sought from among those who have the ability to contribute directly to the work of the DC. This is not always evident at the beginning, and sometimes it is necessary to change some of the members. This should be kept to a minimum, as it can be disruptive. As the work of the DC progresses, each meeting will be built on previous discussions and decisions, and a new member coming in will have difficulty catching up.

—— • ——

The  *(Sponsor's name)*  is planning a conference and inviting carefully selected people to be on the design committee. It would be appreciated if you would fill out this page and return it by  *(date)* , to the undersigned. If you have any questions, please do not hesitate to call me.

*(Sponsor—individual)*
_____

*(telephone)*
_____

**Conference theme**    _____

_____

**Probable dates**    _____

(Please Check)

Yes    No

**Are you:**
1. Interested in the theme of the conference?    ____ ____
   Comments:

2. Able to participate in meetings of the    ____ ____
   design committee? (Here are the details
   on probable time needed and travel
   cost.)

3. Planning to attend the conference?    ____ ____
   Comments:

**Figure 3-2.** *This invitation to join the design committee contributes to a successful conference because it assures that only those interested will be selected for membership.*

Being an active member of the DC takes time. The Sponsor or Coordinator should ascertain that those recommended for membership will be able to give the necessary time, so that attendance at meetings will be consistent. In a membership organization this can be a significant problem. Relationships are voluntary and there may often be overriding factors which lessen the desire of an individual to give freely of limited time. The caution is that the DC should not be composed merely of those who have the time, but very little else, to contribute to its work. Most of us realize that the desirable people are usually the busiest people, and therefore the work of the DC should be carefully spaced so as not to produce an overload. This suggests quite strongly that the DC must be appointed early enough before the conference to avoid hurried, disorganized meetings.

For the ES conference the DC members should be provided with sufficient time away from other duties so that they can actively participate. If the Sponsor of the conference does not communicate strong support for the work of the DC and the necessity for such work, it is unlikely that the task will assume any kind of priority, in contrast with the other needs of the organization. It may be difficult within the system to find rewards for a member of the DC, but there should be a strict avoidance of any punishment. What can we expect if the employee returns from a committee meeting to be confronted by a supervisor whose first remarks are, "Yes, I know you had to attend the meeting, but now let's get back to work and get some real things done in this organization!"

Money becomes a real problem for an MS design committee that does not have sufficient budget to pay for travel and other expenses. This may mean that membership on the committee is restricted to those who have the financial resources, but this does not mean that these are the people who can contribute the most. It would be helpful if one could anticipate the time and money which would be required, so that the Sponsor and prospective members of the DC will know what to expect. It is not always possible to be specific, as we are dealing with a situation with many variables. However, budgets of time and money should be established to give some parameters to the Coordinator and the DC.

Prospective DC members should realize other limitations which exist. Participants come to expect certain things of a Sponsor who has conducted previous conferences. Therefore, roles and behaviors readily become traditional and change by the DC is limited.

This is not to suggest that an organization must be unalterably trapped by its prior experience and can never change. But the familiar saying "what is past is prologue" certainly applies to conferences which are conducted by membership organizations. Organizations which are offering conferences to the general public (PS) are not quite as trapped. However, an organization after the first conference will begin to establish a reputation and this, likewise, must be taken into account by the DC. For an ES, the same attention to history must be recognized.

—— • ——

The ES was a major drug manufacturer who brought in an external Coordinator to design a "different" kind of conference. Previously, the ES had conducted the usual sales conference with banners, entertainment, and general inspirational appeal to the stereotype of the salesman. Somehow, within the Sponsor, the recognition emerged that a different kind of experience at the conference would be more helpful. The Coordinator and the DC recognized that the salesmen would be coming to this conference with the same expectations as in prior years. The DC identified these expectations but designed a totally new kind of conference experience. It was a successful conference primarily because of the sensitivity of the Coordinator and the DC, and their ability to recognize the imprint of the prior conferences.

—— • ——

This was a successful experience because the Sponsor participated in alerting the participants to the changed design, and the DC recognized the need to retain some ritual, but to provide for some change. They did not ignore the past history of the Sponsor and participants.

At the end of this chapter, there will be a discussion of the reports a DC should prepare. If such reports exist from prior conferences, they are valuable inputs for the new DC at the earliest stages of their work. In the absence of formal reports the DC can review programs, announcements, handouts, listings of exhibitors and any other pertinent printed material from prior conferences. Some conferences are audio-taped, or at least some of the more popular presentations are taped for future sale. These can likewise be helpful to the DC. Although these materials may not describe what actually happened, they at least indicate what the participants had expected.

Of course, there are situations where there is no prior recorded history or documentation of earlier conferences. This requires that the Coordinator and the DC reach out to those who participated in prior conferences and endeavor to uncover some of the history from them. This is a difficult and time consuming activity and as a result, may not be done. The result is a high risk situation, particularly when the Coordinator is new to the Sponsoring organization and the DC may not be fully representative of the participants.

### Conference Objectives

The word "objectives" is sometimes a trigger word, which causes people to choose up sides and culminate their discussion in a shouting match. The experience with specific behavioral objectives from the early 1960's to the present is a spotty and erratic story. The pendulum has swung back and forth from doing only those things for which specific behavioral objectives can be written, as contrasted with the other end of the swing, which ignores behavioral objectives completely. Adding to this situation has been the confusion of terms such as goals and purposes.

For the moment we will avoid the use of any of these words, and instead, try to approach the situation from another direction. The Coordinator and the DC should ask the Sponsor, "What is it that you want the participants to know or do after the conference that they did not know or do before?" For purposes of convenience this will be the conference objectives. Whether these are stated in general terms or specific behavioral terms will depend upon the prior experience of the Coordinator, DC, Sponsor, and participants. It may also be necessary to determine the Sponsor's expectations before it is known which words (i.e. goals, purposes, objectives) communicate most effectively. We will use the term "objectives", recognizing that there are many levels at which objectives can be examined.

It has been said that having specific objectives may not be as significant as the process of developing the objectives. This is true for learning situations in general, and much truer for conferences. For the MS conference the process of developing the objectives may prove a boon to the organization by surfacing member needs which were not previously identified. For the ES conference the process can go a long way toward solving problems before they have even surfaced. The greater the amount of time (within reason) spent on developing objectives, the greater the possibility of a successful conference.

Objectives should not be set at a single meeting. It is too easy for everyone to be swept up in the enthusiasm of a particular individual. Rather, there must be the opportunity for the members of the DC to disengage and even return to their regular positions. Then, after contemplation and discussion with others, the DC should meet again and finalize the objectives. This process takes time, but can produce objectives that are more meaningful and to which all will have a greater level of commitment.

To return to the beginning, the first step is agreement on the theme. Now the DC can begin formulating objectives. This should be an unhurried process which allows for the sharing of ideas before getting down to specific words. In some situations the responsibility for this initial step can be given to the Coordinator. This is usually helpful, but can just as easily be counterproductive.

━━━ ● ━━━

The Coordinator was working on a large national conference for an MS. There was a DC of fifteen people, all of whom were fairly sophisticated in the field of human resource development. The Coordinator met with members of the executive board (i.e., the Sponsor) to identify the theme and they all felt they had made adequate preparation for the DC meeting. Prior to the first DC meeting, a member of the board approached the Coordinator with a transparency on which the theme and possible objectives were magnificently displayed. There were excellent audio-visual resources within his organization, and he had asked them to develop and produce the overhead transparencies which would go from the theme to the objectives. At that point, the Coordinator was swept up in his enthusiasm and by the fact that he had taken the trouble to have the transparencies produced. As the DC meeting progressed and went through some of the initial steps to develop the climate, the Coordinator waited for the appropriate moment to show the transparencies.

At what appeared the right time, the Coordinator switched on the projector. There was a moment of silence, and then an outpouring of discussion. At first, the Coordinator was elated at the level of participation. Too soon, however, it became apparent that most of the talk was directed towards criticism of the theme and the possible objectives. Four hours later, the Coordinator found that most of the DC were still attacking the material which had been displayed, and even questioning the theme which had been decided upon by the Sponsor.

It was several weeks before the Coordinator was able to overcome his own emotional reaction, and to try to diagnose the situation. He also contacted several members of the DC and discussed the meeting with them. The DC apparently felt that they were being manipulated.

They felt that they were being asked to acquiesce in a process which had not only fully begun, but was well on the way to its completion. They wanted to have more influence than appeared possible if they utilized the prepared transparencies. There is a danger in being overprepared as well as in being underprepared.

——— ● ———

The Coordinator must recognize where the DC is at, in the process of developing objectives for the conference. Likewise, the DC should have responsibility for their own behavior regarding the development of objectives. It is all too easy to delegate this task to the Coordinator, so that the members of the DC can sit back and shoot down whatever is proposed. There must be a mutuality of responsibility and behavior in evolving the objectives. The clue word is "evolving."

When possible, the Sponsor should not be physically involved (i.e. sitting in on meetings) in the process of setting forth the objectives, although the DC will inform the Sponsor as part of the feedback and evaluation process. This can be done by testing out communications, how closely do the objectives represent what the Sponsor hopes will happen at the conference? It is also desirable to test out the objectives on some of the possible participants. The charisma of the Coordinator, or the climate of the DC can be a trap. They can all like each other so much, and be working together so well that their level of communication is very high. As a result, the objectives may communicate much more effectively to each other than they would to people who had not been part of the evolution of the objectives.

Where the participants are clearly defined, the DC may wish to start with a needs assessment. That is, to go to the participants and determine what they think they need from the conference. For a conference with a learning purpose, this is almost automatically the first step in order to provide sound data for the DC. For conferences with other purposes, the needs assessment may come from the DC members, if they have been carefully selected with this in mind.

We will be returning to the objectives in Chapter 12 to see how they relate to the conduct of the conference and the follow-up.

## Site Selection

The selection of an appropriate site for a conference is a complicated procedure. Chapter 6 is devoted to this process, but at this point, we will discuss site selection in relation to the responsibilities of the design committee.

There is a very close relationship between the objectives, design, participants, and expected outcomes. Sometimes, the site chosen can be a constricting factor. For example, if a conference has many exhibits, there are only certain cities within the U.S. that have the facilities to accommodate such a conference. How the objectives can be accomplished will be influenced by the site. Some Sponsors plan their conferences (by date) several years in advance. As a result, the site will have been selected before the DC has been activated and the Coordinator selected. In such situations, where there is no flexibility, the DC and the Coordinator should visit the site as early as possible. A good deal of what they can do will be predetermined by the site and the location, and the facilities it has to offer.

In other situations, it is possible to do the design work first, and then identify the appropriate site that would be consistent with the DC's work. In either case, what is important is for the DC to determine beforehand whether the site is fixed, or, if not, the limits of their flexibility in the site selection.

## Coordinating Resources

Any conference, no matter what the size, requires certain resources for its implementation. Usually, the greater the expected participation in the conference, the more complicated are the resources required. Almost any conference of the kind we have been describing will use outside resource people (sometimes erroneously called consultants). They will be carefully selected individuals, who are coming to the conference in order to provide some kind of input. This may range from merely listening to conducting a session for all the participants. Some resource people may be conducting sessions at the same time as other resource people (concurrent sessions). They may be used as speakers or as media presenters. In any event, the identification of such resource people should be coordinated through the DC.

——— • ———

For a large MS conference the Coordinator had the DC evolve the objectives. Then, specific objectives were assigned to different DC members and they were delegated the responsibility for developing the appropriate experience to meet the objective. As part of this responsibility, each DC member was to identify appropriate resource people. To involve as many members of the MS as possible, each DC member organized a subcommittee whose major responsibility was to recommend several carefully identified resource people for each of the objectives. The final selection was the function of the Coordinator and the DC rather than the Sponsor or the subcommittees. The coordination of the efforts of all the subcommittees was through the DC.

——— • ———

There must be a specific agreement as to who invites the selected resource persons and what the form of the invitation should be. This step reflects not only on the design, but also on the budget—one of the available resources. The cost for good resource people can range from nothing up to several thousand dollars, depending upon the individual, the time, the location, and how "hot" that particular resource person is at the time of the invitation. Given the usual budgetary limitations, which are a legitimate concern of any DC, it is necessary to weigh the most desirable person against the cost. Sometimes, the cost for a particular resource person may require the DC to rethink the objective or make other modifications, which go beyond the mere identification and selection of the appropriate resource person. If this responsibility is scattered, the design soon begins to fall apart, and the work of the committee is thwarted.

Another resource which must be coordinated by the DC is that of exhibits. At this time, we will only have a brief discussion, focusing on exhibits as resources. There are many reasons for having exhibits, and some possible difficulties are caused by having them, and these will be explored in more depth in Chapter 7.

Small conferences tend to be less involved with exhibits and may limit exhibitors to handouts or swap-shop tables. Larger conferences invariably have exhibits for many reasons. Exhibits can keep members up to date as well as provide income for the Sponsor. But, the DC and the Coordinator should see the exhibits as another resource to be coordinated as they move through the planning process. Occasionally, some of the objectives can be met by exhibitors. Also, the requirements and expectations of the exhibitors may influence the work of the DC. The Sponsor may previously have agreed to provide the exhibitors with completely unopposed time, meaning there will be no programs scheduled during certain hours so that the participants can visit the exhibits. Such prior agreements will seriously limit the flexibility of the design and the DC. To make the exhibits more of a resource than a hinderance, it is desirable to have a relationship with the exhibitors. This is sometimes done by having an exhibitor on the DC, representing all the exhibitors. Another approach is to have the Coordinator develop a direct relationship with the exhibitors to determine their needs and expectations.

For any conference there is the need for what the UN and other international bodies call the *secretariat*. This word sounds pretentious, still, it is most convenient and helps to clarify an important and sometimes overlooked resource. The work of the DC will require a good deal of correspondence, telephone calls, and coordination of meeting schedules. The need for the secretariat develops slowly, but accelerates rapidly as the date of the conference approaches. It is the secretariat's duty to see that mailings go out at prescribed times and to receive communications and questions from the participants, the selected resource people, and the site personnel. The secretariat may start out as a one-person resource assigned to the Coordinator or the DC, but as the process evolves there will be the need for increasing the personnel.

It is likely that an MS would prefer that the secretariat be housed within the membership organization in order to reinforce the fact that it is an additional membership service. Membership organizations are constantly pressed to illustrate that they have observable membership services.

Conferences are rarely conducted without a flood of paper. From the DC comes reports, proposed designs, revisions, and finally the completed design and explanatory materials. Then, there is the flow of correspondence to the proposed resource people, as well as to those at the site where the conference will be held. Some of the resource people may use materials as handouts, and therefore, these must be reproduced in sufficient quantity. Very often there will be other participant materials, some of which must be reproduced by the secretariat, while others will be provided by either the resource people, the chamber of commerce, or the site itself. All of these materials must be prepared, be available at the proper time, and collated into participant packets, as appropriate.

In any event, the flow and production of these materials is so great that unless there is somebody qualified to handle and coordinate this effort (flood of papers), the Coordinator and the DC will be thoroughly inundated. The secretariat will also function *during* the conference and these activities are discussed in Chapter 11.

## Identifying the Participants

Sometimes, the participants are automatically identified by virtue of the sponsoring organization. In such a case the selection of participants is predetermined. It may only remain for the DC to confirm the list so that all concerned are fully cognizant as to who will be invited. However, there are conferences where the participants are not so clearly identified, and the DC must make some educated guesses as to the kinds of participants they hope will attend. It is crucial that all members of the committee have in mind the same general kinds of participants as they go through the planning process.

Frequently, we will highlight the need for congruency among the objectives, the design, and the participants. These three elements must constantly be kept in mind, and adjustments made among them. Once the objectives have been set, the design process can proceed. However, the design must be the effective link between the objectives and the participants. When the participants are known beforehand, as in the case of an ES conference, it is possible to be very specific, and perhaps name the individuals who should participate. When dealing with a voluntary situation, whether a membership or public seminar, it is only possible to make some projections as to the kind of participants one hopes will attend. This may create the need for a change during the conference, and later we will explore one way of doing this through the use of a steering committee. At this point in the planning process, the DC should indicate the kinds of participants they think will attend.

Even when the conference is an annual one, or one that is repeated periodically for the same group, it is not possible to assume that the same people will attend each time. For most national conferences conducted by membership organizations there is usually a 50% participant turnover from year to year, though trade associations do a bit better. This may be a result of the geography, for as locations shift, there is a tendency for the conference to consist mostly of those who are closest. The economy may influence who attends, and a change in theme will bring different kinds of participants. The DC and the Coordinator should develop a profile of the expected participant group. No one should be defensive if, at the actual conference, the participants do not match the profile. However, to the degree that the profile can be specifically stated, it is more likely that the Coordinator and the DC members will have similar images in mind when they refer to the participants.

The DC should develop this profile as specifically as possible. They can list the age range, sex mix, level of schooling, and all the other kinds of demographic information used for analyzing people.

There are times, though admittedly too rare, when it is possible to hand pick participants, even though the Sponsor is not an ES. The following took place at a PS conference.

—— • ——

In an international conference the DC, after agreeing on objectives, listed by name and title those who should attend as participants from each of the countries involved. This was done with full knowledge that the actual selection would be in the hands of the nine participating countries. It was a high risk situation. Yet, by being specific, the Coordinator and DC were able to actually get most of the designated persons, rather than those who were merely available. The result was a much more successful conference than if they had relied on the usual cautious protocol, which leaves it up to the various countries to send whomever they wish, based on a statement of the objectives and a description of the design. Of course, they did not completely achieve their invitation list, but it was close enough to assure a successful conference. It also proved a turning point in conferences that had previously relied on a much looser kind of invitation procedure so as not to impinge on presumed national rights. However, the feedback from the participating countries was positive. Attendance at international conferences is costly, and countries who fund such participation are eager to obtain the maximum return—and one way is to send the appropriate participants.

—— • ——

For an ES conference the selection of participants can usually be highly directive. But in any situation and for any Sponsor the DC should provide as much assistance as possible to enable participants and organizations to make clear decisions about attending, and if they plan to do so, who would be the most appropriate persons. This will help maintain the essential congruency of the objective-design-participant relationship.

## Duration of the Conference

When discussing the desirable length of a conference, one is reminded of the famous response by Abraham Lincoln. When asked how long a man's legs should be, he replied, "Long enough to reach the floor." In a similar vein the duration of a conference should be "long enough to reach the objectives." When the duration is circumscribed by other factors, the DC may have to reduce the number of objectives so that they can be accomplished within the time allowed.

—— • ——

In one conference concerned with improving the use of video tape, the Sponsor (an ES) felt that it would be desirable to start with a unit on the still camera. This would help the participants develop some competency in this form of photography, so that they could more easily see the differences between still photography and the video tape medium. The Coordinator and

DC concurred, and designed accordingly. When the conference was actually conducted, it became obvious that too much was being expected of the participants within the available time. Fortunately, the conference was to be conducted two more times. The Coordinator and the DC urged that the objectives be changed and that those related to the still camera be dropped—not because they were not good objectives, but rather, it was not possible to achieve them within the time available. Instead, a selection factor was introduced, so that participants would be required to show some competency in the use of the still camera before they could be considered for the conference. It worked.

——— • ———

Such compromises are frequently necessary when matching the possible duration against the desirable objectives. The duration of the conference is not only a reaction to the objectives, but also a reflection of participant availability for the particular period of time.

——— • ———

The conference was designed for top-level people from a variety of government agencies. The overall purpose was to inform the participants of a new program which was being initiated, and it was hoped, to get their cooperation for its implementation. The DC was warned that these top-level officials would not come for the full week which the committee thought necessary, though they might attend a two or three-day conference on this same topic. The DC decided to risk the situation. Crucial and important items were scheduled for the first two days. Then, the design was loosened up so that the officials could spend part of the next three days at their offices. However, some important high-level people were scheduled to conduct special sessions during the remaining three days. The purpose of this was obvious, and the result was almost complete attendance by all the participants for the entire conference.

——— • ———

The participants may have an expectation about the duration. When previous MS conferences have been held for three days, the DC should be very cautious as it explores the possibility of changing the length of the conference. Adding days or reducing days may alter the make-up of the participant group. Also, we may find ourselves dealing with an element of Alvin Toffler's "Future Shock." Because people must make a great many decisions each day, there is a tendency for most people to minimize the number of decisions they have to make. To cope with this, we try to reduce certain decision-making situations to habit behavior. It is easier to repeat behavior than to reappraise a situation which may require new behavior on our part. When participants have attended a conference in prior years, they automatically (by habit) expect that conference to require the same number of days each time. To change the duration forces another decision upon them. If it comes at the wrong time (when many other decisions have to be made), it may serve to reduce the possibility of their participation in the planned conference.

A conference is an investment of various kinds of resources. One of them is time. If travel time to a conference is necessary, then the duration has to be sufficiently long to warrant the investment of time it takes to get to the conference and to return. Of course, time has a psychological dimension as well. A participant who may hesitate about taking the few hours needed to fly from New York to Chicago may not think twice about driving a car for an equal length of time to a one- or two-day conference in a nearby city. The psychological dimension of time must be taken into consideration, and we have too little evidence to enable us to fully comprehend it. For some people flying from coast to coast in about four hours is not nearly as traumatic as driving the same amount of time from Washington to New York City. In our western states, it is much easier to travel north and south than east and west because of the mountains. Psychologically, there is more of a tendency to move in the north-south direction. A conference on the other side of the mountains may require a longer duration to justify the additional psychological travel.

## Setting Dates for the Conference

Dates for conferences are sometimes set before the DC is selected, while at other times, the date is negotiable. When a Sponsor has conducted conferences for a number of years, the potential participants expect the next conference to be held at the same time each year. The MS which offers an annual conference is usually locked into a particular time of the year. Usually, there will be general agreement that the conference should be held, for example, the second week of April. To change to the third week of April or the first week of April may not cause too much disruption among potential participants, but to change to early March or late June may result in either fewer participants or a completely different conference mix. Because of pressure and competition for better conference facilities, Sponsors endeavor to keep options open by alerting their potential participants of the possible need to make slight shifts in dates for the coming year. The Sponsor should provide sufficient lead time so the participants can mark their calendars accordingly. Some Sponsors announce their conferences as much as five or six years in advance in order to assure availability. There is little that the DC and Coordinator can do about this but work within these constraints.

When the conference is not a repetitive/annual affair, it is more likely that other factors will influence the selection of the dates. Although the discussion which follows indicates some of the factors to be considered, this is by no means a comprehensive coverage of this element of conference planning. In addition to these general factors, there are also many elements peculiar to a particular group or situation which will likewise influence the selection of the best dates for a conference.

Almost anybody who works has a cycle that must be recognized by those who would offer them conference possibilities. If a Sponsor, either a membership organization or a public seminar, offered a program for accountants between January 1 and April 15, there probably wouldn't be sufficient participation to warrant holding the conference. Likewise, if a conference were to be held in September, and the potential participants were school teachers, it is highly unlikely that they would be available.

This does not mean that we should let ourselves be locked into decisions about dates without further exploration. For example, at one time it was understood that conferences should not be offered during the summer vacation period. It was expected that this was the time when most people would want to get away on vacation and would not want to be concerned with anything related to work. With the acceptance of recreation as a normal part of conference procedure, it has become acceptable, and in some cases, highly desirable to have the conference during what was previously reserved as the vacation period.

The most desirable approach is to schedule the conference during a low work load period or when the participant can make maximum use of the content of the conference.

—— ● ——

The client was a clothing manufacturer who utilized a network of salespersons throughout the country. They were usually called together for an annual sales conference, at which time the company (Sponsor) showed them the new line, the new materials, and covered the various items usually included in a sales conference. The conferences were traditionally held in September, as the Sponsor perceived that he could not get the sales people together during the summer. The Sponsor felt that to bring them together earlier would create too great a lead time for their purpose, which was related to spring sales.

Then, for the next conference, it was suggested that there should be a Coordinator. The new Coordinator suggested the formation of a DC, which was to include some of the salespersons. Because of the distance, the DC relied more on phone calls and the mail than on the face-to-face meetings, which are preferable. The committee developed a short questionnaire which was sent out to all the salespeople. Among other items questioned was that of dates. This step was being taken almost a year before the conference was to be held. The response strongly indicated that they preferred that the conference be held in April or May. That was the time of the year when they were not selling for a specific season. In addition, the salespeople would have just visited their clientele, and would have received valuable feedback as to how the current year's spring line was selling. In the past, this feedback was not shared until September, which was too late to influence the spring line for the following year. By rescheduling the conference, it became possible to get more information for the production and marketing groups, without disrupting the preferred schedules of the salesforce.

———— • ————

It is likely that one of the factors which contributed to the success of the effort just described was the direct involvement of the participants in selecting a new date.

Another factor to be considered in selecting dates is the matter of holidays. At one time, holidays or vacation periods were avoided as desirable conference dates. Although this has changed somewhat, there are still problems when a holiday intervenes.

———— • ————

The conference was in India, but they used an American Coordinator. The first meeting with the DC was in August and agreement was reached on objectives, design, and participants. The conference was scheduled for November. However, the Indo-Pakistan war erupted and the conference was delayed. It was finally rescheduled for the last week in February and first week in March. The new dates encompassed an important holiday (Holi Day) which is celebrated much like the Mardi Gras in Catholic countries and communities, or the Purim holiday of the Jews and Israelis. There is much fun-making, sprinkling of people with colored powders, and general merry making. It is a Hindu holiday, but the Moslems have a similar holiday at almost the same time. As a result, right in the middle of the conference, there was a day which broke the flow and momentum. The work for that day was cancelled and everyone celebrated the holiday. The next day, however, all the participants were back at the conference, working strenuously to make up the lost day, which has not been accounted for in the original design. If the Coordinator had not accommodated to the holiday, and had not rescheduled the work for the lost day and redesigned the flow, it could have been a disaster.

———— • ————

Holidays need not be an interference. There are times when coupling the conference with a holiday will make the participants available for a longer period of time. Of course, it is necessary to have the appropriate site and design to enable the participants to feel they have made effective use of the holiday rather than that they have been deprived.

In addition to national holidays, there are local festival dates which must be identified. The sociologists tell us that the U.S. is not a melting pot but a pluralistic society. This is evident when one examines the list of local holidays in various parts of our country. The variety of national, religious, and ethnic observances makes an exotic and interesting list. Many are specific dates which should be considered when scheduling a conference.

It is horrifying to realize how many organizations sponsor conferences which require the participants to be away from home on election day! This event comes only once a year and is honored throughout the U.S. Of course, the major event is only once every four years, but there are an increasing number of local issues on the ballot, and by sponsoring a conference which in-cludes election day, we are discouraging participants from taking part in fulfilling their regular duties in a democratic society. There is an alternative in the form of the absentee ballot. This is possible, but such a procedure is not available for all elections throughout the country. If there is no choice on the part of the Sponsor but to hold the conference on election day, then the material which goes out to the potential participants should encourage them to seek an absentee ballot.

For the multi-site ES, there can be another situation related to dates. The main office personnel may not be fully aware of some of the local situations in the different sites which affect date selection. For example, many employees participate in annual local conferences known as "career days." These are times when there is an attempt to bridge the gap between the employing sector and potential employees who will soon be graduating from high school. If the participants for the ES conference are asked to attend on the same days as career days, one of the two important activities will lose out. When possible, particularly with an ES, the prospective participant should be queried about dates before they are set.

There may be other local events or situations which influence the date selection. The DC may prefer an isolated spot, so as to use the "cultural island" technique (Chapter 4). But it may be just the time for the opening of hunting season for that rural part of the country. Unless this activity is desired for the participants, the DC must select different dates or an alternate site.

The selection of a site and date must be mutually compatible. A conference in Miami Beach during the summer may look attractive because of the weather-induced low rates. But this may mean that most of the participants are essentially locked into their air-conditioned hotels or adjacent swimming pools. If this fits in with the objectives, design, and participant relationship, then the choice of dates and geography is certainly desirable. However, only certain kinds of conferences would want to discourage their participants from leaving the conference site.

Obviously, the reverse applies to having the conference in the northern climate during the dead of winter, unless winter sports are scheduled as part of the conference behavior.

The winter time presents a further problem in that there are some parts of the country which are made inaccessible by winter storms. The participants may find it difficult to get to the conference site. There is no way of guaranteeing the weather when setting the dates, and the Coordinator and DC can only make an educated guess, and hope.

——— • ———

The client, an MS, had suggested that the dates for this particular conference be in March at a beautiful site in West Virginia. The Coordinator was assured by the site personnel that the weather at that time of year, though not entirely predictable, was usually not too radical.

The conference design called for several of the participants to function as group leaders. It was planned that all the participants would arrive by noon on Sunday, with the opening session to be right after dinner that night. During Sunday afternoon, most of the participants would be free to use the excellent facilities of the site. Those few who were to be group leaders would meet with the Coordinator, who would conduct a brief training session for them on their roles in the conference. To facilitate the transportation to the conference site, the Sponsor had arranged for a charter flight. The scenario started to deteriorate when the chartered plane was delayed in take off, because of mechanical difficulty. This delay brought the plane to the small airport at the site late on Sunday afternoon, just as a predicted snow storm began. There was sufficient deterioration in the weather to raise questions as to the advisability of trying to land at this small private airport. The chartered plane circled the airfield, buffeted by the storm, while there was considerable radio discussion concerning the possibility of landing or going on to a larger airport. The passengers, meanwhile, were becoming very ill. The pilot decided to go on, and several minutes later they landed at an alternate airport. They then proceeded by bus over winding mountain roads, to the conference site. They arrived very late, and in no condition to take part in anything but bed.

——— • ———

This experience provided many lessons. For one, the Coordinator learned that the schedule had been too tight, and had completely ignored the possibility of bad weather in making arrangements. True, if the charter plane had taken off on time, it would have landed safely before the storm. But the plane did not take off on time. Obviously, the Coordinator should have anticipated the need for alternative plans.

As more and more conferences go international, almost every factor discussed in this section becomes even more significant. In addition, international travel rates shift with the time of the year and the direction of major flow of traffic. Those dates are known beforehand, and sometimes shifting the date of a conference a few days, one way or the other, can make a significant difference in conference costs for international travel.

### Reviewing Actions of the Design Committee

The Coordinator and the design committee have now planned

- Conference objectives
- Site selection
- Coordinating resources
- Identification of participants
- Duration
- Dates

It was recommended previously that the Coordinator and/or the DC go to the potential participants and the Sponsor for recommendations, advice, and suggestions. The decision making is still in the hands of the Coordinator and/or the DC. However, before proceeding further with the work of the DC, it is important that there be no questions about the decisions that have been made. This is the time when the Sponsor should be involved, if only for a brief meeting, to get an overview of the work of the Coordinator and the DC and their decisions. To clarify the role of the Sponsor during this meeting, this is not the time for him to ask for new inputs or decisions. Rather, this a checkpoint and the Coordinator and the DC, who have a primary responsibility to the Sponsor, are endeavoring to determine whether or not they have met this responsibility.

In an MS, where members of the organization are also members of the DC, it is probable that the Sponsor is their employee! For example, in many national associations, the Sponsor will be the executive director representing the board of the organization. The executive director is also an employee of the organization, and therefore, of the membership. This can be very confusing! This confusion can also lead to conflicts.

—— • ——

The Sponsor was a large national membership organization. At the reporting meeting, the executive director announced that he was satisfied with the work of the Coordinator and the DC, that they had done their job and need not meet again. The remainder of the work concerned with the conference was to be left to the executive director and the paid national staff. The DC felt that they had not yet completed the design but had only done some basic planning. They confronted the executive director, demanding that they be allowed to continue further with their design work. The executive director finally agreed, but only when the DC agreed to limit activities to one more meeting and then allow the executive director to take over the conference. The DC did have one more meeting, but it was obvious by the low attendance that they were no longer committed to the conference. The executive director, in this case, was more interested in retaining control of the organization than in the quality of the conference. The review process indicated that more than just conference design was at stake, but little was done about it. Maximum use was not made of the review step in the DC operations.

———— ● ————

Reporting sessions can be helpful if carefully organized, and if the respective goals are clarified. It can also surface disagreement or communication breakdowns with the Sponsor which are best aired at this point, rather than later in the design process.

In the case of an ES, the decisions may have to be reviewed by a person highly placed in the sponsoring organization. This could be the same individual or group of individuals who selected the Coordinator and appointed the DC.

## Reports of the Design Committee

One way of simplifying the paper pollution problem is for the DC at this step in the planning process, to stop and prepare a report. Such a report will produce some new paper, but it can also eliminate some of the previous pieces of paper by coordinating and consolidating what has been done into a single document. No report should be produced unless there is a need. At this point in the conference planning process, the need is to clarify the agreements and the plans up to this time.

There is also an historical need. For an ES or an MS that conducts conferences periodically (annually or semiannually), the report of what has happened up to this time is a valuable input for future DCs.

An organization that is offering a public seminar conference has the need to know what works and what does not work during the design and planning process. Months later, after the conference has been completed, it would be impossible to recapture what the DC experienced or to analyze those behaviors and decisions which contributed to the success or failure of the conference. The absence of an adequate report can contribute to a repetition of less helpful actions, and this can be economically disastrous to the sponsoring organization.

## From the Suppliers' Viewpoint

The major suppliers involved in this early phase are site and travel personnel.

### Site Personnel Say—

Why don't Coordinators and design committees come to us in the early stages of their planning? Of course, we are in the business to make money but to do this we have to provide service. We have a great deal of information about preferable times of year, weather conditions, and alternatives, but we are not given the opportunity to provide these resources.

When we are contacted, we are not sure who the Coordinator is. An individual may call us, but gives only his name,. This doesn't tell us enough so we have to probe, and some people resent this. If we know who the Coordinator is, we know whom to contact to provide additional information and help.

The specification of the DC responsibilities is good, but they should share this with us. If they tell us that they are limited only to making recommendations, we won't ask them for a decision. Otherwise, we push for a necessary decision and, in the absence of one, we have difficulty understanding what is happening.

Some of us are real conference professionals, others have some skills, but are probably not as sophisticated as the Coordinator, or even some DC members. Still, we can be helpful if we know more about what is being planned. Share with us the objectives-design-participant situation. Many of us have had extensive experience with various conference groups and we can make this experience available to Coordinators and DC members, if we know their intentions.

Dates are always a problem. There are just so many days in the year. Of course we want to make the best use of our site and facilities that is possible. At times, we have little flexibility, but occasionally various kinds of shifts can be negotiated. Let us discuss the dates with you, recognizing that the final decision is yours. Perhaps we can offer you alternatives that provide other benefits from our site which you had not previously considered.

Please, keep us informed. We know you don't want to be bothered, so after the first contact we hesitate to call you or even write. You may have indicated an interest in some dates, and tentatively we put it into the books. If you change your mind on dates or site, it would be helpful if you would let us know so we can release the dates to other Coordinators who are exploring.

### Travel People Say—

Before locking into dates, why not talk to us? If your participants are utilizing air travel, a few days one way or the other can be significant. Before you decide on the dates, explore alternatives with us.

Rate structures vary throughout the year and schedules are constantly changing in different parts of the country. For domestic air travel, contact us when you are trying to pick the best dates.

    Duration may be fixed in your minds, yet there are so many possibilities when it comes to travel, that you should speak to us. (There is preconference travel and postconference travel. We will talk more about that in later chapters.) But, because of travel packages, you may find that either adding a day to your conference or shortening it by a day, can bring additional benefits to your participants.

# 4.
# Designing the
# Core of the
# Conference

The actual design for the conference can be done by the Coordinator and submitted to the design committee (DC) for their review, recommendations, or decisions based on the ground rules as discussed in the previous chapter. In other situations, designing can be a joint activity by both the Coordinator and the DC. In order to focus clearly on the design elements, it is assumed that the DC is directly involved in designing and this chapter will treat the DC and the Coordinator as a single unit. When it appears that the Coordinator is doing something special or different, this will be so indicated.

This chapter examines

- Flow
- Theme
- General Sessions
- Regular Sessions

## Flow

A good conference design should have a discernible flow and momentum. No matter what its length, a conference has high points and low points; there are times of great activity and times of little activity. The DC must consider these factors as it creates the design.

### Climate Setting

Persons coming together for a conference are establishing a new temporary microculture. That is, there are certain behaviors, ways of dressing, and other cultural behaviors which are appropriate for this particular microculture which would not be quite so appropriate in other places or for other events. The process begins with the first announcement sent out to the potential participants. The form of this invitation/announcement sets the climate. If the announcement is austere and terse, the participant perceives that this is the climate being set for the conference. For trade associations, which endeavor to get as large a participant group as possible, the brochures tend to be more colorful and eye-catching. Where the potential participants are members of an organization and therefore normally would be expected to attend, the tendency is to have a less colorful and more content-oriented initial brochure. The initial notice of an ES conference may merely be in the form of an office memo on company stationery. Each of these messages, both in content and form, communicate to the potential participant some of the expected behaviors. The climate is being set.

When the participants gather for the start of the conference, once again climate setting becomes a factor. The physical environment contributes to this and must be designed accordingly. It is possible for the Sponsor to set the climate by using banners, signs, hostesses and hosts. If the Sponsor's participants are only a small portion of the total population at the conference site there may be limitations as to just how much of the physical environment can be used for climate setting.

The registration procedure is also part of the climate setting. Where the participants have to stand in long registration lines to obtain their materials, they may tend to react negatively. Rapid and comfortable registration contributes to a positive climate. One technique is to have the materials waiting in the participants' rooms or to have the materials delivered to them by the bellperson immediately after arriving at the room. (See Chapter 9 for more detail.)

Usually there is a period of time between the participants' arrival and the opening session of the conference. Some design committees provide for an "attitude adjustment" period, which is a euphemism for a social period, with or without alcohol. When the participants are arriving in the early morning, the refreshments will be considerably different from those of a late afternoon attitude adjustment period. In any event, some kind of early conference activity of this nature can be helpful for climate setting, if that is the climate the DC wishes to set. If not, it is important for the DC to make other provisions appropriate to the desired conference climate.

## Content

The content must be related to the objectives. There are different ways to design the conference to include the selected content.

The *general session* is that part of the conference when all the participants are expected to meet in the same room at the same time. In international conferences, this is called a plenary session. All the participants are gathered together in one place, receiving the same input.

Conference design also utilizes *concurrent sessions*. These are several sessions being held at the same time, but each on a different topic. Participants can attend one or more of these sessions. Variations in the use of concurrent sessions will be discussed later.

There are also *breakout sessions*. These usually spin-off from general sessions. They may be concurrent sessions, but the term is usually used for small group sessions which derive directly from a general session. During the breakout sessions, all the small groups may be working on the same topic.

There are various concepts for organizing the content into a design. We will discuss only three of the more common concepts in use. First, there is the *stimulus* approach. In this situation, the general session uses a speaker, a case study, or a media presentation to stimulate the group about a particular topic. (This is useful when the topic is controversial, or when there are various points of view.) Then, the participants go into breakout groups to discuss the material. It is helpful to have the breakout groups prepare some kind of report which can be presented at the subsequent general session.

The most common form of stimulus session is the speaker. If it is the first general session of the conference, this person may be labeled as the keynote speaker, though this is not necessary. The speaker makes a presentation and plans it so that it can be followed by breakout sessions. Figure 4-1 illustrates an example of this from a conference of the Australian Institute of Training and Development.

Another way of organizing the content into a design is *confrontation-search-coping*. It starts with the participants being presented with a situation planned in the form of a confrontation—a problem to be solved. The confrontation can take place in a general session, or a session can be planned where the confrontation is provided on an individual basis. As all the participants are expected to start with the same type of experience, it is considered a general session and would appear that way in the schedule.

——— ● ———

The Sponsor was an ES and the employees involved were salespersons. The participants received the same information in their packets upon arrival, and were asked to come to a particular room at a designated time. When the participants got there, they found a large ballroom with booths around the walls and an information desk in the middle. There was no podium and no seats. After a while, each participant ventured up to the information desk and was given a diagram which explained that the different booths were each organized around a particular product of the company. When a participant chose a booth and entered, he found a small audio-visual device and a button to push. Upon pushing the button, the participant was confronted by a screen which showed a potential customer who asked a series of questions. The confrontation was designed so that it took no more than three minutes. Then, the participant was told that he could either try to respond to the confrontation or begin a search. That is, he could search for the most appropriate responses to the questions asked. The search material consisted of literature, resource people from production and research, and fellow participants. When the participant felt prepared, an opportunity was provided for him to try out his response and to get feedback from resource people on his ability to cope with the confrontation. Each participant could go through this confrontation-search-coping process as many times as he desired.

—— • ——

### Monday, July 2

**9:00 a.m.-10:30 a.m.**

PLENARY SESSION—Chairman: Keith Stewart
"Developing Human Resources"—Dr. Leonard Nadler

**10:30 a.m.-11:00 a.m.**

MORNING TEA—Viewing of the exhibition

**11:00 a.m.-12:15 p.m.**

VOCATIVE SESSION—The application of Nadler's concepts of training, education, and development in:

1. "The Selling Area": Phil Lacaze, Owen Donmeade, Ralph Keeling
2. "The Management Development Field": Geoffrey Richards, Paul Green, Anthony Power
3. "Supervisory Training": Mike Brereton, Gordon King, John McNaughton
4. "Operator Training": Colin Dunnette, Patric Campbell, Frank Davis

*Figure 4-1. This example, taken from the annual conference of the Australian Society for Training and Development, shows how a stimulus session can be followed by various breakout sessions.*

The third way to organize the content into a design is *information processing*. It is used when a significant part of the conference is concerned with sharing information. This method tends to utilize fewer small groups and more general sessions. The most familiar are those where presenters stand up and read papers. These papers can be either scientific or statistical, as well as generally informative. Unfortunately, too many MS conferences that are professionally oriented tend to use the reading of papers as a major design. Of course, everybody knows that the papers will be printed in some form later on, and therefore they pay little attention during the conference. A paper written to be read aloud to an audience should utilize much different sentence structure and organization than one written for publication. The presenters tend to write for later publication, and then merely read what is essentially a professional article for a journal.

It is possible to deal with large segments of information as the basic content of the conference, but then the design should be different.

—— • ——

It was an international conference with representatives from nine countries. Each delegation had been asked to prepare a report on the conference topic, as it related to their country. The original design called for each of the nine to have one of their countrymen read his report to the conferees during a full day session. The DC realized that this would produce the usually deadly day which many would use for shopping and other nonconference activities. Therefore, the DC redesigned the conference so that each country would prepare its report, according to a suggested format, and bring it to the conference for the opening session Sunday evening. At that time, all reports were collected and duplicated. By the end of Monday, each participant had the nine reports, and was asked to read them all before the opening of the Tuesday session. At the general session on Tuesday, the fifty participants and observers sat around a large conference square made up of many tables. Microphones had been provided so each could speak from his seat. Four discussion leaders had been selected and briefed (each to work with one of the four areas of the suggested format). The discussion leaders were seated at the four corners of the square so that there was no status position. The chairperson made some brief remarks (less than five minutes) and called for questions on any of the nine reports. This process was repeated four times, to cover the four major areas in the reports. The result was a day of stimulating discussion based on questions and twoway communication, rather than on a series of nine readings from prepared papers.

—— • ——

By no means do these three forms represent all the possibilities which are available for conference design, but they are the ones most frequently utilized. As we proceed through this chapter and the next one, many other ways of designing conferences will be suggested and illustrated.

## Scheduling

There is no one perfect way to break up a day for purposes of scheduling a conference. On the negative side there are limits to how long any person should be asked to sit in a seat. There is a saying that "the top of the head can only take as much as the bottom of the seat." Put another way, there is a limit to anybody's interest span no matter how interesting the program. There is also the need for what is euphemistically called the "hygienic hiatus." There are normal bodily functions which also limit the amount of time that participants can be expected to remain in the same room.

Ventilation, lighting, and the lure of outdoors will all have their influence on the preferable blocks of time for any conference. Participants from academic backgrounds are accustomed to the two-hour class, and would find no difficulty with this block of time. Participants who are used to a more active role, might find that one hour is the limit of their endurance.

The degree of involvement will also influence the length of the time blocks. When participants are passive, as in a lecture, they are less likely to want a long time period. When they are involved, as in small groups, the time period can be longer.

The schedule must also allow for movement between sessions and activities. A general session, by definition, involves all the participants at the conference. If there are 1,000 participants in a hall, no matter how many exits are provided, it still takes time for them to leave the hall. Stairways and elevators may limit the speed with which they can proceed to the next session. There must be sufficient time between sessions so that participants can move comfortably from one place to another.

Every conference should have *white space*. This is the term for an unscheduled period of time when participants are free to do what they wish. If the design calls for visits to exhibits, this is not white space, because the participant is supposed to be visiting the exhibits. Some participants make their own white space, if none is provided; they just don't go to the exhibits or some other activity.

The design can handle white space by providing for "individual time." It might even say "free time," though somehow the word free bothers some people. They feel that when participants pay to come to a conference, they want every minute blocked in. There are even some in the ES category who worry that, if the design indicates free time, the Sponsor may question what he is getting for his money. Yet, all of us need white space to cope with information pollution. We need a time when we can legitimately just stop any more inputs and think about what we have already heard.

## Climax

The conference should not be allowed to conclude with a whimper, with the gradual drifting away of the participants. This will happen unless the DC has scheduled some significant activities near or at the end of the conference.

One design is to have a banquet on the evening preceding the last day. For an MS conference the cost of the banquet is usually built into the total conference cost, because participants are more likely to stay on and attend a banquet if they have already paid for it.

Another design approach is to schedule a big name speaker for the final day, usually for lunch. It would have to be somebody who would encourage the participants to remain.

Early departure of participants is a problem faced by an ES as well as an MS. One approach, for an ES, is to schedule an important company official to provide the climax to the conference.

For some conferences, a special kind of activity at the end can provide the climax needed. One such exercise is a "memo-to-myself" whereby the participants go through a goal setting process for when they return home. This exercise will be described in more detail later in Chapter 7.

In many parts of the world, including the U.S., a certificate of completion or attendance is distributed at the end of the conference. This, too, provides a climax, as well as recognition for individuals.

The possibilities for the climax are many and the DC must build some specific and observable experiences into the end of the conference. The choices should be made based on the objective. Is it to encourage the participants to remain until the end, to give recognition, to provide linkage to another activity, etc.? The climax might include presenting certificates to participants, which they can now take home with them. If the group is too large for individual presentations, some symbolic presentations can be made to selected individuals. If materials have been developed during the conference, they could be distributed as part of the climax session. There could be awards for outstanding performance (in the case of an ES) or contributions to the work of the organization (for an MS). The climax might include linkages into next year such an election of new officers, voting on objectives for the next conference, or selection of the conference theme. The climax should be designed to reflect the climate of the conference, the expectations of the participants, and the objectives as stated by the DC.

## Theme

As discussed earlier, most conferences have a specified theme. When the Sponsor is an ES or is offering a public seminar, the theme need not be so apparent. For the MS the theme can be extremely crucial, as it is part of the marketing of the conference. The theme also helps set the climate and contributes to the objectives.

## Special Theme

Some Sponsors who have annual conferences have chosen not to select a special theme, but accept the fact that their members will continue to come without one. It can be more helpful, however, to adopt a theme which communicates the overall purpose of the conference. The theme can be stated in a sentence, a slogan, or in just two or three words. The theme should be as relevant and challenging as possible, so as to encourage participants to attend.

The special theme has many possibilities. It might reflect a significant event, such as the Bicentennial Theme in 1976. A Sponsor may choose to identify a significant trend taking place in the life of the organization, and weave a theme from that. The special theme may honor an individual, or group of individuals.

For an ES the theme might announce the introduction of a new product line or service. An MS might choose a theme which reflects a new direction for the organization. The PS, particularly a profit PS, will try to choose a theme which is attention getting as well as expressive.

## Communicating the Theme

One device that some organizations have used is that of the *logo*. This is a symbolic representation of the theme which is then used for the stationery, brochures, conference materials and anything else related to the conference. Most Americans tend to react to symbols which are related to ideas or products. Just notice the amount of money spent on using and protecting trademarks. The difficulty for the DC is that they may become trapped into using a logo which does not effectively communicate. The development of a logo can be a significant expense and should be avoided unless there is some prior research which indicates that the logo does effectively communicate that which the DC wants communicated. Sometimes, a DC seeks an acronym or some other device, such as a catchy phrase. This too can be susceptible to misunderstanding. The theme needs to be communicated, but the selection of an appropriate method may require the services of people who are specialists in that field.

For a public seminar organization, the use of a logo or an acronym becomes much more important. Such a Sponsor wants something which can be instantly recognized and constantly repeated each time the Sponsor offers a conference. Usually, the communicating device will be geared towards building a Sponsor image. It need not be complicated. For example, if the potential participant is told that the conference is being offered by Scientific Methods Inc., it would probably make little or no impression. However, when the same participants are told that this is the Grid Seminar, they would probably recognize the work of Blake and Mouton.

## General Sessions

For most conferences there will be much time spent in general sessions. The relative amount of time spent in the general sessions and the time used for other sessions will depend upon the objectives and how they can best be reached. It is unlikely that any conference is held without some kind of general session. On the other hand, there are those conferences in which only general sessions are held, and such a design is questionable.

When the group is small, probably under twenty-five, general sessions may still allow for individual involvement. As the size goes above twenty-five, that possibility becomes much more remote, and therefore, there must be a balance between the general session and the many possibilities of small group sessions. Even for general sessions, there are many possible variations. The choice of the design will relate, in part, to the concepts of the design discussed earlier. When designing general sessions, the following need to be considered.

### Resource People

The tendency is to choose a speaker for general sessions. The first general session of a conference is usually the *keynote session* and the speaker for this session is used to provide the keynote of the conference, based on the theme and the objectives. Some speakers have their own particular message, which may or may not relate to the keynote assignment. The more important and impressive the speaker, the less likely it is that the DC will feel that they can influence what the speaker will say. When the DC is selecting a keynote speaker, they should decide if the speaker is being invited because of what he can really contribute to the theme of the conference, or because he has a "marquee name." There are times when it is desirable to have big names, and by no means should we avoid inviting somebody because his name will draw. But, to invite a keynote speaker with only this in mind may prove self-defeating. The speaker may draw a crowd, but not contribute to setting the appropriate climate for the conference.

A well-selected keynote speaker can make a valuable contribution to the entire conference. He can set the tone and climate by his remarks and his delivery. He can pinpoint issues so that the participants are able to make choices as to the kinds of small group activity which will meet their needs.

In addition to the keynote speaker, there are many other kinds of resource people. Some will contribute to content, while others will be related to conference process. Some will conduct general sessions while others will be responsible for some form of small group sessions.

When resource people are being used, they are crucial to the conference and attention must be paid to their selection. When the DC decides to invite somebody to be a resource person, a form similar to Figure 4-2 can be used. The form should be revised to fit the individual situation and the flow of the design process.

The "Title" might become "Proposed Title" if the DC wishes the resource person to make some input on what the session will be called. There are times when the DC has an overall plan for labeling the sessions so that participants have a clearer idea of the topic. The objectives, on the form, might be stated generally, or in specific behavioral terms, depending upon the expectations of the participants. Under "Designed for" there may be actual categories of participants if such information is available and helpful. "Methodology" might contain examples, depending upon the types of resource people and their understanding of the various methodologies available to them. At this

**Name**_____

**Address**_____

**Session:**_____

  Title_____

  Date_____

  Time: from_____to_____


**Objectives:**


**Description:** (might be used for announcements)


**Designed for:** (indicate type of participants who should attend based on factors such as experience, interest, level of previous learning, etc.)


**Methodology:** (including preferred size of group, physical arrangement)

*Figure 4-2. This form elicits information from resource people that is pertinent to the conference design.*

time, the form does not ask for the logistical specifics (e.g., Do you need an overhead projector?) as this is more appropriate after agreement has been fully reached, based on the information received from Figure 4-2.

There are times when the DC will first explore if a particular resource person would be available. At other times, the letter of invitation will include Figure 4-2 as an enclosure. In either case, until this form is returned, the DC should not consider that the resource person has accepted the invitation. There are some resource people who will refuse to complete this form, or anything like it. Then, the DC must decide whether they are prepared to take the person on faith, and record of prior performance, or if the risk is too great. Some prestigious individuals may reject the form and refuse to complete it. The DC must decide when to use such a form and what to do when an invited resource person does not return the form. Even when the form is returned, it may happen that the specific data provided by the invited resource person raises some provocative questions. This is one reason why the form should be sent out as early as possible. The returned form may require that the DC reassess its invitation. In other cases the resource person may make suggestions through this form which will make a positive contribution to the design.

After a resource person has accepted the assignment, a form for gathering biographical data, such as shown in Figure 4-3, should be sent out. The material from this sheet has many purposes. It can confirm the decision of the DC or suggest a reexamination of the invitation. Other information may come to light from this form which suggests how best to use this resource person in the total design.

The biographical information has value for preconference publicity, as well as a help to the hosts and introducers.

### Hosts and Introducers

Linking the DC and the actual conduct of the conference can be a formidable task. To assist in this, the DC can identify carefully selected personnel to serve as hosts and introducers for the resource people. Although these are essentially honorific jobs, they are too important to be left to last-minute decision making or to be given insufficient consideration. Therefore, the selection of these crucial individuals should take place early in the work of the DC. The effectiveness of a good resource person can be damaged by inadequate linkage with hosts and introducers.

The host is selected by the DC to meet the resource person and make him comfortable. The meeting may take place in an airport or railroad terminal, in the hotel, or at the site. The specific place will depend upon the status of the resource person and the nature of the available ground transportation. The host may take care of the registration procedures and other required formalities.

**Name**_____

**Organization**_____

**Address**_____

**Job Title** (if relevant)_____

**Education:** (schools attended and degrees)


**Work experience:**


**Publications:**


**Honors:**


What other information do you think would be helpful to the participants who attend your session?


*Figure 4-3. Biographical information about resource people can suggest how to best use such individuals, as well as provide data important to preconference publicity.*


The host and introducer can be the same person, but the tasks performed are separate. The introducer is responsible for the session the resource person will conduct and should check out the space, signs, materials, and equipment. The introducer should link what has been happening to what is expected of the resource person. Finally, the introducer does just that—he introduces the resource person to the participants at the appropriate moment. The material from Figure 4-3 serves as the basis for the introduction. The introducer must exercise restraint and recognize that the introduction is not the most important part of the session.

## Moderators

As part of a general session, the resource person may plan to follow the initial presentation with questions from the floor. When this is done, there is the need for a moderator. This can be the introducer (sometimes called the chairperson for the session), or another person. The resource person may prefer to keep the floor and microphone and respond directly to the questions. This is possible, but a more effective technique, particularly for a large audience, is to interpose the moderator.

Using a moderator allows for more effective use of the resource person. For example, it provides the resource person with an opportunity to think through the question while attention is focused on the moderator. Additional time can be built in by having the moderator repeat the question. It is awkward to ask the resource person to listen intently to the questioner, while all eyes focus on the platform, and then rush to his feet with an immediate response. This technique makes for good TV press conferences with public officials, but it is a less effective use of a resource person at a conference. Before using the "question from the floor" technique, the DC should determine if the resource person is one who can respond spontaneously to questions in an effective manner. There are people who can write beautifully and deliver brilliant speeches but who have some difficulty when there is the need for spontaneous dialogue with the audience after the speech. It reminds one of the cartoon showing a speaker on the platform, a smoking gun in hand, asking, "Now, does anyone else have a question?"

Moderators should be carefully chosen, right after decisions have been made about resource persons. There should be a matching of the individuals who will have to work together. It is perfectly acceptable to use the position of moderator in an honorific way, giving recognition to deserving participants. But, they should also be people who are capable of handling the high pressure job of the moderator.

As the size of the group increases, there are other techniques which are advisable to increase the possibility of two-way communication. Microphones can be placed at several points in the room, and the participants can be invited to come to the microphone to ask their questions. This eliminates the need for the moderator to repeat the question for all to hear. A disadvantage of this technique is the need for people to leave their seats to come to the microphone. This will appeal to the more extroverted, who may not necessarily have the most important questions.

Using floor microphones with a large audience invites another type of behavior, called "microphonitis." This is manifested in two ways. First, there is the tendency in some individuals, when faced with a microphone, to freeze up, and either mumble or make incomprehensible sounds which they think constitute a question. The other form of behavior is the absolute inability to stop talking when faced by a microphone. (How many of our public officials have shown this behavior?) Having air time, the individual feels compelled to make a speech. He usually starts out with "Let me explain . . . " and follows that up with a long-winded background piece, at the end of which the moderator is forced to ask, "But what is the question?"

There is another alternative to encourage two-way communication in a general session and to make even more effective use of a resource person. It involves using question cards during a general session and requires the following materials and instructions.

## Materials

Small sheets of paper or 3 x 5 index cards. (These may be provided in participant materials placed on the seats before participants enter the room or distributed at the start of the session.)

## Instructions

1. During the introduction of the resource person, the moderator suggests that participants write their questions on the material provided; only one question to a card or sheet. This can be done during the presentation as the question arises.
2. At the end of the formal presentation, provide about ten minutes for participants to discuss the material presented. These are to be small informal groups with no leader or reports. Questions written down should be shared with the group. Out of the discussion, other questions may arise.
3. When a participant has a question for the resource person and it has been written on the card or sheet, the participant now holds this up in the air. Preselected people will pick up these cards and bring them to the resource person.
4. After giving the resource person a few minutes to review the questions, and group them, the moderator reconvenes the session. If appropriate, the participants might be given a break before reconvening. This affords the resource person an additional opportunity to process the questions.
5. The resource person now proceeds to respond to the question cards.

Particularly with large groups, the resource person will probably receive more questions than could possibly be answered in the time available during the general session. The unanswered questions should be retained, for they contain valuable information. The steering committee (see Chapter 11) may find material in the questions helpful in redesigning subsequent sessions. Some questions will indicate other areas of interest of the participants, which can generate follow-up activities or design changes.

## Panels

Another way to combat the problem of one-way communication during a general session is through the use of panels. There are several possibilities.

There is the *reactor panel*. The DC selects a group of participants, probably no more than four, whose function during the presentation is to listen carefully and be prepared to ask clarifying questions of the resource person. The panel so designated should represent different groups within the audience, different points of view, etc. The reactor panel should be carefully instructed to ask questions and not to engage in a direct discussion with the resource person. (That is another technique which will be discussed later under "Dialogue.") The moderator for this panel should reinforce the questioning role of the panel members. During the presentation, the panel members should be seated in the audience, but close to the podium. There are times when the reactor panel might be seated on the platform, but this can take the major focus from the resource person. After the presentation is completed, the reactor members are invited to the platform and introduced. If there is a printed program, it is preferable to put their names and other identifying material in the program. The introduction of the panel members should be very brief, and they should be prepared to start asking questions immediately. All this is more easily accomplished if there has been a prior briefing of panel members as to their roles. Also, the resource person should have been notified that there will be a panel. A preselected reactor panel can be given the following instructions:

1. Before the session, be sure you understand your assignment. Should you be reacting to the entire presentation, or are you to listen for specific points (e.g., as related to sex, race, department in company, etc.)?
2. During the presentation, write down the questions you wish to ask.
3. Review your questions, and make them short and clear.
4. Each question should focus on only *one* point.
5. Avoid questions which might require information which the resource person could not be expected to have, such as statistics, or direct quotes from speeches or papers.
6. Do not engage in an interchange with the resource person, unless the moderator suggests it.
7. Remember, your task is to help the participants get as much as possible from the speaker.
8. Remember, the moderator is in charge.

The DC, or the moderator, on their behalf, should make sure that the panel members accept these ground rules before they agree to serve on the panel. The resource person should be given a copy of the instructions as well.

When the group is not too large, fewer than fifty people, a variation of the reactor panel is to have the participants break out into groups of about ten persons. The groups are then given a period of time, about fifteen to thirty minutes, to discuss the presentation and suggest questions for the resource person. Each group then appoints a representative, and the representatives of the five different groups now become the reactor panel, on the podium, with the speaker. It is preferable to have the panel members (representatives) prepare written questions. If all the questions cannot be answered in the time available for this general session, the unanswered questions should go to the steering committee for further processing and utilization.

Another way to avoid one-way communication in the general session is to use a panel of resource people. This differs from the previous technique in that it starts out by using more than one individual. There are many ways to organize panels, and one used frequently is for the DC to select three or four resource people who can each make a contribution to the topic and relate it to a conference objective. Each of the panel members is carefully chosen because he has a unique or different point of view to contribute to the topic. The panel members are each given a stipulated amount of time, not to exceed five minutes, to make their point. Then, under the leadership of a moderator, the panel members interact around the topic. When a panel of this kind is used, the moderator must be able to control the panel through the respect the members have for the moderator. There should be a meeting of the moderator and the panel prior to the general session. The ground rules for the session should be clearly explained and accepted by all. The moderator's role is to see that there is an adequate balance of input from all members of the panel, and to ask clarifying questions as needed.

The traditional arrangement is to have the panel seated facing the audience, and this does have some merit. However, there are other seating arrangements which may facilitate the interaction among the panel members.

—— • ——

> The panel for this conference consisted of members of different minority groups—youth, women, Black, Hispanic, and a member of the silent majority. Instead of being seated at a table, the stage was set up to resemble a typical living room, with couches and chairs. The panel was asked to have a conversation among themselves, as if they were sitting in somebody's home discussing the question of minorities and the world of work. The printed program had identified each of the panel members, so no formal introduction was necessary. In this setting, the role of the moderator was less significant, as the various individuals conducted an animated discussion, while respecting the rights of the others to express their points of view. There were the usual interruptions one would find in ordinary conversation, but these only served to highlight the spontaneity of the panel.

—— • ——

The *forum* is merely an extension of the panel. It is the process whereby the audience gets involved in the discussion of the panel. It starts with a panel discussion and then moves out to involve the participants. This can be done by utilizing some of the techniques discussed earlier. For example, there can be a reactor panel. This is done by having the main panel speak from one side of the stage and the reactor panel ask questions of the main panel members from the opposite side.

## Dialogue

Usually, a dialogue is thought of as a conversation between two people. In a general session it can involve as many as three people. With more than three the panel format would probably be preferable.

The dialogue can start with the resource person making a short presentation. Then, one or two carefully selected individuals engage in a conversation (dialogue) in front of the participants.

Individuals in the dialogue should be selected because they too have some measure of expertise, although probably not as much as the resource person. The role of the dialogists is to discuss the presentation with the resource person. They can ask questions, but more importantly, it is hoped that their discussion will illuminate the issues. The DC, in selecting participants to serve as dialogists must be careful that such persons do not use this opportunity to make their own speeches. That would be more appropriate for a panel member. For the dialogue technique, the people supplementing the resource person should focus on what was said, and should try to restrict themselves to the substance of the presentation. It is also helpful to have the resource person and the dialogists meet for a brief period, prior to the session. When the general session is the first activity of that day, the resource person, moderator, and the dialogue members could meet for breakfast. It should not be a long meeting, for you do not want the dialogue to take place at the breakfast table. It should just be a warm-up, and can establish a relationship between the resource person and the dialogists.

## Media Presentations

The general session can feature a media presentation, which may serve as one-way or two-way communication.

The media presentation can be essentially for information. It is not expected that the participants will make any direct reaction to the presentation. This does not diminish its value, for if it is a good media presentation, it can still be an important part of the conference by meeting objectives. The danger is that it is too easy for a one-way media presentation to become entertainment. If this is the purpose of the general session, then this is acceptable.

An interesting media presentation can be entertaining, and still be highly informative. An ES can find that a great deal of information on its products and services can be shared using a well-designed media presentation.

In this section, we are also including the presentations known as "industrial shows." They are not only for industry, but the term is used to separate them from the shows presented for audiences who pay for their tickets. Industrial shows are paid for by a Sponsor. They are of extremely high quality, evidenced by the fact that many Broadway and Hollywood stars got their start in industrial shows. There are suppliers who specialize in these shows, and if the DC decides to include one, it is best to seek out the qualified suppliers.

A DC may decide to start the general session with a dramatic presentation—a mock jury trial being a popular device. For a small informal conference, acting by the participants can be fun with poor acting being excused. However, for a large conference with attendant problems of acoustics and lighting, the amateur theatrical can be a farce.

Media can also be used as a two-way communication technique. The media, whatever its form, is designed to serve as a stimulus to the participants. They are informed that they are not expected to merely sit and receive, but will be asked to respond upon completion of the media presentation. This can be accomplished by the panels described earlier in this section, or by some of the regular sessions, described later in this chapter.

## Regular Sessions

The term "regular" is used to differentiate the general sessions (including small groups growing out of the general session) from those designed for other purposes.

In any conference it is possible to use a variety of regular sessions. The more regular sessions that are scheduled, the more difficult is the work of the DC. This sometimes encourages a DC to plan mostly general sessions with only an occasional regular session. This limits the involvement by the participants. Generally, if greater participant involvement is desired, more regular sessions must be offered.

Regular sessions are smorgasbords. As with many conferences, a variety of objectives and participants requires having something for everybody. Despite this, it is likely that there will always be some participants who have difficulty identifying the appropriate sessions. There are ways to help participants make the necessary selections, and this will be discussed in Chapter 10.

## Breakout Sessions

Breakout sessions are those which are scheduled after the general session. It provides the participants with an opportunity to join a small group and discuss the general session content in much more depth. Usually, the membership of the small groups is predetermined, based on some specific criteria set up by the DC. All of the groups are essentially discussing the same subject matter, based on their own area of interest (see Fig. 4-1), geographical considerations for applying the material, or any other criteria which relates to the objectives.

For an ES conference the groups might break out depending upon function in the company, such as sales, production, industrial relations, etc. Or the DC may design so that the groups cut across departmental lines, if that is congruent with the objectives. When using breakout groups, there should be a clear indication of their expected output and what will be done with the results of their work.

For a PS conference there are many more variations possible because of the wide range of the participants. Where the participants are known beforehand, the design can reflect this and utilize the information to improve the possibility of reaching the conference objectives.

——— • ———

The conference started with a general session for medical personnel concerned with quality control. Then, participants went to preassigned small group sessions. The agenda for each group was the same, but the membership was heterogeneous, consisting of a variety of persons from different hospitals and different administrative and medical positions. The group membership was predesignated so as to assure this kind of representation with each group.

——— • ———

Breakout sessions can be combined with the general session by having the resource person assign work to the breakout groups. This may be questions which are asked at the end of the presentation or written material handed out to the participants in the work sessions. It may be a case study by the resource person to give the participants an opportunity to apply what was said during the general session, to a particular situation. During the work sessions, the resource person moves from group to group and is available to respond to further questions and to discuss ideas with the groups. When the general session reconvenes, the resource person can react to questions from the floor, using techniques described earlier in this chapter. It is likely that the resource person will have found, while moving from group to group, that there are certain questions which are of general interest. Some of these may not have been covered during the initial presentation, though the resource person thought they had been. In some work groups other issues may have been raised which were not covered in the general session, but which are important to the participants. The resource person can use the experience of visiting the different groups, the questions which were asked, and the discussions he heard to conduct the "wrap-up" session.

For some breakout sessions the participants will do their own processing. That is, they will decide if they need a leader, how they will get involvement of all group members, and even the form of their report, if one is required. The DC need only provide the time and space. Another format is for the DC to design structure, such as assigning a small group leader, offering a proposed agenda, and suggesting the form of report for the small group. Both designs are acceptable, but the choice should be made based on the objectives of the conference and the level of small group experience of the participants.

If many breakout groups are to be formed, the DC must carefully plan the use of space and the movement of participants from the general session to the breakout rooms and back. Time must be allowed for such movement. Participants must have no doubt about which breakout group they are to meet with. If there is free choice by the participants, the variety of choices should be obvious and clear.

## Concurrent Sessions

At first, concurrent sessions may look much like breakout sessions. However, there are some significant differences. Concurrent sessions need not follow a general session. Even when they do follow a general session, they can have a different content and be completely unrelated to the general session.

Concurrent sessions are chosen so that they represent interests of the different groups of participants who are expected to attend. There is no limit to the number of concurrent sessions, except that imposed by the ability of the DC to identify appropriate resource people, and the space limitations of the site. However, the more concurrent sessions that are offered, the more difficult is the scheduling. Some type of preselection process by the participants would be helpful.

Prior selection by the participants cannot always be made, and the DC must recognize this as they design. On the other hand, reducing the number of concurrent sessions increases the attendance of each session, and thereby reduces participant involvement. The DC must carefully balance these two possibilities, and this is another case where the prior history of the conference, regarding the use of concurrent sessions, can be helpful.

It is possible to have a combination of both breakout sessions and concurrent sessions. After a general session, some participants may wish to follow up the resource person's presentation in much more depth. This can be provided by the breakout sessions on a voluntary basis. Other participants may decide that the general session fulfilled their personal objectives, and they would like to spend the time on other objectives and topics discussed in the concurrent sessions.

Designing for concurrent sessions is very difficult. It is not just a matter of having enough sessions and enough rooms. The balance must be maintained between the topics and the resource people, and the needs of the participants. The DC will have to make some predictions as to which and how many participants would be interested in each concurrent session. The aim is to enable participants to find at least one session, in each group of concurrent sessions, that would be of prime interest. At the same time, the DC does not want to schedule all of its prime resource people at the same time. It will usually take several meetings of the DC to create the best mix for the concurrent sessions.

Hosts and introducers, discussed earlier, are essential for concurrent sessions. If possible, they should be selected because of familiarity with the topic and the resource person. Where there are many concurrent sessions, and therefore many resource people, the linkage provided through hosts and introducers is vital.

### Repeat Sessions

When the Sponsor is an ES or a small MS, it is likely that each concurrent or special session will be scheduled only once, although even in these conferences there are times when it is desirable to schedule the same session more than once. An ES may bring a resource person in from outside the company and this costs money. Therefore, the DC may want to make this outside resource available to all the participants, and not only in a general session. That would not allow for sufficient interaction. One way of handling this is to design for repeat concurrent sessions, particularly where several resource people are involved.

When repeating sessions, there is the question as to whether the groups should move from room to room, or whether the resource people should move. To design for these possibilities, we would have to know several things. For one, do any of the resource people require any special equipment, such as video tape? If so, it may be more desirable to set up the equipment in one room and have the participants move. If there are no special requirements, the DC might want to consider leaving the participants in the same room and moving the resource persons.

There are psychological factors concerned with such movement. They are difficult to identify, but they are present. When the participants are staying in the same room and the resource people are moving in and out, the question of "territorial imperative" arises. That is, the room becomes the territory of the participants and reemphasizes the external nature of the resource person. On the other hand, the converse can be designed, where the resource person stays in the same room and the participants now come to his territory. In some cases this may not be an important factor, but it is one to be considered by the DC. Obviously, moving large numbers of people from one room to another at the same time could produce a great deal of confusion. It may be more desirable to have the participants remain in the same rooms, but with provision for appropriate breaks.

In a conference offering concurrent sessions some participants may choose the "shopping approach." They do not commit themselves to any one concurrent session, but plan to spend several minutes in each. They know they may miss a valuable experience, but they are willing to trade this off by shopping around at various sessions. Sometimes they get trapped by an outstanding resource person who holds their attention, and sometimes by the logistics of the room—they just can't fight their way out!

In a free selection MS conference, it is highly unlikely that this kind of behavior can ever be controlled. However, the DC should endeavor to keep such movements to a minimum. One way is to identify those concurrent sessions which are likely to be the best drawers. These can then be scheduled more than once, and the participants will know that they will have more than one opportunity to attend, and therefore might be more inclined to limit their movements in and out of concurrent sessions.

There are times when it is not possible to identify the interests of the participants, and it may be necessary for the steering committee to make an on-the-spot decision and announce that a particular concurrent session will be offered a second, or even a third time. Of course, the steering committee should first ascertain that the resource person will be ready and willing (it might require additional finances) and space must be available.

**Prerequisite Sessions**

One area frequently overlooked is that of sessions requiring certain prior, or prerequisite experiences. Membership organizations, in particular, hesitate to discourage participants from attending any session they wish. However, this tends to make all sessions function at the lowest level. As more and more conferences are held, and as participants get more sophisticated and demanding, it becomes essential for the DC to design prerequisites for some sessions.

One method is to offer sessions at an annual conference that are extensions of sessions held in the prior year's conference. Attendance at those particular sessions can be limited to participants who attended the prerequisite session the prior year. This allows the session at the present conference to avoid repeating the material presented during the prior year, and therefore allows for a higher level of discussion.

Another method is to require participants to have some kind of credential for a particular session.

———— ● ————

The conference concerned family planning, and the participants consisted mostly of nonmedical personnel, with a small representation of physicians. As the conference proceeded, it became apparent that there was some technical information which the physicians needed, though this was not apparent at the time the DC did their work. A special session was provided, but because of the technical nature of the material, it was agreed that only the physicians would be permitted to attend that particular session.

—— ● ——

There are other ways of screening attendance for special sessions. One of these is a self-test. It should be self-administered and self-scored, so that there is no embarrassment to the participants.

—— ● ——

For an MS conference a resource person was identified who was highly competent in helping others learn how to design simulation experiences. The resource person, recognizing the limitation of time during a concurrent session, did not want to start at ground zero, but planned to work with those participants who already had some knowledge of simulations and would be interested in working at a higher, more sophisticated level. The DC felt that this was desirable, and asked the Coordinator to explore how this could be accomplished. The Coordinator worked with the resource person and they agreed that the resource person would develop a self-administered and self-scored test. Those participants who achieved a predetermined grade on the self-test became eligible to attend and take an active part in the session. Those participants who took the self-test and did not achieve the specified grade, could also attend the session but only as observers. They were to be seated in a different part of the room. Participants who did not want to take the test, or who were moving from one concurrent session to another, were also accommodated in the observer area.

—— ● ——

This approach raises some important policy considerations for the Sponsor as well as the DC. Particularly for an MS conference, there seems to be the implication that any participant should be able to attend any session. Although this is a sound democratic principle, it frustrates many resource people by forcing them to work at a low level. This low level discourages some participants from returning the following year, which in turn encourages the DC to focus their design on those who would return. Thus, the entire process becomes cyclical, forcing out the more mature and experienced participant. The use of prerequisite sessions is a policy decision, even more than a design decision.

### Track Session

A trend in designing large conferences, using concurrent sessions, is to utilize a track system. This is a design which allows the participant to identify an area of interest throughout the entire conference and follow this through related concurrent sessions. For example, a trade association might have different tracks related to the product with which its members are concerned. Five different tracks might be (1) new trends in manufacturing, (2) marketing the product, (3) consumer action, (4) federal regulations, and (5) legal implications. Throughout the several days of the conference, at any one time there would be five concurrent sessions, representing each one of the five track areas. Each time concurrent sessions are held, all five possibilities will be offered with different resource people, but all related to a specific track. If a participant is interested in just one area (e.g. marketing the product), he might attend all the concurrent sessions related to the marketing track. This still allows the participant the option of not tracking through the conference, but choosing those concurrent sessions from each track which are of most importance to him.

The track allows for another element which is not necessary in a conference, but is emerging. This is the Continuing Education Unit (CEU) which can be offered by any Sponsor where the design meets the criterion of contact hours. Extension arms of local universities can provide information on this, though they do not award this credit unless there has been some previous arrangement. We do not want to get too detailed on this, for the CEU is only one form of recognition for noncollegiate learning experiences. At the time this book is being written, there is great ferment in this whole area. In the decade to come, there may be some massive changes relating to such noncollegiate credit, and Coordinators will need to be constantly aware of the movements and the implications for conference design.

The track design lends itself to meeting the requirements of the CEU as well as other forms of recognition such as that sponsored by the American Council on Education. Several employing organizations have their in-house conferences listed in a volume published by ACE. An MS may have its own requirements, frequently labeled as "continuing education for the professions" and the design should relate to the requirements imposed by the organization. A PS desiring to increase attendance should explore all of these possibilities, before getting too far into the design process.

### From the Suppliers' Viewpoint

The major suppliers concerned with the process of designing the core of the conference are site personnel and equipment personnel.

### Site Personnel Say—

We handle many conferences, and each Coordinator and DC seems to have their own special terminology for sessions. We can deal with this, if you will tell us what you mean by a particular session. Instead, some Coordinators test us out by using their jargon to see if we understand. This wastes time and introduces confusion where none is necessary. We can help each other if the terms being used for the various elements of the conference design are clear.

Even the most conservative site is interested in helping the Sponsor get the most mileage possible out of the conference. If banners and posters will help, we will certainly consider appropriate decorations. Before the DC plans any drapery, we should discuss it. Outside some of our sites we have big signs to tell one and all that your conference is at our site. It is also possible to have big banners outside the entrance so the participants know this is the site for their conference.

Inside the site, it depends. If yours is the only conference going on at the time, it is obviously possible to give you much more space and latitude in the kinds of signs which could be posted.

If you are planning to include white space, let us know. Some of our housekeeping, recreation, and entertainment schedules are fixed. Others are flexible, and perhaps we can alter our schedules so they complement your white space design.

If you will need special equipment for general sessions, let us know as soon as possible. You do not have to commit yourselves this early in the design process, but if you do some exploration with us, we can be mutually helpful. If we do not have the equipment facilities, we can refer you to sources we have used and have confidence in. Also, as you design, if you will be in touch with us, we can share what other Coordinators have done with their conferences. This way, you get the benefit of other's experience.

Repeat sessions are always a problem. We know that you cannot give us too much detail on this until the conference is being conducted. In the early design phase, if you can at least indicate that there might be a need, we are then alerted to this possibility.

## Equipment Personnel Say—

Some of us work for a site, while others are independent contractors who service a site. If we work for a site, most of our needs are met by the previous section.

As independent contractor/suppliers we have had experience with many conferences at many sites. If you need equipment, it is usually more helpful to tell us what you want the equipment to do rather than to tell us which piece of equipment you think you need. For example, if you want a cordless mike, tell us how you want to use it. This allows us to make suggestions as to type, for there are several kinds.

# 5.
# Designing
# Related
# Conference
# Activities

In addition to the general sessions and regular sessions described in the previous chapters, there are many other activities which are part of a conference. Usually, employing organizations (ES) focus on the content of the conference, and therefore the design committee (DC) concentrates its efforts on the general and regular sessions. For a membership organization (MS) related conference activities must sufficiently interest participants to attract them to the conference. Recently, the gap between the ES and MS has narrowed significantly. The ES now recognizes the need for a variety of related activities to maximize the value of the conference.

There are two points to watch carefully. First, the DC should not stop its work at the point where the previous chapter ended. The material in this chapter is likewise within the purview of the DC. Some of these activities will require the assistance of persons who have special expertise in areas such as travel, mass feeding, arranging tournaments, etc. However, the DC is still the core group to make decisions regarding these activities. In situations where the DC terminates its work with just the general and regular sessions, there will be conflicts in the implementation of the other related activities. If there is no authoritative body or individual to negotiate the necessary trade-offs and decisions regarding the sessions and related activities, chaos and conflict will result.

The second point relates to the tendency to get "oversold." Some of the related activities to be discussed involve the use of external entrepreneurs who are very interested in selling their services. There is certainly nothing wrong with this, but there is not an equivalent pressure from those responsible for the general and special sessions. Therefore, there are conferences which seem to have general and regular sessions just to provide breaks between the related activities.

This chapter will discuss a variety of related activities, but this does not mean to suggest that every conference must have every one of these. Rather, the DC judiciously decides which of these contributes to the conference objectives. Even in related activities, the basic concept of objectives should not be lost.

This chapter covers

- Special interest groups (SIG)
- Temporary conference groups (TCG)
- Cracker barrel sessions
- Lounge areas
- Job exchange
- Spouses and children
- Field trips
- Recreation
- Banquet
- Recognition sessions
- Business sessions

## Special Interest Groups

An ES may feel that there is no real need for special interest groups (SIG), as the ES does not try to get as wide a range of people as possible to attend, but rather, selects those who are employed by the organization and directly related to the conference objectives. Within the design of the regular sessions, through the use of breakout groups, the needs of individuals with special interests can be met. The ES may find it desirable, however, to make special provisions for SIG, particularly when the conference involves individuals from around the country or the world.

For the MS the SIG is almost a must. During some conferences, the various needs of the participants can be met through the breakout sessions and the track programming described in the previous chapter. However, many of the larger membership organizations are not as homogeneous as in the past. Within one of these organizations, there can be a variety of smaller groups that meet under the umbrella of the parent organization (the Sponsor). This is fairly prevalent in professional membership conferences such as those held by the American Psychological Association, the American Society for Training and Development, and the Adult Education Association. For trade associations there is the same possibility that some are broad enough to have within them various specialties. One way of handling this is to arrange for SIG sessions, which are part of the conference and are integrated into the design.

These sessions are frequently designed by a committee from the SIG and the major responsibility of the DC is to make appropriate facilities available so that the SIG can meet and function as an internal part of the conference. There is no one best way to schedule the SIG, rather, it depends upon the relationship of these groups to the parent organization. Where such groups are highly formalized, usually referred to as divisions within the total organization, there will be a continuing mechanism whereby they can plan from year to year. Where the SIG is not formalized, the arrangements may be a bit more difficult.

One plan is to have the SIG meet either before or after the core conference. This is desirable when the SIG requires more than one full day for its activities. Pre- and post-sessions eliminate the possibility of the SIG conflicting with the design of the core conference. The DC should maintain a constant liaison with the SIG to avoid the possibility of having activities or content areas which may be in conflict with the conference objectives or flow.

Is it better to have the SIG before or after the core conference? There is no unqualified answer, but it is generally more helpful if the SIG meet after the conference. This enables them to further explore subject matter and experiences from the conference as it relates to the SIG's needs. Also, the SIG may wish to schedule some inputs which are different from the conference objectives. Some employing organizations have found that a significant number of their employees from different parts of the company attend the same professional conferences. Therefore, they use this opportunity to reduce travel costs and time by having these employees meet as a conference SIG. The session may be identified by the company name to indicate that attendance is restricted to employees of that company.

The most common design practice is to schedule the SIG within the framework of the conference so as to prevent splinter groups from emerging and scheduling conflicting activities. One possibility is to set aside one full day for just SIG sessions. During this day, no general or regular sessions are scheduled to compete with the SIG. This has the advantage of giving the SIG a significant block of time with no constraints.

This design does have two disadvantages. First, there may be some participants who are not particularly interested in any SIG, or they may have some interest, but are not willing to devote a full day of the conference to a particular SIG. Second, by setting aside a full day in the middle of the conference (a common design for the SIG), the flow and momentum of the conference is disrupted. For example, in a five-day MS conference, the SIG can be scheduled for the middle day. Some participants may attend the first two days or the last two days, inasmuch as they are not particularly interested in the middle day.

A DC can schedule alternatives on that SIG day for those participants who are not interested in the SIG. Among the alternatives are sightseeing or other field trips away from the conference site. This presents the SIG designers with a conflict situation. They are now competing with other activities which can draw participants away from the SIG.

It is not being suggested that the SIG are not helpful or desirable for an MS conference. It is just that they must be well integrated into the design process so as to present additional possibilities rather than distractions or disruptions.

## Temporary Conference Groups

The use of temporary conference groups (TCG) has been an overlooked element of conference design. As conferences get larger, the TCG offers some exciting possibilities. A TCG is a group of participants, usually not more than ten, who mutually agree to meet periodically and informally, to share conference experiences and to discuss conference topics.

Conferences attracting large numbers of participants utilize many concurrent sessions, and it is obvious that no one participant can attend all of them. As discussed earlier, one way that participants cope with this is to move from session to session, never getting the full benefit of any of them, while contributing to general disruption as they move in and out of the various rooms. As conferences get larger, participants find that they know too few other participants, and they wander aimlessly around the conference area seeking companionship. When the conference is an annual affair, participants continue to see only the same people each year, if there is no adequate provision for easily meeting others. The TCG can help meet these needs. Being part of a TCG should be a voluntary activity and the ground rules should be clearly spelled out beforehand. No matter how many TCGs are planned for at the beginning of the conference, the DC can expect about half will have been discontinued by the end of the conference.

The availability of the TCGs should be announced in the material which goes out to the participants, prior to the conference (See Figure 5-1). Participants will be given the opportunity of signing up for them either before the conference or immediately upon arrival. The DC must think through the process clearly, so that participants have clearly identifiable choices. The process should be kept as simple as possible. The DC should delegate the organization and administration of all the TCGs to one particular person (not the Coordinator), who should not make any decisions about the TCGs without getting the approval of the DC or Coordinator. Each TCG should have a designated convener. All members of the TCGs should be provided with specific instructions, indicating how the group gets organized, the prospective members, where the first meeting will take place, and how to reach the convener if any assistance is required.

*(Text continued on page 72)*

—— • ——

## TEMPORARY CONFERENCE GROUPS

In reviewing our past conferences we find that there are needs that can be met in a different way on a purely voluntary basis. They have been expressed by former participants in the following ways:

1. "I can never get to all the concurrent sessions. Yet I would like to know what goes on at some of those I cannot attend."
2. "I seem to meet the same people each year. Is there some way to help me meet new people?"
3. "Our conferences have gotten so large that I don't seem to have any opportunity to sit down with a small group of people just to talk about the conference and things related to it."

We think we have a way to help, if you wish. You are being given the opportunity to join a temporary conference group (TCG), which will meet during the conference, but with no responsibility on anyone's part to continue meeting after the conference.

The ground rules are:

1. There will be voluntary groups of ten persons.
2. The first meeting will be scheduled, but after that, the group will plan for its own meetings.
3. The TCG has no agenda, other than what it sets for itself.
4. There is no chairperson, but we will designate a convener to help organize the group.
5. The TCG can share the concurrent sessions by having members attend different sessions and reporting to the group.
6. Or, the TCG can meet each day to share conference experiences.

If you are interested, complete the attached form and return it with your conference registration. Your preregistration packet will contain the necessary information.

Your Design Committee

—— • ——

(Figure 5-1 continued on next page)

**Yes, I would like to join a temporary conference group.**

My reasons are:



The other kinds of people I would like to be with are:
Geographical area_____
Experience_____
Interests_____
Other_____
No special choice_____


Name_____

Address_____

_____

Organization (or other identifying information)

_____


Would you be interested in being a convener?  Yes_____No_____

*Figure 5-1. Participants should receive an announcement informing them of the availability, intent, and operations of temporary conference groups (TCGs).*


Each person who signs up for a TCG is given a copy of the instructions which indicate the areas in which the members of each TCG can make their own decisions, such as where and when to meet, the objectives of that particular TCG, etc. A form which can be used is shown in Figure 5-2. The DC can give each convener a set of ten forms, or they can be placed in the participant packets which they receive at registration or as part of preregistration. Only the name of the convener, the day and time, and the room for the first meeting need be specified. The other information should be filled out by each TCG member at their first meeting.

If possible, the TCG's first meeting should be on the evening preceding the opening general session. This allows time to review the conference program and to make decisions, such as which members will attend what sessions. At the next meeting, the members can share what has happened at the various concurrent sessions or other regular sessions. The actual conduct and content of each TCG should be set by the members of each group.

## INSTRUCTIONS FOR TEMPORARY CONFERENCE GROUPS

Our convener is_____

Our first meeting will be ___(day)_____

(time)_____

(room)_____

Other members of the group are:


Our purpose is:


Our next meeting is: ____(day)_____

(time)_____

(room)_____

**Figure 5-2.** *This form permits all TCG participants to indicate when and where to meet, objectives of their particular TCG, etc.*


There is a slight possibility that a TCG might separate itself from the conference. The members of a TCG may find their small group meetings of more interest than the regular conference sessions. Such behavior should not immediately be classified as a problem. At least some needs of the participants are being met through the TCG.

The convener might wish to sit in on the meetings as a regular member of the TCG. If the group is not attending any of the general or regular sessions, the convener might determine the reason and share this information with the steering committee. It could be helpful in planning the next conference.

A major problem for the TCG can be finding the time to meet. If the group is going well, the participants may wish to meet more than once a day. They do have meal times, white space time, and perhaps some of the recreation periods. If the TCG is to be an important part of the conference, the DC may consider identifying additional periods of time when the groups can meet without being in conflict with other scheduled conference activities.

### Cracker Barrel Sessions

The term "cracker barrel" may not be familiar to people from outside the U.S. or to some younger readers. Its origin is in the old style general stores which existed in the U.S. before the advent of the supermarket. In small communities and even in some urban areas, the general store served as an informal community meeting hall. People would sit or stand in a particular section of the store and exchange experiences and information. The group usually gathered around a barrel of crackers, which was made available by the storekeeper. People would munch as they talked, and the salty crackers coupled with the conversation produced a thirst. As a result, they would purchase drinks from the storekeeper, which encouraged him to make the space and the crackers readily available.

In conferences the term is used to designate an informal session in which individuals come together to discuss general issues, or sometimes specific predesignated issues. (Note: some prefer to call this kind of conference activity a "swap shop." There is no agreement or disagreement on the terms, so they are interchangeable.)

There are several variations on the cracker barrel session, depending upon need and purpose. One type is the "milk the visitor" method. This responds to the participants' need to meet with a particular person who is at the conference. This is usually a resource person who has been used in a general or regular session, but it could be somebody, not on the conference program, who has something to offer. At the cracker barrel session, the climate is as informal as possible. It is expected that participants will move in and out of sessions when there are several scheduled for the same time, but obviously, the "visitor" will remain at his assigned place. The visitor is advised not to make a speech, but rather to engage in a dialogue with the participants. There are no specified objectives which must be reached other than the objective of providing an opportunity for an exchange between the visitor and the participants.

Given the reason for utilizing the visitor, there will be a specific topic related to his area of expertise or experience. Some cracker barrel sessions draw participants by virtue of the topic, while others draw because of the visitor. These sessions are generally scheduled for late in the day, after the general session and regular sessions have terminated. A favorite time is after the end of the daily sessions and before the beginning of any evening activity. The sessions can also be offered after dinner and terminate whenever the group or visitor feels they have had enough.

Although the session is no longer held around a real cracker barrel, the climate can be created by substituting coffee or soft drinks. It is not advisable to serve liquor, since this produces a different climate, perhaps not as appropriate for this type of session. It creates problems when the behavior of some participants begins to deteriorate under the influence of alcohol.

Cracker barrel sessions are usually held in individual small rooms. This way, participants can go from room to room, visiting as many as they wish. It is also possible to have the cracker barrel sessions in one large room with small circles of chairs in various parts of the room. These must be spaced far enough apart to minimize interference among groups. Some facilities provide portable screens which can be helpful when this arrangement is used. Each cracker barrel session has a sign, indicating either the topic or the speaker in that area, depending upon the design. A single large room has the disadvantage that it can deteriorate into a popularity contest. Some participants may be influenced by seeing groups with large attendance, and tend to move in that direction as well. Some people tend to go with the crowd, even if they don't know why they are going. When sessions end at different times, the groups ending early and moving out of the room can cause other groups to terminate before they are really ready to do so. Both the large and small room set-ups for the cracker barrel have their advantages and limitations, and the DC should explore them while designing these sessions, to see how they may best contribute to the conference.

A completely different approach to the cracker barrel is to plan the sessions without any outside person or visitor. The session is strictly a peer session to enable participants to share. The design suggested above can be used for this, but there is another interesting design possibility. This is the "cracker barrel luncheon."

———— • ————

The DC planned a cracker barrel luncheon for an MS conference. The program listed the ten possible topics as selected by the DC. Participants entered the room where the luncheon was scheduled to take place and found thirty tables set for eight people to a table. Each table had a sign on it indicating the topic for that particular table. Ushers at the door encouraged the participants to enter and seat themselves at whichever table had a topic of interest to them. A few tables had been labled "to be decided" and this was for persons who just wanted to talk to other participants but had no particular topic in mind. As the tables filled up, luncheon was served. There was no formal opening, and no formal closing. The arrangement was merely a facilitating one to enable the participants to meet and talk about topics of interest to themselves with others who shared that interest.

———— • ————

### Lounge Areas

Additional informal information swapping can be generated by a lounge area. The DC must identify an area within the conference facility where participants can meet in a completely unstructured manner.

It is not mandatory that only conference topics be discussed, but a lounge area provides the possibility that this can happen. This should not be confused with the cocktail party or social hour where the focus is strictly on "recharging the batteries," "attitude adjustment" or some other designation for the drinking period. Conference topics may be discussed during those activities, but the primary objective is socializing.

The existence of a lounge area should be announced beforehand, and the room or area clearly designated. Participants are invited to come to this area to meet other participants who wish to talk about any aspect of this conference. For a small ES or MS conference a room can be set aside with coffee available. There should be adequate and comfortable seating. The room should not be available during the general or regular sessions, but only when there are no conflicting activities.

The lounge area is sometimes set up in the exhibit area, as one way of encouraging the participants to visit the exhibits. This requires a designated space in the exhibit area where participants can sit down and talk with others. Some exhibitors may not be enthusiastic about this, as they would prefer that the participants remain on their feet, going from exhibit to exhibit. Exhibitors are usually agreeable about paying for the coffee and cake when the lounge is set up in the exhibit area. The DC should explore the situation with the exhibitors (essentially through an exhibitors' committee) so that there is mutual understanding of the purpose and operation of the lounge area, when it is within the exhibit hall. There are other variations of the lounge area idea:

——— ● ———

The Sponsor was an ES and the participants came from various parts of the organization. The conference was held at an excellent site with a swimming pool (it was summer) and other recreational facilities. The Sponsor and DC insisted that there should be evening sessions. The Coordinator suggested that it was unlikely that the participants could possibly go for four days continuously, from 8:00 a.m. to 10:00 p.m. He recommended a "self-renewal period." This was from 4:00 p.m. to 6:00 p.m. each evening just before the social hour was scheduled. During the self-renewal period, there were certain ground rules. If a participant was in his room, it was a signal and he did not want to be disturbed. A special lounge area was designated, and it was agreed that participants who came to this area wanted to discuss some aspects of the conference. When participants were in any of the recreational areas, there was obviously no restriction on their conversations. This allowed the various participants to meet their individual needs.

——— ● ———

For the MS conference the lounge area can provide an easy way for participants to meet each other. The announcement describing the lounge area can note that participants should wear their name badges to gain entrance, and that they should feel free to approach and talk to strangers in the lounge area.

## Job Exchange

Helping people find jobs may not be a stated objective of a conference, but it certainly ranks among the not-so-hidden agendas. Even if not planned for, it will take place. The DC can plan for this inevitable occurrence and build the job exchange into the conference design.

For an ES conference the job exchange is almost as important as for an MS conference. A small conference for a small ES may not need a job exchange. For a large multi-site Sponsor, the job exchange will be happening even if nothing formal is planned. Depending upon the objectives of the conference and the personnel practices of the employing Sponsor, there may be formal job exchange possibilities. For an ES the job exchange will have to conform to the personnel practices of the organization. If the organization uses a post and bid system, this can be built into the conference. There might be a posting of job vacancies at the different sites, and the bid can take the form of arranging meetings with designated contact individuals to discuss the job possibilities. A formal or semiformal arrangement is more helpful than relying on the inevitable grapevine. By being too informal, one runs the risk that the information about a job vacancy may not reach those who are really interested and qualified.

The job exchange should not be so highly developed that it becomes a major aspect of the conference, unless this is one of the objectives. For some multinational companies, a job exchange is one of the objectives of their international meetings.

The job exchange is usually not one of the objectives of the PS conference, though some of the larger public seminars have served this function, even when it has not been a stated objective. As participants come from a variety of organizations, there is always the possibility of talk about job opportunities which have not been broadly advertised.

When the MS is a professional organization, it is highly likely that the job exchange is an expected aspect of the conference. In the past the job exchange has assisted younger members in making the contacts so essential to movement in their field. The older members usually have other contacts and do not need to rely on the job exchange, unless economic conditions warrant it.

The DC should notify the participants as early as possible that the conference includes a job exchange. Both potential employer and employees will have to make some preparations. The employer (whether participant or not) must know what forms, if any, are to be filled out, and should provide some written statement of the job, qualifications, etc. The employer must also indicate how contact is to be made. Are applications to be forwarded to the potential employer, or will the applicant be contacted? Will there be somebody at the conference to conduct interviews?

The participant seeking a new position must have some kind of resumé. Where volume is expected, the person handling the job exchange should develop a form to provide for some kind of comparability. For some professions, e.g., newspaper, the participants will bring clip books or other indications of professional accomplishments.

There are two essential elements in setting up a job exchange, particularly for a professional MS. The first is that there should be a qualified individual handling the files. Frequently, the job seeker wants to avoid any publicity about the process. Likewise, there are employers who do not want to be too obvious in their search for new employees. Of course, the Equal Employment Opportunity Act requires that the employer advertise as widely as possible. The person responsible for the job exchange should know the EEO law, as well as other legislation regarding discrimination. This underscores the need for a qualified person to handle the job exchange.

The person responsible for this activity may also be expected to meet with the job seekers and provide at least a minimal amount of job counseling. If so, the person selected for the activity needs the experience and qualifications of this particular area of human services. Recognizing these requirements, the DC tends to rely on a commercial search organization. Although this provides the required professional assistance, the DC faces the decision as to how they will choose one organization over another. The decision is a difficult one, particularly when there are competing search organizations.

Where the DC does build in a job exchange, there also has to be the appropriate physical facility, not only for controlling the various documents, but also for conducting interviews. The selection of the facility is based on factors such as the stature of applicants, the practices of employers, and the kinds of discussions which must take place.

### Spouses and Children

In past years it was customary to talk of "wives" sessions. The DC must be cautious, for such a title is not only archaic, but could be misleading. There is a need to change the title and the thinking to spouses.

Because more women are entering the work force and joining professional societies, it is becoming more common to find a woman attending a conference as a participant, and her husband as the extra person, the spouse. Adequate provision is required for spouses, where the Sponsor is interested in encouraging spouses to attend.

The DC must decide the relationship of the spouses to the general and regular sessions. One option is to open the general sessions to the spouses, where space is available and it does not pose a problem.

—— • ——

The DC agreed with the recommendation of the Coordinator that spouses should be invited to attend the general sessions which were scheduled for 8:30 a.m. During the discussion which led to this decision, several members of the DC commented that the spouses would not want to get up that early unless there was an outstanding speaker or presentation. The Coordinator noted that the DC had done an excellent job of selecting resource people for the general sessions and therefore could anticipate a turnout from the spouses. Planning conservatively, the DC selected a site which could accommodate the expected participants with only a limited amount of extra space for spouses. Unfortunately, the Coordinator was more accurate in his estimate than the DC. The resource people proved so attractive that many spouses did attend the general sessions, and there was a consistent shortage of space. The limitations of the site did not allow for obtaining a larger room even though the first of the four general sessions showed that with the attendance of the spouses, the room was too small.

———— • ————

Another decision to be made is whether spouses can attend the regular sessions. Minimal spouse attendance is expected at regular sessions and concurrent sessions because of their specialized nature.

If the DC anticipates that spouses will attend these sessions, they can be accommodated. If the design calls for participants to be assigned to regular groups during the breakout sessions, provision can also be made for the spouses. When the small group membership is assigned, the DC can set up special groups of spouses. The spouses' groups can also discuss the material presented during the general session but from a spouse viewpoint rather than the participant viewpoint. It usually is not necessary that these discussions be fed back during the wrap-up general session, as is suggested for regular participant small groups. Making provision for spouses is also important for an ES conference.

———— • ————

The conference was for regional representatives of a major company. During the conference, the participants were being informed of management decisions and operational plans for the coming year, new management policies regarding community relationships, and information on new product lines. Each day was devoted to one of these topics. The general session consisted of a presentation by one of the corporate level people involved in that topic. This was followed by breakout sessions based upon the function of the participant within the company but crossing regional lines.

The Sponsor suggested that most of the participants, who were men, might want to bring their wives. There was a fairly good turnout, generally wives in two categories. Many were quite young, without children or jobs that might inhibit their attendance. The others were wives whose children had already left home and who did not have a job. Therefore, the DC designed for these two groups. The younger wives, as might be expected, had husbands who had been working for the company a short time. These wives wanted information about the company so they could more fully understand the presentations at the general sessions. The older wives, whose husbands had worked for the company longer, had less need for such information. (Of course, these were generalities and the DC risked not meeting the needs of the few who did not fall neatly into these categories.)

The DC, during its planning, selected company officials appropriate to each group who could lead the discussions following the general sessions. The result, as measured by written and oral feedback, was a better understanding on the part of the spouses (in this case, wives) of the problems their partners would be confronted with in the year to come.

——— • ———

In this experience it should be pointed out that attendance by spouses at the general sessions was not mandatory. No attendance list was used nor was there any attempt to encourage or coerce anyone to attend. However, attendance was quite high. The company officers who conducted the spouse sessions were surprised at the level of interest and understanding. Recent literature in the field confirms that many wives are interested in becoming more involved in their husbands' work life, particularly at the white collar level. It is doubtful if the same behavior would be found where the husband has a blue collar job. It would also be interesting to find more examples where the spouses are men and to determine how interested they are in their wives' economic role.

Where the spouses are predominantly women, there is still the tendency to treat them as frivolous and unconcerned with real issues. Too often a DC provides for shopping tours, talks on cosmetics, and other topics unrelated to the conference objectives. Although there are many women who prefer these kinds of sessions, their number appears to be decreasing. Even women who are not committed to women's lib still want to be involved in the part of their husbands' lives which takes up so much of their waking hours.

In certain cities where conferences are frequently held, shopping is a different experience from what may be available back home, wherever that may be. In such a case, special sessions devoted to shopping possibilities would be appropriate. Special shopping tours might be organized where the products are so "foreign" that help would be welcomed to make the shopping tour a pleasant and rewarding experience.

What about including the men on shopping tours? If the shopping area is unique, or the products available are not just for the female shopper, why not include the men? "Shopping" should not be equated with "women," nor vice versa. If there is the possibility that there will be many participants interested in shopping, the DC should determine the possibilities as well as the hours most desirable for this out-of-conference activity. In some cities, the shopping hours may conflict with the usual conference hours. The DC will have to decide which is to take precedence at given times or risk losing some of the participants, with or without spouses, to the temptations of the market place.

It is much easier to discuss spouse activities for women than it is for men. We have too little experience in providing for men who are spouses of conference participants. It has been suggested earlier that the DC develop a profile of the kinds of participants they expect will attend the conference. Likewise, the DC needs to develop a profile of the spouses as to sex, interests, etc. Some programs designed for women can just as easily be designed for men, that is, to enable the husband to understand what his wife is doing, either as an employee or as a member of the Sponsoring organization.

A realistic factor which confronts the DC is budget. Where the Sponsor is an ES, and spouses are invited, adequate budget should be provided for the spouses. If not, the invitation proves to be meaningless if the participant cannot afford to bring the spouse. Or the participant may feel a pressure to bring his spouse even at the risk of upsetting the family budget. The Sponsor should clarify the economic side of the invitation. For an ES conference it can be assumed that the Sponsor is paying the expenses for the participant, but are the expenses for the spouse likewise to be covered by the Sponsor? If so, does this mean all expenses, or only part of them? For public seminars, there is less tendency to bring spouses, therefore, the provision for them is usually minimal. It should be clarified beforehand that if spouses are welcome, they still cannot attend the sessions without payment of the fee.

For an MS conference there is usually one fee for the participant and a reduced fee for the spouse. The extent of the reduction is influenced by a variety of factors. For example:

- Will spouses be allowed to attend *all* sessions?
- Will spouses be admitted into the exhibit hall?
- Will spouses be able to partake of any free meals or services provided by the conference or the exhibitors?
- Will spouses require special tickets for any of the activities?

As more conferences are held in or near parks and other family type attractions, participants are bringing along their children as well as their spouses. In recent years, suppliers have emerged who will provide children's programs to complement a conference. The DC should make an initial decision whether to encourage participants to bring their children. If so, then some of the same factors discussed in relation to spouses will also apply to children. Also, having children along with some participants will influence their participation in some related activities such as field trips, recreation, and entertainment. If having children is desirable, there are excellent alternatives in all related areas.

A much more difficult problem is what to do about a participant who brings a companion who is not a spouse. This situation will not arise during an ES conference. It could during both the PS and MS conference. There are many kinds of problems which arise, including emotional and legal ones. There are places where it is illegal for two single individuals of the opposite sex to share the same bedroom in a public facility. The DC can do little about this, but should turn it over to the site personnel to handle. There are probably other problems related to this issue, but it is doubtful if they could be helped by any further discussion in this book at this time.

## Field Trips

There are various kinds of travel related to conferences. Although not usually classified as field trips, the DC should also consider the growing practice of pre- and postconference package tours.

When the participants may be taking a tour on the way to the conference, the DC must plan for adequate time between arrival and the first opening session or other conference activity. This is not only to provide the opportunity for the participants to relax after the travel and excitement, but also to allow for any delays which can occur. Where unscheduled airlines are used, this is a distinct possibility. It is not that unscheduled airlines are any less efficient or safe, but they may lack the back-up equipment or personnel to allow for departure and arrival at the designated times.

If a postconference trip is available, the DC should plan for linkage between the close of the conference and the subsequent trip. If sufficient time is not allowed, the participants may spend their time packing and otherwise preparing for the postconference trip instead of attending the closing sessions.

Even after the participants arrive and the conference has started, there can be travel outside the site. This occurs during the regularly scheduled conference period, and the DC must plan for these field trips in a variety of ways. The planning should occur very early in the design process, while seeking the appropriate conference site. The DC should look for what has been termed "site relevance." That is, a site is chosen because it has something special to offer. The DC can provide for the appropriate field trip within the design. It is unfortunate and frustrating to be at a conference with many interesting sites outside the door, and to have a design which does not allow for the trips. Of course, for an MS conference the participants may vote with their feet and not attend some conference sessions, thereby negating the prior work of the DC. The following sections describe the various types of field trips.

### Conference Related

A conference site may have been chosen because of something in the area which is of interest to the participants such as a factory. Therefore, the DC should make provision to visit the factory and perhaps even for participants to receive VIP treatment while there. Many factories have special provision for tours, particularly if the number in the party is not too great. The DC can make all the necessary arrangements beforehand with the prospective host, even though it may not be possible to identify exactly the number of participants who will take part in the plant tour.

When the host for the tour is an operating site, such as a factory or school, the most appropriate times for the visit should be ascertained, as well as the number which can best be accommodated. Then, the DC makes adequate provision by requiring prior sign-up, or uses some other control mechanism so that the conditions set forth by the host can be met. There should be sufficient notice of the field trip given to the participants, so that they do not feel they have been deprived of the opportunity to decide whether or not to take advantage of the activity. It may be necessary for the DC to arrange for more than one prospective host in order to meet the varying needs of the different participants, or the large number who may wish to take advantage of the field trips.

A conference related field trip should be scheduled within the framework of the conference design. This includes adequate briefing of the participants before the trip, so they know what to look for and have some knowledge of the host before the trip begins. On his return from the field trip the participant should have an opportunity to rethink what happened in order to maximize the experience.

### Historical

The bicentennial year in the U.S. encouraged the development of previously historical sites and aroused the interest of Americans in historical field trips. Some of the historical sites are extremely interesting, and when the conference is being held near an historical site, the DC can make provisions for a field trip. This field trip is not conference related, unless the participants are teachers or travel agents, but the activity still comes within the purview of the DC. Early planning can assure that the historical field trip does not become a competing activity to some essential part of the conference design.

As a nonconference related activity, it has merit in providing a break in an otherwise very full conference program. The DC may wish to provide for the historical field trip in the middle of a conference which last four or more days.

The DC need not get involved in the actual conduct of such a field trip. The local chamber of commerce, patriotic societies, and government agencies have ample resources to identify places of interest and can help make arrangements. The DC looks to these resources for the planning of the field trip. The decision regarding scheduling the field trip should be made early enough to allow for planning at the local level and integration of the trip into the conference design. The DC can expect to find that local holidays and festivals will vary from one part of the country to another. If there is a government operated historical facility, it may be free of charge, while a private facility usually has an entrance fee. In either case, the DC needs to know this beforehand so as to arrange for the financial side of the trip, and to inform the participants. When transportation is needed, this too must be arranged for, prior to the conference. The DC coordinates this with local traffic flow and similar conditions, as related to the conference design for other activities. All of this reinforces the need for the DC to rely on local resources for arrangements, but always, carefully coordinated through the DC so as not to dilute the conference design.

### Entertainment

Many conference sites provide in-house entertainment. This can range from room service to a very elaborate night club with a bar and a dining room. When the participants of an MS conference anticipate that there will be entertainment available, the DC should explore the possibilities. (They may even want to take a trip to the site prior to the conference to study the possibilities.)

Usually, the site management expects the participants to utilize the in-house entertainment facilities. This may be the basis for making some meeting rooms available at no cost, or at a very low cost. It may also be the basis for special, low rates for bedrooms for participants. If the DC arranges field trips to take the participants away from the site for entertainment, the management may consider this as a show of bad faith by the Sponsor. The mutual expectations about entertainment should be clarified.

The U.S. is so vast that the possibilities for entertainment are worthy of a book, but patterns continually shift and a book would quickly become dated. If a conference is being held in some part of Texas, even in large cities like Houston or Dallas, the DC can arrange a field trip to a ranch outside the city. The city dwellers among the participants would get an interesting view of ranch life in Texas. There are ranches which provide horse shows and mini-rodeos, and follow this with the traditional Texas barbeque. The experience is unique to that section of the country, and participants coming from other parts of the U.S. would welcome this kind of entertainment provided by the DC.

In urban areas the entertainment field trip might consist of providing tickets, purchased on a bloc basis, to a Broadway show in New York, or a baseball or football game in other cities, depending upon the season and the stadium. The cautions raised earlier are still valid—where the entertainment is built in as part of the conference, and it should be, the DC takes action before the conference design is locked in.

The ES has discovered that a conference for employees longer than two days can be improved by providing for some entertainment. Where the cultural island approach is being planned, an entertainment field trip can prove a welcome diversion. Some of the participants may feel uncomfortable having their physical movements limited to the conference site. Providing a field trip for entertainment contributes to self-renewal which is helpful to any participant. Some company-owned facilities prohibit the sale of liquor, or do not allow liquor on the premises. Still, there are some participants who like to have a drink. The entertainment field trip can be, for them, just a few hours in a nearby town or village where a bar is available. Once again, the DC makes this a voluntary activity, so those who do not wish to drink are not forced to spend several hours in a bar.

## Providing Alternatives

Where the Sponsor is an ES, it is likely that whatever field trip is planned will be attended by all participants. A possible exception, as noted above, is when the field trip for entertainment is solely directed towards drinking.

A PS usually does not include field trips, unless there is something special about the surrounding area. Even here, the DC makes the information available to the participants, but does little else. Therefore, providing alternatives is not necessary.

For an MS conference the range of participants is usually so great that it is unlikely that any particular field trip would be of interest to all the participants. Therefore, the DC provides alternatives. One is to schedule nothing at all and to allow the participants to seek out their own field trips. In most places one can find local ticket agents and travel agents who are pleased to arrange for field trips. Generally speaking, these agents are experienced and cooperative, but there is always the possibility that there are some who would exploit the participants and not give fair value. Although the Sponsor is not involved, a negative climate can be engendered. This would affect the conference as well as the Sponsor. Therefore, it is necessary for the DC to exercise some control in involving organizations and individuals who will provide alternatives to field trips for the participants.

Another alternative is to make provision for the participants who do not wish to leave the conference site but would prefer to stay and talk informally to others. The cracker barrel/swap shops discussed earlier can be scheduled at the same time as field trips. This should not be the only time these sessions are scheduled, as many who go on the field trips might also want to attend. Using this design approach as an alternative to the field trip suggests that the topics for discussion should arise from those who choose to stay at the conference site.

## Recreation

Much has been said of the Protestant Work Ethic, and it has influenced many a DC. For an ES it has been customary for the DC to schedule for almost every working moment, to avoid the criticism that the participants were vacationing and enjoying themselves. It is now recognized that recreation is not only helpful, but almost mandatory. Particularly when the conference is to go for more than two days, recreation is most desirable. The form the recreation takes is circumscribed by the available facilities and the interest of the participants. The next chapter will discuss site selection, but we must consider it here as it relates to the design process.

As with field trips, recreation should be available, but not required. The recreational activities relate to the site and the age and background of the participants. Executives who are out of shape should not be persuaded to become actively engaged in recreational activities for the first time at the conference. Care should be exercised when recreation consists of highly competitive sports, so that the emotion generated during the recreational activity does not influence conference behavior. A softball game in which the teams have become highly competitive, and where side money bets are being placed, may seem to present no problems. A close call on one of the plays that is challenged by one group of players can be followed up by someone seeking "revenge" during the conference. If this sounds overly cautious, watch the behavior of some people during and immediately after a team sport. Not too many years ago, in South America, the tension aroused by a soccer game produced a war between two countries.

The DC seeks recreation which minimizes the competitive factors unless there is a fair centainty that the behavior will not be carried over into the conference. The DC cannot assume responsibility for the behavior of all the participants. When individuals organize their own recreation, there is little the DC can or should do.

Often, participants need to legitimately disengage from the verbal communication that is the basis for the conference. The DC should schedule half days or other designated periods of time when those who seek exercise and recreation can easily find it.

If the conference design does not allow for recreation, some of the participants may choose to miss sessions in order to seek the recreation they desire. Once this has happened, the participants may find it difficult to reenter the conference flow, and therefore, choose either to leave early, or to spend much of the remaining conference time in recreational pursuits.

There are some recreational activities over which the DC has no control and should not seek control. For example, there are the poker and bridge players who need this activity as much as the jogger needs his. The DC allows the mature participants to make their own arrangements for card games. This is one of the several elements of conference behavior which is outside the purview of the DC. The exception is where the laws prohibit gambling of any kind. The DC should alert the participants to this, but does not have any role in enforcement.

Where the site has a casino, as in Puerto Rico, the DC must know the hours of operation to avoid conflict in conference scheduling. Not everybody will go to the casino, but when this recreational activity is available, the DC is advised to avoid competition. Some participants may opt for the casino rather than the conference sessions.

## Banquet

A banquet serves many functions in a conference design, and the least of these is eating. When the objective is mass feeding, the DC merely negotiates this with the facility, but when there is a banquet, it is expected that there is some kind of activity before and/or after the food.

For the ES there may be some company protocol which the DC knows or must ascertain. This information may automatically decide the factors which will be discussed in this section. The PS may avoid the banquet as being too cumbersome and unnecessary, though eating together is common in public seminars. For the MS the banquet can become a traumatic element of design, but a necessary one.

The banquet provides a confrontation in two areas. The first is the seating arrangements, to be discussed later in this section, and the second is that the banquet should be consistent with the climate of the conference. The work of the DC can be destroyed if the banquet is merely handed over to the site personnel with little relationship to the total climate set by the conference design.

Coordinators are frequently asked "When should the banquet be held?" There is no easy answer to this, as it must reflect the total design. Some Sponsors have requested that the banquet be held early in the conference, so it becomes part of the keynote activities. Other Sponsors have requested that it be scheduled as close to the end as possible, to encourage participants to stay.

A banquet includes both luncheon and dinner activities, though it is more commonly associated with the latter. By having it in the evening, there is the flexibility of time and content, including entertainment. Usually, an evening meal costs more than a luncheon, and this too must be considered by the DC. Of the many variables to be considered, the three which provoke the most concern are formal or less formal, seating, and program.

## Formal or Less Formal

In the past, banquets at a conference tended to be formal affairs. It was expected that formal attire (i.e., dinner jackets and long gowns) was required. Styles constantly change, and at this time the trend is away from formal attire, with people generally doing their own thing. For some participants, however, the annual banquet is the time to bring out their formal attire and they bring this with them to the conference. If this is the case, the DC should confirm this in the material being sent out to participants before the conference. If the decision is to allow less formal attire, then the DC makes this known to the prospective participants.

A banquet, by definition in conference design, requires some degree of formality. There is a wide range of possibilities, and the DC should make decisions about these. If not, these decisions may be made by the site personnel to the detriment of the activity.

A trend which contributes to informality is the growing tendency towards having a buffet banquet. This has come about more because of the cost than for any desire to be less formal. Still, the effect is the same. When the participants go through a buffet line to get their own food, the climate will be less formal, but it can still be a banquet. In such situations, the head table (if there is one) either goes through the line first or they do not use the line, but are served while seated at the head table. In either case, the banquet will be less formal than if there is regular service by waiters. The degree of formality will also influence the seating and program arrangements.

### Seating

Seating at the banquet may require some preconference planning. If so, the DC assumes this responsibility. If there are no prior arrangements to be made, then the banquet seating may be left to the steering committee or Coordinator.

For an ES banquet the seating is not overly significant. Usually, the group is small and free seating is appropriate. (Free seating is the term used to describe the situation where participants choose their own seats.) If there are status needs within the organization, seating can be a problem which the DC must consider. This can be handled by having name plates designating the seating. The DC may not actually lay this out but has responsibility of seeing that the task is delegated to a specific individual. When the Sponsor is a very formal, hierarchal organization, the seating arrangements have to be explored before the conference, as it may determine which company officials are to be invited and where they are to sit. The DC should not wait until the conference begins to send out invitations and ascertain who is likely to attend.

For a large MS banquet seating becomes important, if only because of the numbers to be seated. Physical arrangements must be considered. Will there be a head table? This is traditional and common, but this means that those who are to sit at the head table must be notified before the conference. If the DC does not do this, the time for the banquet will arrive, and the make-up of the head table becomes a major crisis. The selection of those to be seated involves internal politics in the sponsoring organization, and the DC must explore the possible ramifications. The DC also provides for the appropriate gathering of the head table guests, so they can enter the banquet hall at the prescribed time in the correct order. If there are to be introductions, the DC determines who will be responsible for obtaining the necessary biographical material and suggests ways of limiting the introductions.

When there are many people at the head table to be introduced, the DC should select an individual who is capable of making the necessary introductions without accompanying speeches. If possible, the introducer should have a sense of humor so the introductions are entertaining and hold the interest of the audience. For straight introductions, the protocol within the organization may determine who is to do the introducing. It is, however, not absolutely necessary to have a head table.

——— ● ———

The DC expressed dissatisfaction with the traditional head table and the parade of the dignitaries, because it was not congruent with the conference climate of trying to emphasize the mutual responsibilities of members and officers of the Sponsor. The DC arranged to have the banquet hall set up with tables, each seating ten persons, and no head table. At each of the tables, one or two seats were designated as reserved. The participants entered the hall and picked the table they wanted to sit at, leaving the reserved seats open. The DC arranged that the house lights be dimmed, and the officers and major employees of the Sponsor entered and were identified. Instead of going to a head table, those introduced went to a predesignated table and took the reserved seats. Each table had one or more of the national figures, people whom the participants knew by name but had probably never met. The feedback from the membership was very enthusiastic. Subsequent feedback from the officers indicated that they found it extremely helpful to be able to sit and talk with participants during the banquet, rather than being isolated at the head table with no possibility for interaction.

——— ● ———

## Program

Should there be a program at a banquet? This depends upon the objectives of the activity. The DC should decide if the major purpose is to provide mass feeding, to have the participants hear a leading speaker, to distribute awards, to be entertained, or some combination of all of these. If there is to be a speaker, then the DC must decide if he is to be entertaining or informative.

The ES can have a speaker from some part of the organization with which the participants do not usually have direct contact. If the group is small, an opportunity is provided to interact with a selected company official.

An MS may use the banquet to encourage attendance for the entire conference. In that case the banquet is scheduled for the last night before the day the conference is to end. It is hoped this encourages the participants to stay for the banquet and at least part of the following day. For this purpose it is best to have a speaker who is either a big name whom everybody will recognize and want to hear, or one who is known as entertaining.

A resource for banquet entertainment is that which is found in the local area. The DC is not expected to know of such resources, but there are organizations and individuals in all parts of the country that can help. Providing entertainment for banquets has become big business and there are firms that specialize in this.

A banquet can be the appropriate time and place to present awards. The style can be similar to that used for the Academy Awards ceremony. The usual MS banquet cannot be expected to equal the appeal that the Hollywood activity does. When awards are to be part of the banquet, the DC should explore the possibility of making the ceremony congruent with the style and objectives of the conference. The ground rules should be carefully set forth as to whether the recipients are to make acceptance speeches or just murmur their "thank you" into the microphone. The awards may be accompanied by scrolls or certificates setting forth the reason for the award, but reading them aloud is not a good idea.

Some awards are appropriate for distribution at a banquet. For example, when one or two outstanding individuals are to be recognized, the banquet can be the place. The DC decides if there will be acceptance speeches, and if so, suggests guidelines as to length and content. The DC may notify the prospective recipients in advance, or the notification may take place at the banquet. The recipients should be advised to forego any listing of those who have been helpful to the recipient in the task which merited the award.

There are other times and places for awards, and the DC should utilize these rather than the banquet. In rare cases, when the recipient may also be a good banquet speaker, the DC can combine the award with a speaker at the banquet.

## Recognition Sessions

The range of recognition sessions can go from just reading off names to a multimedia presentation. The DC should decide at what point in the conference design recognition is best given and in what form. There can be more than one session.

The selection of recipients for awards should be made by a committee, other than the DC. Organizations that give awards usually have some mechanism for identifying the deserving individuals or groups; the most common device being an awards committee. This committee should forward the necessary information to the DC. It is even possible for the awards committee to design a session and submit this to the DC for their final decision.

For some MS conferences the recognition ceremonies have been repeated so often that they have become rituals. It may merely remain for the DC to identify that individual who will have the responsibility for conducting the session.

When possible, the DC should reexamine the recognition ritual. The passage of time suggests that forms of public recognition change. The recipients are usually members or organizations related to the Sponsor. An ES can utilize a conference to recognize particular employees or units of the organization that have done outstanding work.

For an MS the recognition of members is important. When the officers are elected annually, there is some kind of recognition for the outgoing officers. This may take the form of a memento, scroll, or plaque.

The Sponsor may choose to recognize nonmembers who have made a contribution to the goals and purposes of the organization. Honor is frequently accorded to legislators at the national and state level for their legislative activities which relate to the Sponsor. When the DC is notified that the recipients are important political figures, appropriate protocol is identified and followed. This includes titles, forms of address, and seating at the session.

There are other non-members who can be granted some form of recognition. The committee making the selection should keep the DC informed of their decisions. This should be done as early as possible in the design process, to minimize confusion and conflict. The situation may arise where a nonmember is being recognized for some speech or writing which is in direct contradiction in principle to a session scheduled at the conference. It is perfectly acceptable and even desirable to present varying points of view at a conference. However, what is the result when the spokesperson for one point of view receives recognition, while a resource person with an opposing point of view is forced to sit passively in the audience?

Earlier, it was suggested that awards and recognition given at the banquet should not be accompanied by speeches. When a special session other than the banquet has been designed for recognition, speeches are possible and desirable. The DC should work with the awards committee to make the recognition session as meaningful and important as the rest of the conference.

———— ● ————

During the conference, an award was to be given for the winning industrial design for that year. The awards committee met and made their decision. They also proposed an agenda for the awards session. The chairperson would briefly read the criteria for making the awards, and another committee member would then tell why the committee made the awards they did. Then, the winning design would be projected on a screen, using slides. There would be several so the design could be observed from many angles. The recipient would then be given a plaque and allowed to make a speech of under five minutes pointing out highlights associated with the development of the design.

———— ● ————

An ES may give a particular unit of the company an award for some out-standing activity. This is common in sales organizations where a region has outstripped all others or in some way exceeded its goal. But recognition need not be limited to sales units. To the degree possible, there should be some description of the activity which has won recognition for that unit. If it is a small conference, then a model, replica, or handout might demonstrate the reason for the award. Where the conference is larger, there is much in the way of media which can enable the participants to share in the reason for the award.

The reason for the award, or the recipient, can be of interest to more than just the participants at the conference. The Sponsor may wish press, radio, and television coverage. The DC usually does not get involved in public rela-tions. Larger conference sites generally have a PR staff to handle such mat-ters. The ES may have a PR office which would be pleased to handle the details, if they receive sufficient prior notice. The DC needs to explore the possibilities of media coverage as this may influence the exact form of the recognition session as well as its placement in the flow of the conference design. Where mass media is involved, it is necessary to prevent distorting the session to satisfy the needs of the mass media rather than the participants. The DC is responsible for providing for an equitable balance.

## Business Sessions

This section is exclusively for the MS, because the business sessions re-ferred to here are required of membership organizations by law or practice. These sessions are usually included as part of the annual conference. The DC determines the law and/or practice and designs the session accordingly. Some state laws require that there be at least one annual meeting open to the membership and even sets forth the minimal agenda for such a meeting. Where this is the case, it is easy for the DC to build the requirements into the conference design. The constitution and by-laws of the organization likewise detail other activities, such as election of officers, passage of resolutions, etc. Where this is to be part of the conference, the DC should organize the business session, or delegate this to a member of the executive board, or the paid staff.

It is likely that not all the participants are interested in the business details of the Sponsor, and many will not attend the business session. This en-courages a DC to schedule business sessions at the least desirable times, whenever that happens to be for a particular conference. A more positive alternative is to schedule the business session at some mid-point of the con-ference. Those who are not interested can utilize the field trips and recreation opportunities. Of course, those interested in the business session must deprive themselves of the alternatives, but this is a decision which each participant must make.

In an effort to attract larger numbers of participants to the business sessions, a DC can build in a "Report to the Membership" session. This is carefully staged and may require professional assistance. The DC focuses on the content and objectives, but identifies the appropriate resource to design the specifics. A multimedia presentation may be appropriate. Some organizations have even contracted for professionals to act out a prepared script related to the report.

A membership organization celebrating an important birthday (25th year) or an event (new headquarters building) can stage a pageant to make the business session more interesting and appeal to greater numbers of participants. By using audiovisuals, it is always possible to make the business meeting interesting.

The DC should determine the possibilities for design as related to the objectives for the business session. If the Sponsor merely wants to conduct the routine business as quickly as possible, then the design may be left to the officers or the parlimentarian. If the Sponsor wants broader involvement from the participants, then the DC seeks other design possibilities, such as some of those discussed under general and regular sessions

## From the Suppliers' Viewpoint

As the design process evolves, more suppliers are involved. The following are typical comments by suppliers about what has been discussed in this chapter.

### Site Personnel Say–

The temporary conference groups are a good idea, but let us know where you want them to meet. These are small groups, and they can easily meet in the bedroom of one of the group members. We can make this available by having our housekeeping people make up the room while the guest is at breakfast. In some of our rooms it is even possible for us to rearrange the furniture so as to get better space for a small group to meet. All of this can be done if our housekeeping personnel can be notified at least a day in advance. Usually, if we are notified after 5:00 p.m., it is difficult for us to make the necessary arrangements for the following morning. We need either more notice or charge you extra for bringing in housekeeping personnel early the next day. We would prefer not to have to make an extra charge, so give us sufficient notice.

The cracker barrel and lounge area activities are excellent and we would like to support them. Let us know about these ideas during site selection and we can explore with you some of the various locations. During this early stage of the design, if you let us know what you have in mind for these activities, we can help you think through some of the alternatives.

What can we say about "singles?" In some places we are restricted by law as to how to register guests. It is a situation with which we have little experience, but it is growing. If you anticipate there will be mixed singles, with either one or both being participants, let us discuss this beforehand and perhaps have fewer difficulties at check-in time.

If you are planning an extensive program with your banquet, please let us know. We can handle it, but it can take some rearrangement of our usual schedules for setting up, serving, and cleaning up for a banquet. At this early stage of the design, we do not expect you to commit yourselves. But, if you do share your thinking with us we are better able to give you cost estimates and make suggestions.

### Travel Personnel Say—

Arranging field trips is our business. We do it for individuals or groups. We can recommend places to go in the nearby area that you may not be familiar with. If you rely on a committee of local persons, they probably are not too familiar with what is available. How many people have ever been a tourist in their own neighborhood?

There are packaged tours, and we have brochures we can send you on these during your early design phase. This can help you make some decisions as to days and times. We can also provide data on costs. Package tours which include pre or postconference travel are possible, and these can be arranged for individuals as well as for groups.

We are prepared to set up tables in the registration area, or any other appropriate place, to help your participants arrange individual travel. Working with some airlines, we can also provide confirmation service for return trips right at the conference site.

### Entertainment Personnel Say—

Our business is to provide entertainment for your conference. This ranges from an individual speaker to a mini-Broadway show. There is no limit to the kinds of entertainment we can provide. We are far beyond the stage where the biggest thing done was a semi-nude girl jumping out of a cake.

Some of us have a particular list of clients who are entertainers, and you can choose from them. Others produce shows, or help your people put on their own show. We realize that entertainment is not the main purpose of a conference, but we hope you recognize that good entertainment can be an asset for most conferences.

Children at conferences are new, but some of us have special personnel who are highly competent in this area. Perhaps we can work together to design activities for the children which reinforce their parents' participation during the conference.

## Local Convention and Visitors' Bureau Personnel Say—

Our business is to help make your conference as successful as possible. If you are pleased, you will come back to our city again. If you are a Coordinator, you will bring other conferences to our city if we make your task easier. We have much in the way of materials and services and most of it is free of charge. Our expenses are met by the city or by suppliers and merchants in the city.

If you are looking for local attractions for field trips, we are the people who probably know more about this than anyone else. In some cities, we will make all the arrangements for you. More often, we will be able to provide you with a list of travel agents and others who could provide the service you need.

We want to hear from you as early as possible. We know that we are in competition with others until you decide on the site. During the design phase, we can provide information on our local resources for recreation, entertainment and field trips. We want to help, so why not contact us during the design phase.

# 6.
# Selecting the
# Conference Site

Selecting the best site for a conference is a complicated and sometimes exhausting experience. This chapter will explore some of the many variables that the Sponsor must consider when searching for a conference site. The term "site" will usually include the total provision of the space for the sessions, as well as the bedrooms and eating arrangements for the participants. At times we will differentiate, for not all facilities provide for the entire conference, requiring several related sites to handle some conference activities.

The actual process of site selection should be handled by the design committee (DC) or the Coordinator on behalf of the DC. However, there are circumstances where the Sponsor, particularly an MS and sometimes a PS, has to make a commitment to a particular site several years before the DC is activated. The larger the conference, the more limited the range of possible sites, resulting in advance bookings of two to three years and more. The ES may have their own facility (to be discussed below) and therefore the site selection is automatic. Even so, this chapter can be helpful in relating the site and the elements of conference design.

The lead time for a PS conference tends to be less than one year, and the qualifications regarding the size and nature of the site are not as demanding as those of an MS. Also, the range of sites for a PS conference will be much larger than for an MS conference. The objectives for a PS conference will usually be in the direct area of learning. The facility sought by the PS will emphasize these learning objectives and the core design elements discussed in Chapter 4.

Unlike the MS and the PS, the ES may have sufficient space for their conference in one of their company buildings. It may be space currently utilized for staff conferences or activities by their human resource development group, or it may be a site which the company has built specifically for conferences and learning activities, such as Xerox, Leesburg, Va.; Eastman-Kodak, Rochester, N.Y.; and IBM, Binghamton, N.Y.

An ES can also have an agreement with an existing site. A contract is usually signed for a given period of time in order to assure the Sponsor that the space will be available. The agreement may commit the Sponsor to using all the space, or it may provide only for accommodating the Sponsor along with other users of the site. There are some special sites that provide for this possiblity, such as Hillsdale Conference Center and Harrison House.

Of course, an ES can also utilize hotels and motels just as the MS or the PS. One has only to look at the "Events of the Day" listing in any hotel or motel in a large city to see the numerous ES conferences being conducted.

The factors we will discuss related to sites are

- Types of sites
- Sponsor and participants
- Relation to design
- Transportation
- Logistics

## Types of Sites

A conference can be held almost anywhere, but we'll examine the more traditional places.

## Conference Centers

Some sites have been built specifically for handling conferences, or contain buildings that, though built for other purposes, have been modified for conference use. These conference centers differ from the hotel/motel in that they do not accept people who are not in some way related to the conferences. Examples of such facilities are Airlie House, Warrenton, Va.; Arden House, Harriman, N.Y.; and Harrison House.

The term "conference center" is used to advertise and describe so many different kinds of sites that the label is no longer helpful. The range of facilities and arrangements possible at conference centers cannot be described in a book, as they change continually. This is good, because the needs of individuals and organizations are also constantly changing. The DC must determine if the change in a prospective conference center site is an advertising ploy or reality. Most conference centers are managed by responsible persons, but the field is so lucrative that it has attracted some questionable individuals.

There is such a lack of agreement on what constitutes a center that someone suggested the formation of an association of conference centers. Such an organization could develop standards to enable a Coordinator to receive comparable information from several sites when endeavoring to make a selection. At present, this is impossible, and reinforces the need for a walk-through before making a site decision.

Generally, a conference center has a major advantage. Its main business is conferences, and therefore the site personnel and facilities are geared for that kind of activity, rather than the conference being a secondary activity.

## Higher Education Institutions

This category includes any postsecondary institution from the community college through the graduate university. University conference sites can be part of the regular campus with the attendant benefits and limitations. The academic environment may be helpful in climate setting, if that is what the DC desires. Using an on-campus facility may also make faculty more available, if they are to serve as resource people. Timing is crucial, because if the conference is being held during regular semesters, there may be a limitation on the use of facilities which are primarily for the student body. During semester breaks (recess or vacation), the DC will find that universities are most eager to accommodate conferences, for they have underutilized facilities. This can include bedrooms, as well as food service.

There are universities that have on-campus sites specifically designed and constructed for conferences. These have some of the advantages discussed in the previous section.

Some universities have an off-campus conference site. This may have been purchased by the university, or obtained as the result of a bequest from an alumnus. Such sites tend to be remodeled mansions which are quaint but may not have the range of facilities required by a DC. Once again, for some conferences, the ambience of a former estate and mansion house may be just the thing.

The emerging community colleges (sometimes referred to as junior colleges) have recognized their unique role in their communities and have endeavored to put conference sites into their building plans. Where the funds were available, special conference buildings and facilities have been erected. Where space and/or building funds are limited, the community colleges have erected multipurpose buildings that serve as student centers, flexible classroom buildings, or conference sites. The community colleges have recognized the financial returns of conference sites and have responded accordingly. The community colleges are also interested in providing conference opportunities as part of their mission of community services.

Using educational institutions as conference sites can be a mixed blessing for Sponsors. The institutions offer not only the site, but also the assistance of a Coordinator. Some institutions will not make their site available unless the Sponsor will utilize their Coordinator. This can provide an additional resource, but some of the Coordinators lack the necessary experience required by many Sponsors. Some institutions have a highly qualified staff that can provide a Coordinator, a secretariat, and the other support services that contribute to the success of a conference. Therefore, although such a site may be more expensive, the cost can be offset by the additional services provided for the same charge by an institution which has these resources.

## Hotels and Motels

Older hotels and motels tend to have inadequate facilities for conferences, unless there has been extensive remodeling. Those built before the 1960's did not incorporate provisions for conference activity of the nature that we are describing. Many of the larger hotels did have provision for conventions or conferences that utilized only general sessions for large numbers of participants. Owners of older facilities, in some cases, have spent large sums to modify their buildings and rooms to be more acceptable to those seeking a site. Coordinators are warned not to rely on the publicity or brochures of such facilities, but to make an on-site visit. Behind the elaborate appointments there may be very thin walls and inadequate lighting. In large buildings the elevators may be unable to handle the flow to and from a general session, as compared to the usual flow of room traffic for which they were originally built and programmed.

In the last few years the number of hotels/motels built for conference business has increased. These facilities are specifically built to appeal to Coordinators seeking conference sites. There has been an increased awareness of how the needs of participants differ from those of the usual guest, and some chains have provided special training for their personnel who handle conference business. Hotels and motels seeking conference business also have helpful tie-in arrangements with various kinds of travel agents, including local people, who can coordinate field trips.

Recognizing the increased awareness of the relation of recreation and entertainment to a conference, many of these facilities have also built in such resources or made arrangements to make them locally available.

## Cruise Ships and Theme Parks

A more recent phenomenon is the cruise ship or the conference at sea. In some instances the conference will contract for the entire ship, while in other situations, the conference group will be only part of the passenger list. Of course, the former situation is much preferable. At first, the cost may seem exhorbitant, but a careful comparison with "land" conference costs that can be incurred by Sponsors and participants may indicate that the difference does not rule out consideration of the cruise conference.

The size of cruise ships varies, but a Coordinator would need 750-1,000 participants in order to contract an entire ship for a conference.

Cruise ships offer a greater range of bedrooms than most land-based conference sites, and this has advantages and limitations. It can produce additional revenue in the form of charges for the more elegant rooms and suites, but such luxury accommodations can generate class consciousness and hostility. However, this situation is not too much different from a hotel that has a range of rooms and charges.

The cruise ship will provide entertainment and recreation and the Coordinator will have more control over these elements than is usual in a land based facility. Spouse programs are easily arranged, and of course field trips will be coordinated with the ports of call of the cruise ship.

The Coordinator anticipating a cruise conference should work through a reliable travel agent, as the arrangements can be overwhelming if they are an additional chore. There are travel agents who specialize in cruise ship arrangements and the Coordinator should turn to them.

The cruise conference can be used effectively by any Sponsor. It opens up new possibilities which the Coordinator and DC should explore carefully with the Sponsor before proceeding too far with the design.

Another recent development is the *theme park,* the best known of which are the Disney enterprises in Anaheim, California and Orlando, Florida. At the time this book is being written, there are about thirty-five major theme parks, and the prediction is that there will be many more developed in the next few years. Sometimes, they originate with the entertainment side, as with the Disney activities. A newer trend is that exemplified by Marriott in their plans for a theme park in northern Virginia. The entrepreneur is a hotel/motel chain which is building, with recreation and entertainment as a significant element. In most theme parks conference facilities are available.

Such a site has many possibilities, but also limitations. As with the cruise conference, it has the advantage of a single package arrangement with everything being provided by the site. There are many opportunities available in one place and they can be offered in a coordinated fashion. An obvious limitation is that a participant may not like what is being offered and does not have any readily available alternatives.

### Sponsor and Participant

In addition to considering the site and specific design elements, the DC must also consider the nature of the Sponsor and the probable participants. Both have certain expectations, though these are seldom stated specifically.

A conference site will have a reputation which tends to establish the climate. As can be expected, a reputation is a very vague element, yet it must be considered when selecting a site. The following indicates one aspect of this, in the case of a PS.

—— • ——

During the early days of the war on poverty program, the Coordinator was designing a conference for participants (the poor) who were engaged in developing and conducting programs as part of the war on poverty. The participants were to be brought to

Washington, D.C., as some of the conference objectives could best be achieved by having the participants meet with various government officials.

The Coordinator recommended a facility about forty miles outside of Washington, which could provide some degree of isolation. It was far enough away so that they could not lose participants too readily to the attractions of the city, but close enough to make the Washington resource people easily available.

When the design and site were being discussed with the DC, there was stinging criticism, for the site suggested was one usually used by high-level government officials. The DC felt that using such a site for a poverty program might indicate that they were squandering funds. They suggested an inner city site. The Coordinator gathered the financial data which indicated that the cost of the out-of-town site, though somewhat higher than an inner city site, was not that far out of line, considering the types of meeting rooms, logistical support, equipment, etc. The inner city site would need to be supplemented by renting equipment and purchasing some supplies which were included in the cost of the out-of-town site. Actually, the out-of-town site had the reputation of catering to high-level persons and therefore was considered to be much more expensive than it really was.

After much discussion, the DC and the Sponsor suggested that there might even be some program benefits in having a conference of "poor people" in a status site. This proved to be the case. The participants felt (as determined by the evaluation process) that they had been given treatment equal to the avowed purpose of the war on poverty—to enable them to enter the mainstream of society.

——— • ———

Not only does a particular site communicate an image, but also certain parts of our country evoke particular images. Mention "Las Vegas" and both participant and Sponsor are likely to think of gambling and shows, forgetting the excellent conference sites that are available. It may become difficult to convince participants that the DC is planning a serious working conference in that city.

In selecting a site, the DC must consider the financial arrangements for both the Sponsor and the participant. What is the range of costs? Who will be expected to pay for what? For example, if the DC makes special arrangements for bedroom rates which are below the advertised rate, how is this communicated to the participants? At this time, we are not so much concerned with the actual rate as with collecting and disseminating correct information. The DC will be asking questions like:

- What are the actual room rates to be charged to the participants?
- Will the cost be different if the charges are made directly to the participant rather than to the Sponsor?
- What is the estimated cost per participant for other items such as food, recreation, entertainment, tips, etc.?
- What other costs can be expected to be incurred at the site?

At sites where much conference work is done, there is usually someone available who will have these figures readily at hand. Sometimes this information is included in the very informative brochures the sites produce. More recently, because of rising costs, some of this information has been supplied on a duplicated form and inserted in the printed brochure. Of course, individual differences and preferences make an absolute estimate unlikely.

The ES usually pays all the cost of the participants, either by direct reimbursement, or by having all costs charged to the appropriate department. In this case, it is solely the concern of the Sponsor and not the participant. If the ES is not paying all costs, then those which the participants are to pay should be stated as clearly as possible. It is doubtful if this will deter any participant from attending, but it will assist in maintaining a favorable climate. There is also the question of trust. If the participant is not given correct or sufficient information prior to the conference, and then finds that there are additional costs that could have been anticipated, he may well wonder what other surprises are in store. A good conference design can be damaged because of inadequate information. One can imagine the unspoken (but behavior influencing) thoughts of a participant at an ES conference who finds that he must pay significant sums in order to keep up with the others. The question of spouses must once again be considered. It makes a difference if spouses are *welcome* or *invited*. If merely welcome, then the participant should clearly understand that the expense for the spouse is a personal one and that the Sponsor has no financial obligation. If the spouse is invited, it is implied that the Sponsor will assume either all or part of the cost. The DC cannot rely on the nuance of the words "welcome/invited," but must spell out the specifics to the extent possible.

For the PS the cost of the facility can be one of the most crucial items in the budget. Whether or not the PS makes a profit depends upon participant attendance. An extremely expensive site may require a larger attendance to just break even. This will influence the kind of design that can be developed. An alternative is to raise the fee and to make a profit with fewer participants. This introduces a high risk element, as the higher price may also mean fewer persons who are interested in attending. There is a range of cost possibilities available within any site, and the DC must explore these to see what kind of mix is most likely to produce the quality and quantity of participants desired by the PS. A common practice in PS pricing is to include the meals in the total conference cost rather than making them a separate factor. If the DC selects a fairly isolated site, this becomes a necessity. An alternative is for the

DC to select a site close enough to other eating facilities so that the participants can arrange for their own meals. The trade-off is that the site may then require a charge for the meeting rooms, which are usually offered at either no charge or a low charge, when it is expected that the participants will eat at the site.

The DC must explore, both from cost and design perspectives, whether the participants should be eating together or separately. In addition to cost, there is a question of the conference flow. If a PS conference is to have luncheon or dinner speakers as part of the program, then obviously the participants must eat together, and there is little choice but to build this into the fee structure.

The MS must also watch participant costs, as the expected range of costs influences the possible number and kinds of participants who might attend the conference. By selecting a site which seriously alters the cost as compared to preceding years, the DC may be appealing to a different range of participants than those who have attended previously.

Cost is an obvious and concrete example of the need for the DC to relate the site to the Sponsor and to the participants. What should be sought for each situation is the most desirable mix of site-Sponsor-participant.

### Relation to Design

The most important reason for careful site selection by the DC is the direct relationship of the site to the conference design. If the DC has control over site selection, then it should have some idea of how it will design for the factors discussed in the two preceeding chapters. For example, if they plan to use breakout rooms, then the site must have that possibility. As has been pointed out, there are times when the DC must design within the limits of preselected site. Then, the site needs to be considered in terms of what limitations it puts on the design possibilities. It is also possible that the site will open up other design alternatives by virtue of the facilities it has which the DC had not even considered. In relating site and design, the DC must explore rooms, equipment, and exhibit area.

### Rooms

The size and type of rooms available is important information for the DC. Almost all conferences have a general session or some point at which all the participants are together in the same room. Therefore, there must be a room of sufficient size to handle them. An ES has less difficulty with this concern, as the number of participants can probably be more closely predicted. The PS usually establishes a maximum number of participants, and therefore can be specific about the room size for the general session. There are times when a PS does not allow for additional participants arriving on the day of the conference, and in this case the size of the room available becomes an important factor. It is unlikely that the number of participants for an MS conference can be determined exactly. The selection of the room for the general session, therefore, becomes critical. The MS will have some estimates that they hope are accurate and will produce a good fit between the number of participants and the size of the room. It is equally as distressing to reserve a large room and have a small group attending as it is to reserve a room too small and be faced with an overflow.

The need for other rooms will depend upon the design, as discussed in earlier chapters. If breakout rooms are to be used, the DC should have some idea of the number and types of rooms which would be desirable. This may require visiting several sites to identify the one which can accommodate the design. If the site has been previously selected, or if one is preferred by the Sponsor, the DC design options may be influenced by the availability of rooms for breakout and concurrent sessions.

Earlier chapters have discussed design considerations, and these must be linked to the site. From the design viewpoint the DC may be looking for rooms or space which can accommodate

- Concurrent sessions
  How many will there be at one time?
- Special interest groups
  Will rooms be available for them on the day(s) required?
  How many special interest groups will need rooms?
- Temporary conference groups
  Will they meet in a participant's bedroom or will a meeting room be required?
- Cracker barrel sessions
  What kinds of space or rooms will be available for this activity?
- Lounge areas
  Is space available for special participant lounge areas or will they have to share with outsiders?
- Job exchange
  If a room is desired, where will it be in relation to the rest of the conference activity?
- Spouses
  What kinds of rooms will be needed for spouse activities?
  What kinds of facilities will be available for spouses who are not attending any activities?
- Field trips
  If these are being planned, can they be conducted from the site? (Can the buses reach the site easily, or does it mean going in limousines and then transferring to buses?)

These questions are by no means all that need to be asked, but they indicate some of the concerns the DC must have while seeking a site and relating it to design.

A site which is conference oriented will provide diagrams illustrating the exact footage of the rooms, their locations, etc. These diagrams will vary from a simple, one-page mimeographed sheet, to a multicolor, many-paged brochure. The DC must examine the printed materials carefully and discuss the possibilities before making a site visit. By no means should a review of printed materials take the place of an on-site visit. This is not to suggest that there is any chicanery on the part of the site management, but experience has shown that some of the diagrams and pictures do not communicate the total reality of the situation.

—— • ——

The DC reviewed the motel brochure and the rooms appeared to be just the right size and number to be compatible with the design. Expecting a brief and rewarding visit, the DC arranged to see the motel. They were met at the door by the assistant manager, who was also in charge of conference arrangements. The DC had been invited to arrive at lunchtime so they could experience the type of food they would be served at their conference. After a pleasant and filling lunch, they proceeded to examine the facilities and found that the room for the general session was exactly suited to their purposes. The DC then accompanied the assistant manager to the smaller rooms which would be used for other sessions. The size was perfect, but the rooms were designed for social functions. They were lit by beautiful and ornate chandeliers, none of which could provide sufficient light for a work session. The DC questioned the assistant manager who finally admitted that there was no way to make the chandeliers produce more candlepower. He offered to bring in additional floor lamps to illuminate those sections of the room which were in virtual darkness. This was tried, but to no avail. The DC had to seek other sites, but at least had avoided scheduling their conference into rooms which were unsuitable.

—— • ——

Another factor related to meeting rooms is the possibility of setup costs. Usually, rooms are set up in the morning and are not varied during the day. If this is the design, then setup costs will not be a factor. If the DC has not explored this possibility, they may find that costs and logistics lock them into one setup for the entire day, no matter what the requirements of the different resource persons.

—— • ——

The DC had visited the site, walked through their design and found everything compatible. It was to be a large conference, and the DC planned for many concurrent sessions. The resource people had been queried as to their methodologies and facility requirements. Some were using theater style, some conference style with tables, and others just chairs with no tables. Presumably, this had all been checked out with the site personnel. Therefore, the DC spent two days planning for the most effective use of the rooms, given the needs of the resource persons and the anticipated size of each session. Then, they considered the flow of participants from one set of concurrent sessions to another. They related all this data and finally designated room assignments which appeared to meet all the requirements. When this information, particularly the setup of the individual rooms, was communicated to the site personnel, the DC was informed that there would be additional charges. The reason was that some rooms had to be changed from theater style to conference style and in some cases tables had to be removed from the rooms. The DC had planned for the time necessary for the changes (by using breaks, exhibition area time, general sessions, and lunchtime) but the site management insisted they would have to use extra personnel and therefore there would be an additional charge. The only alternative was to set up the room in the morning, and schedule sessions based on the room setup. It required extensive negotiations with the site management, because the possibility of setup cost had not been investigated during the initial site visit.

━━━ ● ━━━

## Equipment

Many conference sites indicate that they have all kinds of equipment available. The DC is cautioned to check this out most carefully. If the conference is to use audiovisual materials, one of the first questions to ask is if union projectionists are required. Without arguing the merits for or against unions, the reality of conference life is that in some cities no projection equipment, including an 8mm projector, can be operated by other than union operators. This can be a significant cost factor. If the DC has explored this beforehand they can avoid disputes and disappointment and provide the necessary budget. Or, resource persons may be encouraged to use other methods of presentation. There is no national contract, so the DC must ascertain the status within the particular conference city and site.

In addition to projection equipment, a conference can be improved by the effective use of other kinds of equipment. One of the most useful is the "easel and newsprint," sometimes also called a "flipchart." There are many names and variations of the basic equipment. The term "easel" is obvious, but the "newsprint" may be confusing. In the early 1950s, when the use of this equipment was evolving, the first paper used was that purchased from newspaper plants, which would have some of this blank, almost white paper left on the ends of newsprint rolls. It was necessary for the user to cut up the sheets, but the cost was minimal. Today, the whole process is much more sophisticated, with various kinds of paper available. Many people still refer to the paper as newsprint, but other terms used for the paper are butcher paper, and artists' pad.

No matter what it is called, if this particular piece of equipment is needed, the DC must check very carefully before the conference begins. There are many types of equipment called "easels" that would not really be suitable for the usual conference needs. Also, given the design of a particular conference, there may be the need for more easels than are available at the site.

———— • ————

In the initial site visit the Coordinator asked the site personnel if easels with newsprint were available. Five of these would be needed during the conference. The request was met with a strong affirmative, and the Coordinator did not check further. When the conference began, the Coordinator discovered that the site had only two easels, and one of these was being used by another group. The site personnel agreed to obtain the additional easels, and they did, but after the conference had begun. Some groups had to work without the planned easels and newsprint. The site billed the Sponsor for the additional easels at a high cost, which they explained was the cost to them. Subsequent bargaining, with attendant loss of time, reduced the cost but did not eliminate it.

———— • ————

A common difficulty is to find that the paper available is of the small artist size, which is not as useful as the full-size sheets. Also, markers may be of poor quality, or dry, as site personnel frequently forget to test them before making them available. Asking for masking tape results in blank stares, or at best a role of cellophane tape with the admonition that this is not be used to post newsprint sheets on the wall!

Whether easels/newsprint or projection equipment, the DC should determine not only the availability but also the condition of the equipment. This should be done during early negotiations. A look at this equipment at the earliest possible time may indicate something of the perception and practice of the site personnel regarding equipment. Of course, it is also important to do a final check just before the conference opens, with sufficient time to obtain replacements, as may be indicated.

Reproduction facilities are also important to a well-run conference. These can range from a spirit duplicator (the jelly type which actually turns out a blue copy) to a comprehensive photocopy machine which copies on both sides of plain paper. The availability of such equipment should be determined, as well as the attendant cost factors. The DC should not normally expect the site to provide such equipment or service without some additional cost. An ES may find that it is more economical to bring reproduction equipment from their own offices rather than rely on that available at the site. If distance and size of equipment are factors, then renting locally may be an appropriate option. A PS might choose to provide their own reproduction equipment, depending upon what they have available in their own organization and what can be committed to the conference. A PS that conducts many conferences within a reasonably small geographic area may find it more economical to obtain equipment which is easily transported and set up. An MS has many options, depending upon budget and need. As the MS tends to deal in larger numbers than the ES or PS, it is usually more economical for them to provide their own reproduction equipment and operator.

Efforts will have been made by the DC to determine the reproduction needs of the resource persons prior to the conference. Generally, most reproduction can be anticipated, but there are some items which are only possible to reproduce at the time of the conference. Among these are

- Rosters of participants with name, home address, organization, room at the conference site and similar useful information.
- Reports of particular sessions that will be discussed in the general session.
- Press releases in conjunction with significant resource people, important speeches, awards, and recognition sessions.
- Daily bulletins listing changes, announcements, and other material of interest for the day.

## Exhibit Areas

At this point in our discussion, we will only touch briefly on exhibits. The next chapter will go into much more detail. Conference site must include consideration of exhibits. Such considerations may involve anything from providing a rack with literature that is to be picked up by the participants to accommodating 200 commercial exhibitors. Particularly when the Sponsor is a trade association, it can be expected that exhibits will be an essential element of conference design. The DC should have some feel for the nature and type of exhibits to be accommodated.

During the designing process, and until arrangements are made with the exhibitors, it is not possible to indicate the full range of possibilities. In the early stages, the DC should be asking questions, such as

- What are the purposes of the exhibits? Are they to provide information or to produce income?
- How many square feet should be made available to the exhibitors? Does the site have sufficient clear footage available?
- Where will the exhibits be located, as related to the participants' involvement in the exhibits, and as related to other conference activities?

Individual exhibit areas usually consist of curtained-off areas of about nine by twelve feet. If exhibitors have equipment, other requirements may be necessary. There is the need for an adequate electrical supply. Where the conference site has been designed to accommodate exhibits, the need for special electrical circuits will probably not cause any difficulty. The site will have the required electrical lines. When the site has been remodeled, or has not been built specifically to handle exhibits, the electrical supply can be a severely limiting factor.

Moving exhibit material in and out of the site must be considered. This includes the necessary entrances for large containers or unusual size equipment. If elevators are required, can they handle the bulky equipment the exhibitors may be bringing in?

Time is also a factor. If the site has a crowded schedule, setup and knockdown times may be severely restricted. Exhibitors need to know in advance how much time they have at the beginning of these activities. The DC must know when the exhibits can be opened and when they must be closed (as it may affect their design).

In these days of expensive equipment and "light-fingered" individuals, security of the exhibit area is very important. Potential exhibitors need to know what kinds of security provisions can be made at the site. If the exhibits include consumer or marketable items, this information is essential in providing security.

It is rare to find an MS conference without exhibits. The PS exhibits will vary because of the wide range of Sponsors and objectives possible within the PS category. The ES conference tends to have fewer exhibits, usually only when the ES is trying to introduce new product lines or to inform the participants about the Sponsor's activities.

### Transportation

If the conference is being held in the same city where most of the participants are located, transportation may not be a significant factor. Most conferences which draw persons for more than one day tend to draw them from wider geographical distances and therefore transportation is a vital factor.

### Air Travel—Domestic

Airlines offer a variety of package offers available for group travel to a conference. One approach to minimizing transportation difficulties is to have the conference right outside the gate of the airport. In the last few years there have been motel chains that have purposely built sites near or adjacent to airports and have advertised that participants can fly in and be right at the airport for their conference. This allows for easy arrival and departure. This has proven extremely attractive to many an ES, for it allows for a one-day conference (fly-in a.m., fly-out p.m.) thereby eliminating the cost for the overnight stay and additional time lost at the job.

Even where there is provision for an overnight stay, proximity to the airport reduces ground travel time. It eliminates the often lengthy trip by taxi or limousine to a downtown site—a trip that can consume more than an hour each way in travel time. Though this is not a great deal of time, it does add possible discomfort to additional travel time. Particularly, if the ground travel time coincides with rush hour, it may mean fewer taxis at the airport and long tangles of bumper to bumper traffic on the roads. A limitation is that being near the airport may mean that the conference is a considerable distance away from other facilities that might be of interest to the participants.

Participants who arrive at an airport and have an unfortunate experience on their way to the conference are not likely to start the conference in a favorable frame of mind. For example, the participant who takes a taxi for $15, not knowing that a limousine was available for $3.75, can be expected, understandably, to be hostile towards the Sponsor who had not given him sufficient information.

It is also possible for the participant to find that it costs only $3.75 to make the trip from the airport to the conference site but that the airport limousine makes so many stops that it becomes a gruesome and nauseating experience. However, if two or three participants had grouped together and taken one cab to the conference site, the average cost would have been less and it would have been a much more pleasant trip. Each airport has its own system of ground transportation and it would be helpful for the DC to give participants this information so they do not have to stumble around at the airport with the possibility of making poor and costly choices and therefore starting the conference in a negative frame of mind.

Where the Sponsor is an ES, and paying the entire cost, the participant is less likely to be concerned with cost and more with the physical ease aspect. For the PS, it depends on how the conference has been priced as to whether the ground transportation will be an additional cost. Cost is usually an important factor for the MS, but physical comfort may be a more significant element. In many cases, participants at an MS conference expect that the Sponsor will make the entire event as comfortable and convenient as possible. If this expectation is not fulfilled at the first event, airport arrival, the Sponsor can expect negative feedback during the early days of the conference.

International conferences have utilized a technique which has proven useful. Arrangements can be made to have a host at the airport meet the incoming flights. It is helpful if the participants have notified the secretariat of the specific arrival time. Even without this information, it is still possible to set up such a service at the airport. It is likewise possible to arrange for group ground transportation for the participants from the airport to the conference site, or their hotels. Planned ground transportation eliminates the necessity for the participants to identify or negotiate with the transportation people and face the previously discussed problems. Ground transportation can be provided, and the participants can be on their way to the conference site very quickly, comfortably, and usually quite economically.

For VIPs, such as speakers and resource people, such provision should be made even if it is not done for all participants. By providing for some host service at the airport, it is possible to determine if the resource people have arrived and if they are comfortably and safely on their way to the conference site. Meeting resource people at the airport has multiple advantages. The obvious is that the Sponsor will know that the resource person has actually arrived. If the flight comes in without the resource person, the Sponsor can begin to implement alternate arrangements for covering the assignment of the no-show resource person.

If the resource person does arrive, and is met by preselected host, they should drive to the conference site together. During the ride, the host can brief the resource person on any changes or pertinent up-to-date information, which might influence the planned presentation.

## Air Travel—International

Where the conferences cross national borders, air travel is probably the only means of attending. Of course, U.S. participants might drive to Canada or Mexico—and the reverse is also a possibility. For some Caribbean Islands, travel by boat is an alternative. Generally, air travel is the most frequently used method. In addition to some of the factors discussed earlier, there are the additional cross-cultural and legal apsects which must be considered.

Participants arriving in a foreign country will be landing at an international airport. Most of these have bilingual signs. At least one of the languages will be English and this would provide for most of the particpants, as international conferences are usually conducted in English.

There are some legalities and concerns which must be taken into account when landing at a foreign airport; for example, foreign exchange. It is not the practice for travelers to convert their money into the local currency prior to arrival. This is even truer now than in previous years, because of the constantly fluctuating exchange rates. Some countries, particularly in Eastern Europe, require that a specified minimum amount of foreign currency be exchanged for local currency at the port of entry. In some countries, the amount of money (cash and traveler's checks) must be declared upon entryand accounted for on departure. Whatever the currency regulations, the DC should determine these beforehand and be sure that all arriving participants are notified so they can make adequate currency provisions.

At most international airports, banks will be open during times of expected arrivals. However, difficulty has been experienced by travelers in some countries where the banks are not open on some religious and legal holidays. Some banks are not open twenty-four hours a day, and late night arrivals are possible. The DC should explore the times of expected arrivals as related to banking facilities, or perhaps have the participants met by a host who is supplied with sufficient local currency for tipping, etc.

Usually, there is no problem for foreign travelers going through the customs procedures, but each country has its own regulations which may not be known to the incoming participants. They should be informed of this so as to avoid difficulties and duties. Also, provision can be made for ground transportation to the hotel or conference site with no currency outlay by the participant.

—— • ——

The participants were coming from Japan to a conference in the U.S. They had informed the Sponsor of their plans which included a postconference trip to Europe before going home. The Sponsor sent appropriate information, but did not emphasize an obvious point. Japanese tend to bring gifts to their hosts and others who might render a personal service, such as taking them sightseeing. As the participants would be going home through Europe, they had brought additional gifts with them for that part of the trip. They had been informed of U.S. Customs regulations that make special provision for this, but the arriving participants were to make the necessary arrangements at their port of entry. As this had not been highlighted, it required delay and complicated discussions until the situation could be settled without the Japanese participants having to pay duties on the items they had brought with them to be taken to Europe. With more attention focused on the Japanese gift-giving custom, and the U.S. Customs regulations, the embarassing airport incident could have been avoided.

—— • ——

Arriving participants will have passports, but there is also the question of a visa. These regulations can be somewhat confusing and when the conference relies on international participation, visa information is a must. There are no generalities concerning visas as this is strictly a legal step which is at the discretion of the receiving country. Some countries grant "tourist" or "social" visas which are usually valid for a stay of up to fourteen days. In some countries, visas are granted at the airport, whereas others require a formal application some time prior to entry. The participant usually handles the visa situation in his own home country prior to departure, for some airlines will not board a passenger for specific countries unless a visa has been issued. It may take several weeks or even months to obtain some visas, and the DC should anticipate this when inviting participants from other countries.

The tourist visa will generally be sufficient for most conferences. If the conference is to go beyond the limited period for which a visa has been granted at the airport, the secretariat will have to make provision for obtaining the necessary extensions. If this is not fully explored before the conference, some participants may have to spend valuable conference time visiting immigration offices to obtain the required extension.

In some countries the secretariat will also have to check out what can be brought in by foreign travelers. Some goods are absolutely forbidden or are suspect, such as transistor radios or tape recorders. In other countries items such as stuffed animals or agricultural products may be forbidden. Lists of such items are available from the customs officials and it is helpful if the participants are made aware of these regulations during the preconference planning state.

There are some less exotic articles necessary for a conference that may also provide entry difficulties. In some countries printed materials, slides, etc., are allowed in, but only on payment of a duty, which can be quite expensive. It is unfortunate if the participant has brought specially prepared materials and then must pay a duty to carry them into the conference. Or, particularly where there are some restrictions on freedom of information, it is common to find that the printed materials will either be confiscated at entry or held in customs until they can be read, evaluated, and cleared. This process may not be completed until long after the termination of the conference.

An ES, particularly a multinational company, will employ persons who specialize in international air travel and its complications. The DC should identify this resource and communicate with this person as early in the design stage as possible. The PS who is involved in international air travel should have somebody in the secretariat who has the necessary qualifications to handle the tasks indicated above. The MS who has many international conferences will likewise have identifiable resources. Most difficulty is experienced with an MS who has never been involved in international aspects and broadens out to include foreign participants. Without attention to the complications of international travel, the MS will probably receive fewer foreign participants. Some participants may not attend because of the lack of concern for individuals who must cross borders.

### Drive-in

Not all conferences involve participants arriving by air. In larger cities and surrounding geographical areas drive-in conferences have evolved. These conferences usually last from one to three days, and weekends are often utilized (Friday through Monday). Weekend drive-ins are intended to encourage participants to attend who live within reasonable driving distance and who can't be absent from work. It is used by an ES for management retreats. The PS finds it helpful when the participants do not want to lose time from their jobs, or where the purpose of the conference is to assist persons in finding other jobs. The MS uses the drive-in conference for local and regional conferences rather than national conferences. It is helpful for the MS, which is a social or fraternal organization. The weekend drive-in combines the conference with some form of recreation or entertainment.

Drive-in conferences need not only be for weekends, but when the DC designs for a drive-in conference during the week, there are some transportation difficulties. The site selected must be accessible to automobiles, or convenient to public transportation. As most people will drive their own vehicles, emphasis should be placed on providing for those who drive rather than those coming by public transportation. If the conference site is in a congested area there may be many kinds of problems which the DC must consider.

The starting time of the conference should be coordinated with probable arrival times of participants, considering traffic flow, etc. In some of our larger cities, the traffic pattern changes after 4:00 p.m. to accommodate those leaving the city. Although those entering will possibly not encounter traffic jams, they will find that the usual streets which were two-way earlier are now one-way outgoing and this can necessitate detours. For participants coming into an unfamiliar city this can be a negative experience and result in late arrival.

With participants driving in, parking is required. The DC must explore with the site personnel the kinds of parking that are available. Also, cost becomes a factor as charges in our metropolitan areas for parking spaces keep soaring. When participants are paying their own way, with a PS or MS, information about parking costs should be included in mailings to participants. If the DC can negotiate for a reduced fee for participants, a distinct possiblity, this too should be part of the information which goes out to the prospective participants.

If the site is a motel, parking is probably a minimal problem. By definition, a motel is for automobiles, but the term is used so loosely that the DC is advised to check out the parking. If it is a hotel, it may have a parking facility adjacent or nearby, or the participants may have to seek out their own parking in the surrounding area. Some hotels provide valet parking (i.e. the participant leaves the vehicle in front of the hotel and it is parked by hotel personnel. Likewise, it is retrieved by hotel personnel). If the anticipated attendance is large, the DC should check to be sure that the hotel had adequate staff for retrieving the vehicles within a reasonable period of time. Likewise, there should be the staff to rapidly move the vehicles from in front of the hotel to the parking facility. A large number of unparked vehicles in front of the hotel can result in traffic jams, accidents, and other unfavorable incidents.

The DC may have to choose a site which only provides for the conference, and parking is left to the individual participants. It is probable that information about parking is available from the hotel or the local chamber of commerce. The DC should assemble this data and send them to the participants so they can plan accordingly. The DC should not be satisfied merely with a statement from the hotel personnel that "there is plenty of parking in the area." This is too vague and can present the DC with problems at a later date. Also, if the conference is being scheduled for a weekend, the site personnel may state that "on weekends there are different parking rules, and your people can park any place for as long as they like." It is probable that the site personnel have never parked in the area on the weekend and really have no personal knowledge of the parking regulations. Some large cities have parking restrictions which apply every day but Sunday, so Saturday is still restricted.

If on-the-street parking is used, auto safety is an additional factor. Participants may be worrying during the sessions if their cars will be in one piece by the end of the conference, or their cars will be there at all! This uncertainty can lessen commitment and involvement in the conference. It may even deter some individuals from attending.

In these days of our energy crisis, the DC should encourage car pooling for a drive-in conference. They may even assist in the arrangements. This can be helpful not only for energy conservation purposes, but it can also stimulate additional participants to attend the conference. By encouraging car pools, the cost for individual participants can be reduced. By arranging for car pooling, prospective participants will be making a commitment to come together and this can reduce the last-minute cancellations.

## Cost

In addition to the previously mentioned items, there are other cost considerations related to travel. Travel cost is always a factor which must be considered by the DC. It can be handled in a variety of ways. One is to identify a travel agent or have one officially designated for the conference. It would not require that every participant use the "official travel agent," but it does make a resource available to those who do not have their own. There are times when groups of participants may be leaving from a major city to fly to the conference. This makes it possible to arrange for charter flights or group fares which can considerably reduce the cost to the participants. This has the added advantage that when participants make a monetary deposit, often required on charter flights or group fares, they are more likely to attend. For an MS this would be extremely helpful. For the ES and PS, group travel may be less significant.

Most major airlines provide services for conference related travel. The DC can explore this, particularly for the MS, as the rates and other benefits may influence the design possibilities. The time of year, and even the day of the week, can make a significant difference in travel cost.

### Logistics

Some Coordinators concentrate only on design and leave the site selection to others. Some may be involved in site selection for the elements previously discussed, but then abandon the process and leave the rest to other people. Either way, the Coordinator may lose valuable parts of the design, becoming overwhelmed by some of the logistics factors to be discussed. The extent to which any particular Coordinator will be involved depends upon the complexity of the design and the variables at the selected site. When possible, the Coordinator should at least be cognizant of and make inputs to the logistical side, even if the decisions are to be made by the DC or the Sponsor.

## Mobility

Movement of participants during the conference must be considered in selecting a site. Although the design may not be completed while the sites are being explored, the DC should have some general parameters which indicate room needs and possible movements of participants.

After the general session of a conference, there will be movement of large numbers of participants at one time. Depending upon the anticipated size of the participant group and number of available exits, the DC may find that it must provide additional time to allow for participants to get from the general session room to the breakout rooms or the concurrent session rooms. Similarly, moving from the smaller sessions into the general session may require the use of elevators. If a large group of participants all attempt to use the elevators at the same time, it can be anticipated that movement will be slowed.

Where many small rooms are to be used, it is unlikely that they will be adjacent to the general session room unless the site has been specifically constructed with this in mind. Therefore, the DC can anticipate that some groups may need ten or fifteen minutes more than other groups to return to a general session, depending upon proximity to the general session room. This may require special instructions to the small group leaders or session conveners.

Mobility also relates to exhibit areas. Generally, exhibitors prefer that participants be encouraged to move through the exhibit areas as they go from one session to the next. Accordingly, the DC might have the general session room on one side of the exhibit area and the smaller rooms on the opposite side of the exhibit area. While this will encourage participants to visit the exhibits, it also disrupts the movement of the participants to scheduled sessions. If the participants must move through the exhibit area going to the next sessions, the DC should anticipate that some participants will arrive late at following sessions, and some will not show up at all.

The DC may have to use more than one hotel to accommodate a large number of participants. Usually, the hotels will be either adjoining or close by, although this is not always possible. The DC should endeavor to avoid a site that requires providing transportation between hotels, because such additional movement will inevitably result in complaints about the size, availability, and comfort of the transportation. If sufficient transportation is not provided, the participants will come late to the sessions, and some may never make it from one hotel to another but rather opt for other ways to spend their time at the conference.

The anticipation of the usual weather is a factor that, though outside the control of the site, must be considered when using more than one hotel for a conference.

——— ● ———

The conference was held in a southern city, and the number of participants was great enough to require two hotels. The DC had arranged for two adjacent hotels with a short walk between them. It was anticipated that the major inconvenience for the participants would be in having to leave one air-conditioned hotel, walk through the summer humidity and heat of a southern city, and then into the nearby other air-conditioned hotel. In order to obtain the most reasonable rates, the DC had split most of the meetings between the two hotels. It was a four-day conference, and the first three days were peppered with intermittent and heavy showers. The movement of the participants became restricted, and they would choose sessions in a single hotel rather than risk getting wet and then having to sit in damp clothing in an air-conditioned room. The feedback to the Sponsor was somewhat negative based on the restrictions the participants imposed on themselves as a reaction to the weather. There was little that the DC could have done about this situation, once the decision had been made to use two different hotels rather than one big one for the conference.

——— ● ———

When it is impossible to schedule only one hotel, or when the conference requires a larger site, there is little the DC can do but alert the participants to the possibilities. It may be that some elements of the design can be planned to accommodate the negative effect of weather, but this is very difficult.

### Bedrooms

There is usually a range of bedrooms provided in any conference facility, such as single beds, twin beds, double beds, and suites. Even within these categories there is a range of prices. The DC must identify this information so as to be able to allow the participants to make the necessary choices. For all kinds of Sponsors this information is important, either to plan budgets or inform the participants of anticipated costs. Frequently, the site personnel will take care of the reservation process, and they may prepare a special card indicating the title of the conference and the types and rates of rooms available, with the special conference rates. These cards are either mailed directly to prospective participants or enclosed in other mailings by the Sponsor. The participant is requested to return the cards, usually directly to the site facility. This releases the secretariat from having to handle it. A weakness of this approach is that the secretariat has no idea of how many rooms are being reserved. Such information would give the DC some idea of the number of participants who plan to attend.

The ES will probably have one person on the staff making all the necessary reservations for the participants. The PS usually finds that a designated staff person to handle the reservations is an effective approach, though this can increase the work load on the PS staff. The MS tends to rely on the hotel (or hotels) and this does not provide any difficulty.

An all too common problem is that hotels and motels tend to overbook. Of course, booking is the responsibility of the hotel/motel. As overbooking has become all too common, some localities penalize those facilities that do not honor their confirmed reservations. The Coordinator should determine the legal steps that can be taken in case the overbooking disrupts the conference. To do this, the Coordinator must be aware of the local regulations before the crisis, which can force hundreds of participants to sit on their luggage in the lobby and wistfully look at the hotel registration desk. Where there is even the remotest possibility that this can happen, the Coordinator should have a member of the secretariat on duty in the lobby to provide for someone to talk to the participants and negotiate on their behalf. This secretariat member should have direct access to either the manager or the assistant manager on duty, so that alternate accommodations can be provided, at no additional cost to the participants.

The DC should not overlook the possibility of utilizing bedrooms as meeting rooms, as with temporary conference groups. The membership of such a group will usually be ten or fewer. They could arrange to meet in the bedroom of one of the group members. Other small groups can likewise utilize bedrooms for small group meetings. Where such meetings are to be held early in the day, the DC should check during site selection if the housekeeping personnel can make up some of the rooms earlier than others.

### Eating Facilities

Some conference sites pride themselves on providing a "stuffed mind in a stuffed body." If the participants are locked into the site and have no options as to where to eat, the kind of "stuffing" becomes important. Generally, most conference sites do a good job on the food, both in quality and quantity. Of course, there will always be those participants who have special perferences, and it is unlikely that they would be satisfied by anything served at any conference site. For the ES conference this does not present too great a problem, as the participants are attending for business reasons and will normally not comment on the food unless it is unexpectedly poor. When the conference site is a center which the ES owns, rents, or uses frequently, it is likely that the food tastes of the sponsor will be evident and the gastronomic needs of the usual participants will be readily met.

For PS and MS conferences, where participation tends to be more voluntary, the quality and quantity of food can be important in encouraging attendance. If all meals are included in the conference fee, the participants need to know this and know if they have any options. When participants are free to choose their own eating places, it is less critical for the DC to examine provisions made within the site.

Sites are in business to make money, and the Sponsor is one of their customers. The site personnel (e.g., conference manager) may agree to provide meeting rooms at no cost with the understanding that the participants will be eating all their meals at the site. If this is the agreement, then the DC must carefully consider field trips or other activities that might take the participants to other places during mealtimes.

There are many ways to serve meals, and generally the DC need not get too involved in the process. However, if meal times are to involve some planned conference activities, then the type of service does become a concern of the DC. Earlier, we have discussed activities such as the cracker barrel luncheon, and awards lunches or dinners. When these are planned, then the DS should explore the type of serving, the number to be seated at each table, etc., during the site selection visit. The major options are the buffet and the plated service (i.e., the whole entree on one plate). Butler service (i.e., waiters bringing the different items and serving each diner individually) is usually very expensive and time consuming. Each type of service has its advantages and limitations, and the DC will need to decide the most appropriate, given the purpose of the meal and the relative costs.

Hotels or motels which engage in mass feeding often use the plated service, and the quality of the meals served is variable. If the food service is an important part of the conference, the DC might identify a person who is competent in this area to negotiate on behalf of the Sponsor. Conference managers are reliable, but they are protecting the interests of their site and employer, which is completely understandable. The DC might need an equivalent individual for this aspect of the negotiations.

If the participants are to eat at the site, additional information may be needed. A conference center may reflect the mores of its surrounding community rather than that of the Sponsor. In many southern cities it is expected that ties and jackets be worn by men in the dining room after 6:00 p.m. Rather than risk embarrassment, the DC should be sure that participants are notified if this is the case. The notification should be early enough so that the participants will bring the needed attire. Where the Sponsor is the sole user of the conference site at a particular time, it is sometimes possible to negotiate so that the Sponsor can determine the appropriate attire. If the site is catering to several conferences at the same time, the Sponsor will usually be unable to alter the norm.

In hotels and motels there is usually a wider range of possibilities for eating, and each dining room may have its own dress requirements. The DC would have less responsibility in a hotel or motel for making any arrangements, except for mass feedings.

### Staff Support

It is probable that the DC will be working with an individual designated by the site as the conference manager. Sometimes, this will be a fully qualified individual who is very much aware of the implications of the various kinds of conference designs. In too many cases, it is more likely that the conference manager will be an employee with a variety of duties, of which only one is related to conference activities. The DC should not accept the title at face value but should determine the kinds of support which the conference manager, and others on the site, can be expected to provide.

When the site has a "professional" conference manager, the DC will find that this person is most helpful and raises concerns which the DC might not even have considered. Although such personnel are working for the site, these conference managers want the participants and Sponsor to have the best possible conference. If Sponsors are satisfied, they are more apt to use the site repeatedly and will pass the word about the excellence of the site on to others. The participant of today can be the Sponsor of tomorrow's conference, and it is to the best interest of the conference manager to see that all concerned are aware of the positive support of the site staff.

Even if there is no professional manager, the designated site personnel will try to be helpful. The limitation is that they may not have the background to be able to anticipate the situations which arise when matching design with site. (One reason for writing this book is to help site personnel relate more effectively to the Coordinator, DC, and Sponsor.)

There are other site support personnel who can be involved, in addition to the conference manager. The list would include, at a minimum, all of the regular employees of the site, such as front office personnel, bellmen, housekeeping, maintenance, and food service. An effective conference manager can facilitate relationships with each of these individuals and groups, so that all is well planned and functions smoothly. If there is no conference manager, or a weak one, the Coordinator may have to make some other arrangements. At the very least, the Coordinator should designate a liaison person (usually from the secretariat) to work with the site personnel during the conference so that all requests can be funneled through one source. This will eliminate the possibility of confusing and contradictory directions being given to the site personnel.

### Site Relevance

A factor in site selection may be the relevance to the conference of some of the elements discussed earlier under field trips. For example, the site may be near the home plant of an ES or it may be a preferred vacation spot. Whatever the reason, if the site is to be selected for site relevance, the DC should determine that this relevance actually exists!

The site may have been chosen because it has certain offerings for a particular time of the year, such as ocean bathing. But, what if the weather is bad, sharks are reported, there has been an oil spill, or some other unexpected situation? The site should have some alternatives other than letters of apology delivered to the room of each participant. The Sponsor and the participants have certain expectations which have been aroused if the site relevance has been proclaimed in the preconference material. If the negative occurrence is unavoidable, the site personnel cannot be held responsible. But, if the DC, during site selection, has not explored alternatives, both the DC and the site personnel are open to severe criticism by the participants and Sponsor.

Whatever the nature of the site relevance that prompted the selection of the particular site, it should be clearly identified. Then, the benefits should be utilized. It would be unwise to select the conference center at Anaheim, California—just outside the gates of Disneyland—without making provision for the participants and families to visit that famous place. Otherwise, the participants will be forced to miss sessions and can legitimately question the conference design.

Entertainment and recreation are an essential part of many conferences and should be planned as the site is being selected. The DC may consider a golf tournament, but find that nobody on the DC is really a golfer. Rather than doing a poor job of organizing the tournament, they should rely on the site personnel. If the site has been selected because it does offer a recognized golf course, there will be a golf pro or some site staff member who can efficiently organize the tournament. Of course, this should be coordinated with the design so that sessions and the tournament are not in conflict.

## From the Suppliers' Viewpoint

Up to this point, the Coordinator and DC have been shopping around, and this is necessary and legitimate. Now, they must make some specific decisions. To do this, they must become involved with the following suppliers.

### Site Personnel Say—

We welcome visits from the Coordinator and the design committee. We realize that they would want to see the actual facility and even some of our personnel before making a decision. This is time consuming, but it is part of our job and what we have to do if we want to get contracts for conferences.

To help all of us, there are several things that you can do. Please let us know beforehand when you plan to visit. It is not that we will do any special clean-up or preparation (as you might at home for a prospective purchaser or tenant), but it will allow us to schedule times so that you can have our undivided attention and even meet others of our staff who would be supporting your conference. We are a seven-day-a-week operation, twenty-four hours a day, so we have to schedule days off during the week. The day you arrive may be one when an important member of our staff is not available. If you give us some notice, we will be glad to reschedule.

Share your possible design with us. We keep saying this, but still find that Coordinators look upon us only as booking agents rather than a resource. The more we can understand your design, the more we can relate the site to it. We have brochures and pamphlets, but they never tell the whole story. We are constantly changing our facilities, usually expanding and adding. There are also many variations possible and we could not put all of it in a book. Some of us have tried to develop planning books which you can use to relate our site to your design. Even these cannot tell the whole story. They are helpful, but must be supplemented by direct inspection.

If you have a large conference, we know the problem of movement. This can be one of the most annoying aspects and we would like to work on this problem with you. We realize that you are an MS, and even for some in the PS category, you cannot tell us exactly how many participants you will have. If you have a general idea, and tell us that, we can work together to minimize any movement problems.

Obviously, there are unwritten and sometimes unspoken obligations on both sides. We usually provide some courtesy rooms at no charge for the Coordinator and perhaps the Sponsor. Beyond that, we are open to negotiation as to how many other persons we can accommodate at no charge, or at a greatly reduced rate. Also, there are many variations on the kinds and numbers of rooms we can provide free.

A major problem is finding out from you who really has the authority to sign the contract. For some small conferences, we do not use written contracts, though we do like to have a letter of agreement, so both sides know what to expect and are clear on the costs. For a conference that will use a significant portion of our facilities, a written contract is essential. There are many who speak with an authoritative voice, but may not be the ones who can legally bind the Sponsor to an agreement. When we have dealt with a Coordinator in previous conferences, we know something about how each of us operates. For a first contract, reconize that at some point we need to know "who is in charge?"

Those of us who operate *conference centers* have a unique product. We do not take in transients, and our major purpose is conference work. We recognize that this is the major concern of the Coordinator and want to support him to the fullest extent. Obviously, there are differences if you contract for our entire facility or only part of it. In the latter case, we may not be as flexible regarding meal times and the use of some specialized facilities and equipment. This can all be worked out, and our personnel are geared to working with conferences.

If we are a *higher education institution*, recognize that our major function is not conferences. This does not mean that we cannot do an excellent job for you, but that it requires a bit more coordination than in some other types of facilities. Usually, we can be highly competitive on costs, as our overhead is borne by other parts of the institution. Also, we have facilities that are always there whether used or not, so the more we use them the lower our overhead. Some of us have special facilities, located either on campus or nearby. We even have special equipment for some professional conferences, which may not be readily available elsewhere. It is important the Coordinator visit us and spend time with us. We can make a significant contribution to many conferences, which is different from that available at some other sites.

There are many *hotels and motels* throughout the U.S. and not all of them can really handle conferences. If the group is small, and all that is needed are some bedrooms and a single conference room, almost any chain facility can handle that. Recognizing the growth in conference business, our larger installations have special rooms and personnel for conference work. It is rare that any single conference will take over an entire hotel or motel. Our regular commerical guests must be accommodated. But, we are always willing to explore possibilities, though it is less likely that we can provide the type of "cultural island" that is available at some of the other sites. However, we have advantages in the range of options and facilities that some of the more specialized sites lack.

*Cruise ships* and *theme parks* have not been adequately utilized for conferences. On cruise ships, we have possibilities that many Coordinators never consider. Some of our ships are small enough that a conference of even a few hundred participants can have the entire ship. This allows for scheduling of shipboard activities and ports of call in relation to the conference objectives and the needs of the participants. We have a range of supplies and services that enable a conference to be selfcontained. We also make provision for spouses and children so that they can come along but not lessen the impact of the conference.

Theme parks are not primarily designed for conferences, but we have found them attractive to participants. Therefore, we are expanding our facilities to accommodate conferences as well as transients. We recognize that we will appeal more to the MS which is a social and fraternal organization, rather than to those that are professional organizations. The PS and ES will find us helpful, if they are encouraging participants to bring families. Our appeal is mostly to conferences that will have a family attendance.

## Travel Personnel Say—

When you are choosing a site, think of travel. There are all kinds of positive possibilities, and we can be helpful if you contact us early enough.

When using domestic air travel, recognize that the energy crisis of the early 1970's caused many airlines to curtail services. This may not be apparent from their advertising, but the reality of the schedule is what we have to deal with. This can be expected to change, but it could be for either better or worse.

We have had Coordinators tell us that travel was not a problem—they flew to the prospective site with no difficulty and left just as easily. It is dangerous to generalize from one flight or from the experience of one individual. Discuss travel with us and avoid difficulty later.

There are various fly-and-drive possibilities, as well as other combinations which can enhance the attractiveness of your conference. Give us a chance to plan this with you while you are selecting your site.

Few of us have any illusions about the problem of ground transportation at airports. We can make suggestions to lessen this difficulty, if you discuss it with us beforehand. This would not be a crucial item in site selection, but perhaps we can offer some advice when you are considering alternative sites in the same general location.

For international air travel, see the experts. Flying internationally is much different from domestic air travel. Seeing the information in the airline schedule books does not communicate the whole story. If we specialize in international travel, we usually have people on our staff who have been there. They can tell you from personal experience some of the advantages and limitations of different cities and different modes of travel. We can also help you charter flights as well as individual travel. There are so many variations in rate structures, constantly changing, that this is a job for a reputable travel agency, and not a member of the secretariat.

### Local Convention and Visitors' Bureau Personnel Say—

Why not visit us first? If you are interested in our area, let us know and we can give you detailed information on available sites. We are not selling any of them—our interest is in our general area. We have the information on all of them and can give you a starting point in you search for the best site.

You may not know too much about us. We are local, nonprofit organizations that provide many of the resources you need to select a site and conduct a conference. In some cases we are part of the local government structure, while in other situations we are supported by the various suppliers. Most of us are members of the International Association of Convention and Visitors' Bureaus, an organization which was organized in 1914.

If you plan a large conference, see us as early as possible. Large numbers mean more income for our citizens, and that is our business. The larger the conference, the more we can help in getting special rates and other economic advantages for the Sponsor and the participants. We can also link together various kinds of services and suppliers whom you might need without your having to go out to find them.

After you have selected your site, let us know. We would be particularly interested in the reasons for your choice. This will help us improve our service to other Coordinators in the future. It can also help us when we advise our local sites as to what they should be offering and how to relate to site seekers.

If you are planning a drive-in conference, you must see us. We can advise on parking, one-way streets, etc. Sometimes, we can even put you in touch with the police to arrange for special parking and security.

## Equipment Personnel Say—

If the site does not have the necessary equipment, then come to us. We can all do a better job if you come to us during site selection. We know what we can provide, when, and how. If the site personnel make promises regarding equipment, without involving us, we cannot guarantee delivery. It is not important to find out who is to blame. What you are concerned with is having the best conference possible. Anytime the site personnel tell you that you will have to go outside for equipment, involve us in site selection.

We know that some Coordinators are bothered by unions. We have even had union conferences complain about using union projectionists. Usually, union equipment operators ensure quality performance. We police our own people and if you find union operators who do not perform well, let us know.

If equipment is a significant part of your conference, then the appropriate suppliers should be directly involved in site negotiation.

The delivery, setup, security, and knockdown of equipment are all important. If the site cannot accommodate to this, the Coordinator should know about it before signing the site contract.

## Catering Personnel Say—

Most sites do their own food service work. Some rely on outside caterers, but these are usually the "convention center" sites. They provide space for the conference, and nothing else. The participants are housed at local hotels, but mass feeding is done at the conference site. For this, the outside caterer is a source. There is usually only one caterer who has the contract for any food service in that site.

Our prices are usually published and the site personnel know what they are. Therefore, some site personnel may actually arrange for food service as part of the contract. All they can really arrange for is the price as related to the menu. It is important for the Coordinator to work with us to arrange for the type of serving, etc. If there is a large number to be fed, which is the usual case, much coordination is needed. We need to speak directly to the Coordinator, or any person designated by him, to arrange the logistics, so the mass feeding we supply is directly related to the flow and design of the conference. Even the type of food is important. We need to know if the Coordinator wants local food (grits in the South) or a more general menu. We neeed to know how to serve in relation to speakers and other activities during food service. There is much to be discussed, and this should be directly between us, not through the site personnel.

We can help, but we need to be involved during site selection. Otherwise, we can almost anticipate negative comments during the conference evaluation.

# | 7.
# i Exhibits

This chapter explores exhibits as an adjunct to a conference, rather than as an exhibition with a conference component. Initially, the Sponsor must focus on why exhibits are desirable for this particular conference and how they will contribute to the conference goals. It is rare to find a conference without exhibits of some kind. The term "exhibits" is used to describe a range of possibilities which can vary from a small table with literature, to multiple and complicated displays involving participants. It is unfortunate that exhibits are sometimes considered a necessary evil when, for most conferences, some kinds of exhibits are necessary and the evil aspect can easily be avoided. The aspects of exhibits which we will discuss are

- Purposes
- Exhibitor's committee
- Relationship to design
- Getting participants to the exhibit area.

## Purposes

If there have been exhibits at prior conferences, it is likely that the Sponsor will decide to have exhibits again, unless the feedback from participants and exhibitors has been overwhelmingly negative.

If the prior conferences have not contained exhibits, then the DC must explore the reason for this absence. It may be because they could not contribute to conference goals, the exhibitors were not interested, or there had been a decision at an earlier time not to involve exhibitors. It is important for the DC, which feels that exhibits would be helpful, to fully explore the past history of the Sponsor in relation to exhibits. It may merely be that the Sponsor had not previously explored having exhibits in conjunction with the conference.

There are four major purposes for having exhibits, and in any particular conference there may be exhibits for one or more of them.

**Financial Return to the Sponsor**

Exhibits can be a significant source of income for the Sponsor. Indeed, many an MS looks forward to the annual conference and to the exhibits as a way of balancing the budget. There is nothing wrong with using exhibits to provide a financial return to the Sponsor. If this is the sole or major purpose, there could be problems for the DC. The Sponsor will tend to favor the exhibitors' demands over those of the DC. In the event of conflict, the DC will be the one to lose.

An ES is least likely to have exhibits for financial purposes, because it does not usually use a conference as an income producing activity.

If the PS is offering conferences as an income producing activity, it is highly improbable that they would want to have exhibitors who could provide competition. Still, a PS might choose to have carefully selected exhibitors who would supplement what the PS has to offer and to whom the PS could allocate some of the conference expense. If the PS wants to conduct a conference for purposes other than financial return, then income from exhibitors may be necessary in order to fund the conference and to enable the PS to charge a lower fee to participants.

——— • ———

For several years in the Washington, D.C. area there has been an annual audiovisual workshop. One year the conference was cosponsored by three professional organizations and a university. The Coordinator had been the Coordinator and the moving force of the three previous conferences. The DC was composed of the Coordinator and a representative of each of the four sponsoring organizations. The conference was open to all who wished to attend, and was not limited to membership in one of the Sponsor organizations. The Coordinator sought firms in the Washington, D.C. area who might be exhibitors. The income from these exhibitors enabled the DC to set a fairly low fee for participants, and even provided some income to the Sponsors.

——— • ———

As noted earlier, the MS may be highly dependent upon the income from exhibitors at the annual conference. This requires that the DC identify inducements to encourage exhibitors to participate, and then design accordingly. Some of the possibilities for designing will be discussed in the "Relationship to Design" section.

**Interest of Participants**

The participants of any particular conference will have interests which they hope to satisfy by attending the conference. If the Sponsor provides exhibits which meet the needs and interests of the participants, then the exhibits perform a significant function. This also serves to encourage further participation at future conferences offered by the Sponsor.

An ES shares its new developments with the participants by using exhibits. When the participants are employees of the Sponsor, the exhibits may show the products or the latest concerns of the employing organization. For a large multisite ES, exhibits are significant to communicate what is going on at some of the different company sites. For a multinational company, the value of such exhibits is even more apparent, because too often employees in distant lands are not sufficiently aware of the newer movements in the company.

A business organization may sponsor a conference for sales persons or dealers. The sales persons might be employees, but not in all cases. The dealers certainly are not employees of the Sponsor. But both groups attend the conference because the Sponsor invites them and wants to encourage them to feature and sell more of the Sponsor's products. Both the sales people and the dealers attend because it is to their benefit to learn as much as possible about the products they are to sell. Exhibits are crucial in keeping the participants up-to-date on the new products of the Sponsor and on modifications of existing product lines.

A PS can use exhibits to keep participants informed of new developments in their field of interest. These may be exhibits about other activities of the Sponsor, or activities of related organizations and groups. Of course, the exhibitors must be carefully selected so that they reinforce the Sponsor.

The MS will arrange for exhibits which reflect the interests of the participants, and these depend on the kind of organization which is doing the sponsoring. When the Sponsor is a professional organization, it is likely that the membership will expect that, by attending the conference, they will be able to experience exhibits which will keep them abreast of the latest developments in their field. If the MS conference is composed of persons who are in the same trade or industry, the participants can use the exhibits to update their information about what is happening in their common field. An MS whose focus is on social or fraternal purposes may not have quite the same interest in the exhibit area. It is probable that the only exhibits in this case would be those related to what the organization itself wants to tell its members about programs, paraphernalia, etc.

**Sales by Exhibitors**

Up to this point we have been exploring why the Sponsor and participants would want exhibits. It is also important to explore why exhibitors would want to become involved in conferences, which frequently require a significant outlay of personnel time and financial resources. If the exhibitors cannot have their needs met, it is unlikely that they will be willing to participate in conferences by purchasing space or utilizing "free" space. (It is never really free, for the exhibitor must pay for the materials and personnel, even if there is no charge for space.) The DC must identify what the exhibitors can expect to gain from the conference if they are to be encourged to purchase space.

## Commercial Exhibitors

There are probably two major reasons why commercial exhibitors do buy space at a conference. The first is that the exhibitor hopes to make sales at the conference. This does not mean that the goods will actually be delivered at the conference, although this can happen in the case of some small consumer items, books, etc. Principally, an exhibitor is hoping to take orders for goods which will be delivered at a later date. The exhibitor wants the participants to have sufficient time to explore the exhibits, to examine the products, to question their uses, and to have the opportunity to talk at leisure and at length with exhibitor personnel.

The exhibit area is a high-pressure situation, although every effort may be made to make it appear as a low-pressure one. The evaluation by exhibitors may be based on how many sales resulted, or how many contacts were made. The DC needs to know what criteria the exhibitors are using to determine whether their presence at the conference has been successful.

Another different goal of some exhibitors may be to make contacts at the conference which will be followed up later. For this objective, the organization of the exhibit area tends to be more relaxed and more conducive to conversations and interaction, with less emphasis on closings (as used in sales terminology). Exhibitors will still want to show their products or services, but will expect a different set-up in the exhibit area.

It is possible to have a mixture of both sales and contacts within the same exhibit area. A large conference, with many exhibitors, will undoubtedly serve both purposes. The DC needs to know the exhibitors' expectations so that design elements can reflect the needs of the exhibitors, to the extent possible.

## Noncommercial Exhibitors

Noncommercial exhibits can also be found at conferences. These are for general information purposes, and are usually sponsored by organizations which may or may not be commercially oriented. For example, there is a type of advertising called "missionary" where the advertiser/exhibitor is trying to contribute to building its image in the eyes of the participants though no effort is being made for any direct sales, and perhaps not even contacts.

More common are noncommerical exhibits provided by government agencies that find it beneficial to have exhibits at carefully selected conferences. Chief among these are the Department of Labor, Department of HEW, Department of Commerce, and Internal Revenue Service. There are also state and local organizations that provide exhibits to encourage companies to move into their jurisdiction for economic and tax purposes.

### Exhibitors' Committee

Over the past few years, exhibitors have become more sophisticated and demanding. Those who participate in conferences for sales purposes have taken long hard looks at the cost of exhibiting and at the possible return. One result has been the decision by exhibitors to seek more involvement in the whole conference process. In many cases exhibitors have formed a committee to work with the DC. This should not be an adversary relationship, but it can move in that direction if the exhibitors' committee and the DC do not clarify their respective roles and relationships. On the other hand, there may be times when a DC will urge the formation of an exhibitors' committee in order to provide a direct line of communication between the many exhibitors and the DC.

There are many ways for exhibitors' committee members to be selected. For MS conferences there is usually a core group of exhibitors who participate from year to year, although, because of changes in product lines, new companies forming, and old companies changing, it is likely that each year will find new exhibitors who are interested and old exhibitors who are no longer interested. Therefore, one approach is for the DC to encourage the exhibitors to form a committee which can represent them, but whose membership will change from year to year. The exhibitors' committee can consist of individuals who have participated as exhibitor personnel, or who are company representatives. Obviously, it would be more helpful to have personnel who have also been exhibitor personnel at prior conferences. They are more likely to know the kinds of participants to expect, as well as the probable design thrust, which may not change significantly from year to year.

The exhibitors' committee should be initiated early enough so that they can make inputs to the DC during the early states of its work. The suggestions from the exhibitors' committee will relate directly to the work of the DC. The DC can react to the input and contact the exhibitors' committee with suggestions for its members. The exhibitors' committee can then go back to all the exhibitors with ideas from the DC and can encourage suggestions from exhibitors. In any event, the DC should not use the exhibitors' committee to control the exhibitors. Exhibitor personnel are generally experienced and sophisticated, and will resent manipulation just as they will respond positively to the opportunity for involvement.

It is helpful if the exhibitors' committee does not change completely from year to year. Continuity facilitates the work of the DC, as well as being more representative of the general trend of those exhibiting. However, it must be possible for a new exhibitor to make some input to the exhibitor's committee.

This can be accomplished when the DC sends out material encouraging exhibitors to participate in the conference. The material can include reference to the exhibitors' committee and if possible, the name of the individual to be contacted for more information about the work of the committee.

### Relationship to Design

Whether there is an exhibitors' committee or not, it is important that there be as close a relationship as possible between the design and the exhibits. All too frequently, the participant finds that moving from the sessions to the exhibits requires a significant shift in thinking and behavior. It is almost as if two different conferences were going on simultaneously. This should not be the case. Unless the DC relates to the exhibits, this can happen. In some cases, the Sponsor sees the DC as functioning only in the design area, and as the exhibits are income producing, they should be under the direct control of the Sponsor. This produces a dichotomous conference, and results in confusion on the part of the participants, and even conflict between the DC and exhibitors. It also results in the loss of a valuable resource to the DC.

### Coordination with Design Activity

Any exhibitor can organize his exhibit many ways for a specific conference. Of course, there are some exhibitors who have packaged exhibits with little or no flexibility. More common is the exhibitor who has complete flexibility or, if using a packaged display, tends to make it modular, so that a module can be pulled out and another substituted, depending upon the particular conference where it will be used. To enable the exhibitor to make the selection of the appropriate module, the content of the exhibit, and the personnel, the DC should notify exhibitors as early as possible of at least the theme of the conference. Then, as the design process moves ahead, the exhibitors should be kept informed of the thrust the DC is proposing. In some cases, the DC may already have made decisions and will inform the exhibitors. There are times when the DC may merely wish to inform the exhibitors of some directions they are considering and ask for suggestions from the exhibitors much as they would from potential participants or potential resource people.

An important reason for involving the exhibitors early in the design process is to afford them an opportunity to respond to being a resource to the conference. The exhibitors will have materials and equipment that may be useful for resource people who are conducting particular sessions. Of course, it is important to avoid having the exhibitors use a regular conference session to market their products, unless this is an objective of the conference. Some Sponsors are extremely cautious about this possibility as the policy statement of the American Society for Training and Development indicates. It is included here as an example of the steps Sponsors should take to ensure that there is a clear distinction between the exhibit area activities and session activities.

## SUBJECT: ETHICAL PRINCIPLES FOR ASTD ACTIVITIES AND PROGRAMS*

Statement of Purpose

ASTD provides a unique forum for open dialogue and creative exchange of ideas among professionals in our field. Consequently, it is essential that every Society activity and program represent the highest standard in decorum, mutual understanding and conscientious adherence to ethical principles on the part of *all* participants.

1. Unless specifically designated, ASTD programs and seminars are a *noncommercial* forum. Individuals should refrain from the use of brand names and specific product endorsement whenever practicable and under *no* circumstances should the Society podium be used as a place for direct promotion of a speaker's product, service, or monetary self-interest.

*Abstracted from the ASTD Policy Statement of January 10, 1975.

There may be some sessions in which resource people will be referring to items in the exhibit area, and with appropriate coordination, materials could be made available to the resource people. A case in point is one where a resource person is speaking about a product and how it was used by him, but does not have the product readily available. This frequently happens in the case of audio-visual materials, and the best the resource person can do is to indicate to the participants that they can go to a certain booth and see the equipment. It would be just as easy for the exhibitor to provide the resource person with his product and still avoid being involved in marketing to the audience at that session.

There are many ethical problems to be considered in this kind of coordination, and the DC should be aware of these and avoid conflicts such as favoring one exhibitor over another, or allowing the sessions to be used essentially for marketing the products of any exhibitors.

Of course, if the purpose of the conference is to sell, and the participants have come for that purpose, then the DC must design sessions which serve as showcases for exhibitors' products. For this kind of conference the DC must still be cautious about ethical conflicts, such as degrading competitors, offering extra benefits, staging special selling sessions in competition, and offering material or information that conflicts with sponsor policy. A conference designed as an exhibitor showcase will probably have a significant number of exhibitors as members of the DC.

## Integrating the Design and the Exhibits

The exhibits should be integrated with the conference to the greatest extent possible. Exhibitors can assign the personnel and choose the products or services that most closely relate to the theme and the participants, and, if notified early enough, the exhibitor can choose whether to relate exhibits to the general conference theme, or to a particular objective, session, or track. This is a decision that must be made by the exhibitor, not the DC, but it requires that the exhibitors have sufficient notice of the objectives and aspects of the design so they will have the data on which to base these important decisions.

We have previously discussed the danger of ethical conflicts, when a resource person sells a specific product from the platform. There are exhibitors for whom this can be appropriate. For example, in the case of noncommerical exhibits, when the intent is information giving, this would be highly desireable. In such cases, the exhibitors might even be offered platform time so they can reach participants in a more organized manner. However, the line between these situations can be so unclear that the DC would do best to err in the direction of not having any exhibitors on the program, unless every exhibitor can be offered the same opportunity.

These precautions should not prevent exhibitors from integrating with the sessions in other ways. For example, it would be acceptable for an exhibitor to advertise a particular session at the exhibit booth. If a resource person is going to be covering material that is related to the exhibitor, but not advertising the product or service, such additional publicity is expected and accepted. For example, an exhibitor who is a book publisher may find that one of "their authors" is a resource person at the conference. The author may not even be speaking about the published book, but still the publisher wants to draw attention to the caliber of author they have. A notice of this relationship at the exhibitor's booth would certainly be ethical, and it is hoped, done in good taste.

## Special Exhibition Sessions

As mentioned earlier, there is the tendency on the part of some Sponsors to separate the design activities from the exhibits. Yet, there are excellent reasons why the DC should be involved with exhibits and in communication with exhibitors. Through careful coordination in designing sessions and the scheduling of activities in the exhibit areas, it is possible to improve the quality of the involvement and the opportunity for communication.

One design possibility is the *film festival*. Many exhibitors have films which describe their product or service, and some exhibitors will be marketing films at the conference. The DC can have a booth set aside which is adequately darkened, where exhibitors can show their films on a regular schedule. This space usually will be a booth within the exhibit area, so that more participants will be attracted.

Another alternative is to have the film festival outside of the exhibit area in one of the rooms where regular sessions are being scheduled. Films are listed and shown on a prearranged schedule. The DC needs to explore with the exhibitor or the exhibitors' committee which arrangement is preferred. Having the film festival in the exhibit area might bring more participants in to visit other areas. Having the films shown in the regular session room area might reach more participants who might otherwise spend little time in the exhibit area. Of course, participants seeing a film of interest in the regular session area might then decide to visit the exhibit area to seek more information about the film, or the product or service. To do both at the same conference might be oversaturation.

The DC might also consider an *exhibitors' general information booth*. This is helpful when the exhibit area is quite large or if it is expected that the participants may not take the time and energy to cover the whole area unless they can identify booths of interest. Space is set aside, usualy close enough to the entrance to encourage participation, but far enough inside the area so that the participant actually enters the exhibit area. The purpose is to give the participant a taste of what is available in the exhibit area and perhaps even help him plan which exhibits to visit. In addition, it can help those exhibitors who feel that they have less than desirable space and might not attract as many participants as they would like.

Each exhibitor is given fifteen to thirty minutes, depending on what the DC and exhibitors mutually decide, to present pertinent information or have a prepared audio-visual presentation. The schedule can be repeated as many times as possible within the time the exhibit area is open.

A variation of this is to have the exhibitors' general information booth near the registration booth, but this can present some traffic problems. If the registration area has sufficient space, this exhibitors' booth can offer a welcome diversion during early registration and then be a constant resource during the time the exhibits are in place, even though the exhibit area itself may be closed.

Another possibility involves using participants, rather than exhibitor personnel. This is sometimes called *show and tell*. A booth is provided in the exhibit area, with a prearranged schedule. The exhibitor is given a period of time, usually not to exceed forty-five minutes, and during this time the exhibitor's product or service is shown, described, or demonstrated depending upon which approach is more appropriate. This is *not* done by exhibitor's personnel, but by a regular participant who describes to other participants how he has successfully used the product or service.

———— ● ————

The show and tell booth was set up in the exhibit area. Many of the exhibitors at this conference sold films to the participants. A schedule was posted indicating that, while the exhibit area was open, each film company exhibitor would have forty-five minutes. The exhibitors were briefed beforehand by the DC and each decided to show one film within their time block. Each film was introduced by a participant who had actually used the film in a real situation (not just a preview). After the film was shown, the participant described how he had actually used the film, including a discussion of its advantages, and its limitations. The participant also responded to questions from other participants.

The ground rule was that no film could be shown by an exhibitor unless a participant could be identified who had used the film and was willing to assume responsibility for the session. Obviously, this limited the films to be shown in this booth to those which had been previously used, thus preventing the introduction of new films in this particular session. The booth was continually booked, and the feedback from participants who attended was very positive.

———— ● ————

In this example there was no additional fee required from the exhibitors for the use of this facility. Of course, the exhibitors who did not have films and were not included did express some dissatisfaction. They too would have liked some additional exposure to participants. Similar sessions for nonfilm materials or services can be designed.

### Scheduling

The hours that exhibit areas will be open sometimes creates great conflict between the DC and the exhibitors. This is aggravated by the previously mentioned tendency of some Sponsors to keep the DC and exhibitors apart. Problems occur when the DC designs a full program, involving the participants in session or nonsession activities continually, while the exhibitors want the participants to spend large blocks of time in the exhibit area. This does not have to cause conflict between the DC and the exhibitors, as the needs of both have a legitimate place in the conference design, whether the Sponsor is ES, PS, or MS. There must be sufficient coordination and joint planning so that the design will reflect the inputs and compromises of the DC and the exhibitors.

The first decision relates to which days the exhibits will be open. There are various possibilities, depending upon the length of the conference, as to how soon the exhibitors can set up and how late they must knock down. As indicated in the previous chapter, this has to be determined early enough so that the DC is aware of whatever limitations the site imposes. A common approach is to have the exhibits open the second day of the conference. In a four- or five-day conference, the exhibits usually terminate a day before the end of the conference. When the site books many conferences, one right after the other, there must be some time for cleanup by site personnel, in addition to the hiatus needed between the knockdown of one conference and the setup of the next. However, many sites apparently have enough space for both storage of incoming exhibits and for exhibits to be shipped out, or they are not booked so solidly that other possibilities are available to the DC.

One possibility is to have the exhibit open on days that coincide directly with the conference. Therefore, if the conference is starting on Monday, the exhibitors would have to arrive with their exhibits either on Saturday or Sunday so they are all set up and the exhibit area can be opened in conjunction with the conference opening.

Another possibility is to have the entire exhibit area open either just before or just after the conference. This may be more attractive to an MS that is a trade association. The exhibits for a trade group could be crucial enough so that participants arrive before the opening of the main part of the conference and stay after the close. Sometimes a DC attempts to bridge this by including the exhibit days as part of the program design. For example, the DC may announce a five-day conference, but design it so that the first two days are exhibits and the last three days are sessions. This kind of scheduling is high risk, as participants may not arrive early enough or stay long enough to visit the exhibits, which will produce extremely negative feedback from the exhibitors and probably dissuade them from participating in future conferences. Generally, exhibitors prefer that the exhibit days be integrated with the session days so that the participants will be at the site.

Another aspect of scheduling is the number of hours the exhibit area will be open. This, too, can provide a conflict, in which some exhibitors find themselves trapped. Exhibitors may want the exhibit area open for many hours, but at the same time they recognize that staffing an exhibit can be an extremely debilitating activity. If the exhibits are open for many hours at a stretch, it may require staffing with additional personnel, thereby raising the cost for the exhibitors. If the exhibit is not open a sufficient number of hours, it may not warrant participation by the exhibitor. This is another instance where the exhibitors' committee is extremely valuable in communicating their desires on hours to the DC. This may require negotiation.

In addition to the total number of hours the exhibit area is to be open, the time of day is significant. There is no best time for an exhibit area to be open. This decision relates to the nature of the sessions, the length of the sessions, the proximity of the exhibit areas to the session rooms, and the lure of the recreation and entertainment activities that are available. All these are variables, and there is no exact formula that will guarantee success. The best that can be hoped for is that times of day and number of hours will meet the needs of the DC, the exhibitors, and most important, the participants.

The availability of the exhibit, as to both days and hours, must be directly related to the other design elements being planned by the DC. The prime activity, of course, is the sessions. It is too easy to have conflict between these sessions and the hours the exhibit area is open. In such cases, both the DC and the exhibitors must realize that there are conflicts and reach some agreements. For example, the exhibitors may want the exhibit areas open during lunch time, because the participants would probably have some free time to spend in the exhibit area. However, the DC may be planning on some luncheon activities such as an awards ceremony or a cracker barrel session. Obviously, these activities could prove a better draw than the exhibit area. On the day when these activities are scheduled, it would probably be more advantageous to close the exhibit area. Some exhibitors find little difficulty in competing with these other activities, as not every participant goes to the awards luncheon or the cracker barrel sessions. However, if the cost of these luncheons has been built into the conference fee, attendance is more likely, and the result will be a rather empty exhibit area.

There are other activities which can create conflicts without adequate planning. Field trips may be planned which would draw off large numbers of participants, and the exhibitors can expect that at that time the exhibit area might be closed. Of course, exhibitors may contend that not everybody goes on the field trips and they might prefer to remain open to provide an additional opportunity for those who stay behind. This should be discussed, and decided upon before the conference starts, in light of expected participant behavior. If time has been scheduled during the conference for recreational activities (the golf tournament) or for special entertainment (the Texas Bar-B-Que), then these periods might be less desirable for keeping the exhibits open. Some of the exhibitors might even wish to take part in the recreation and entertainment which is offered. This can best be determined by open communication between a DC and the exhibitors, prior to the conference.

## Getting Participants to the Exhibit Area

Exhibit areas are of no use unless paticipants visit them. Earlier we discussed the difficulty of scheduling so as to minimize conflicts between sessions and exhibit hours. There are, however, some positive approaches that can be taken by the DC, with the cooperation of the exhibitors, which will encourage participants to visit the exhibits.

## Opening Ceremonies

Just as the opening of the conference is a significant activity and is highlighted by a keynote speaker, the opening of the exhibit area can also be such an event. There are several reasons for making the opening of the exhibit area one of the highlights of the conference. The exhibit area may be in a different place from where the participants are lodged. In order to maximize the use of the exhibit area it is important for the participants to know, as early as possible in the conference, exactly where the exhibit area is located. By highlighting the opening ceremony, attention is focused on the physical location of the exhibition. If the particpants visit the exhibit on the opening day, the location becomes familiar and they will be able to find it comfortably at future times.

There are many ways to conduct the opening ceremony. It should be conducted in good taste, consonant with the climate of the conference and the expectations of the participants.

—— • ——

The exhibit area was located in the same hotel where the participants were lodged, but a distance from where the sessions were being held. To focus attention, a ribbon-cutting ceremony was planned, with the president of the MS dramatically cutting the ribbon with a large pair of golden scissors to signify the opening of the entrance to the exhibit area. When participants arrived at the ribbon-cutting ceremony, they found the president, other officers, and a bevy of scantily clad females (professional showgirls) mingling with the participants and encouraging them to enter the exhibit area upon completion of the ceremony. The ceremony went as planned, and many of the participants did follow the girls into the exhibit area. But this was rapidly followed by a demonstration and boycott of the exhibit area by female participants who resented the use of scantily clad females as a device to highlight the exhibit area.

—— • ——

The opening can be more than just a ribbon-cutting ceremony. More attention will be given later to prizes, but a brief discussion is appropriate here. The object of a planned opening is to encourage maximum attendance by participants at this time. Special inducements can be offered in the form of prizes, refreshments, or other "freebees" which could attract participants. When consumer goods that participants can take with them are being exhibited, exhibitors can provide special offers in conjunction with the opening ceremony. Some exhibitors might announce that they will have a small gift for the first fifty (or any given number) participants who come to their booth.

The opening must not conflict with regular conference sessions, but it should be early enough in the conference to reach the objective of familiarizing the participant with the nature of the exhibits.

## Location of Exhibit Area

To the extent possible, the exhibit area should be located close to the sessions area. This could present some participant movement problems, but the closer these two areas are, the more pertinent the exhibit will appear, and the less possibility that participants will be dissuaded from attending by having to go to a different part of the facility to see the exhibition. In some sites the exhibit area is located in the basement or some other less desirable part of the building. Participants may hesitate to wander into these less known areas.

The exhibit area must be designated clearly enough so that a participant does not start to attend a session only to find that it is an exhibitor's room. The two should be clearly marked, but close enough to each other so that distance does not become either a physical or psychological barrier.

If space permits, another possibility is to have the exhibits near the bedrooms of the participants. If a conference center is being used at which lodging is provided, the participants may have their bedrooms in one wing, with the session rooms in another wing of the center. There may be large hallways or lobby areas between the two that could be used as exhibit areas. There would probably be less floor space and that could mean smaller booths or fewer exhibits. But this placement provides much more involvement with the participant. Whether this is desirable would depend upon the nature of the site, and the purpose of the exhibits.

The DC can also explore other parts of the site to house exhibits, areas that would normally be in the path that participants can be expected to use. The closer the exhibits are to normal participant movements, the greater the attendance at the exhibits, to the satisfaction of all concerned.

## Prizes

The use of prizes to encourage participant attendance is a delicate matter. Some professional groups might resent being offered prizes to encourage them to visit a particular exhibit. The term "prize" can be avoided and some other appropriate term used. The gift (or some other euphemism) should be directly related to the self-image of the participants and the conflict can then be avoided. For example, if a professional magazine is exhibiting at a professional conference, then giving away free copies of the current issue of the magazine to those who visit the booth would not be in conflict with the professional image of the participants.

A common form of prize giving is through the use of drawings. When participants visit booths, they are given cards to fill out. At a later date, winners are drawn from these cards. There are many possible variations for handling a drawing, and we will limit this discussion to some of the major practices.

Each exhibitor can have his own drawing. When participants visit the booth, they fill out cards, which are retained by the exhibitor. At some place in the booth area an announcement of the prizes and either the time of the drawing or the time when the winners will be announced should be posted. Obviously, the exhibitors will make this as late in the life of the exhibit area as possible to obtain maximum participant involvement.

There can also be a single drawing for the entire exhibit area with individual exhibitors pooling their prizes, but without losing identity as to the source of the prize. For a single drawing the cards are filled out at each booth, but then the cards are returned to the original exhibitors after the drawing.

The DC needs to be involved in order to coordinate the drawings with other conference activities. Also, the list of prizes may be part of the preconference publicity arranged by the DC. The DC may also have appropriate cards printed and make provision for their return to individual exhibitors when there is a single drawing.

Some DCs lose the value of the drawing by insufficient planning and publicity. The drawing should be a public affair, held in the open, with sufficient fanfare to attract participants to the exhibit area. It is the counterpart of the opening ceremonies and can have a role in encouraging some participants to stay for the entire conference in the hope of winning one of the prizes.

The type of prize can be important. If there is much publicity, the participants should be able to expect significant prizes to be awarded. The DC might have several exhibitors pool their contributions to the prize so as to be able to offer several expensive prizes, such as cruises, or costly equipment. These can then be supplemented by several less expensive items or some of the exhibitor's products or services.

The cards which the participants fill out have uses other than just being the basis for awarding the prizes. Each exhibitor will want to use the cards for a mailing list to allow for postconference follow-ups.

The whole process of the drawing should be planned by the DC so as to be done in good taste and to reflect the climate of the conference. Drawings and lotteries are a part of American history, going back to prerevolutionary days. Announcing a drawing raises expectations on the part of the participants, and it is important for the DC to recognize these expectations and to plan the drawing accordingly. If the exhibitors are not prepared to offer significant prizes, perhaps the DC should discourage this activity entirely.

There are other forms of "prizes" which do not involve drawings. The most common is the discount. This is utilized when the exhibitors are showing commodities that the participants can purchase directly, including such things as books, clothing, and films. In some situations the purchased item can be picked up by the participant during the conference. Or, the order can be placed at the conference with the appropriate "conference discount" and be delivered at a later date. When there may be significant items available at a conference discount, the DC might want to include this information in the preconference publicity as another inducement for conference attendance. Primarily, this is true of MS conferences, though it might also be of interest to a PS.

## Meals and Refreshments

Another way of encouraging participants to visit the exhibit area is to offer free food and drink. Not only does it reduce the conference costs for the participants, but the Sponsors as well. The participants might be offered a continental breakfast (i.e. juice, coffee, and hot roll or cake) in a different part of the exhibit area each morning, prior to the first session of the day. It encourages the early bird participant to come to the exhibit area as the first activity of the morning. The participant partakes of the continental breakfast, which can be eaten while walking, and allows for movement from one exhibit to another.

If there is a large exhibit area, the continental breakfast can be made available in different parts of the area so that participants are encouraged to move about. They will be inclined to visit more exhibits, which is the purpose of offering the breakfast. The DC should work with the exhibitors in planning this so that the continental breakfast is terminated in sufficient time to avoid conflict between those seeking a late breakfast, but who should be attending the sessions.

It is also possible to offer light refreshments (coffee and donuts or soft drinks) at different times during the day to encourage participants to visit the exhibit area. If this is to be offered, it should be announced in such a manner so that all participants are aware of these amenities. Provision must be made to replenish food supplies as they become exhausted. It is bad business to announce the availability of cold drinks in the exhibit area during the afternoon, only to have the drinks gone when the participants arrive a little late. This will dissuade the participants from taking advantage of other offers made by exhibitors.

Some exhibitors dislike the serving of food in the exhibit area because of the possible damage to their exhibits by spilled coffee, sticky soda, or piles of crumbs. The DC should work with the exhibitors to ascertain if they are all in favor of food (for which they will be expected to pay) in the area. There might be some suggestions as to which parts of the area might be more desirable for the food service.

Generally, exhibitors view the offering of light meals and refreshments favorably, as it is part of the American tradition of "visiting" and being "homey." Participants are more likely to stay and talk with exhibitor personnel when they realize that these people have paid for the coffee they are drinking. It is one of the climate setting elements.

Less common, but still a factor, is the cocktail party of exhibitors. Sometimes, these are held in the exhibit area as an additional encouragement for participants to visit. This activity tends to be more expensive than those previously mentioned, but for some conferences, the cocktail party may be expected.

In addition to these activities in the exhibit area, exhibitors tend to have receptions in their suites or in some other place outside of the exhibit area. The DC need not be concerned with these, but should concentrate only on those meal and refreshment activities that are designed to bring the participants into the exhibit area.

## Social Area

Previously, we discussed a lounge area or a place where participants could sit down, and meet, and talk with other participants in an informal way about the conference or anything that concerns them. One possibility is to set up the lounge or social areas within the exhibit area. If this is done, exhibitors should accept the ground rule that this is neutral territory and the exhibitor personnel should not occupy the space. The participants should not feel trapped while in this area but, rather, as relaxed as possible.

The need for a social-lounge area is also a reflection of our changing population. With the declining birth rate, and with people living longer, the average age of participants at conferences will tend to rise. Older persons are more likely to want a place to sit and relax. If the social areas are provided at convenient spots around the exhibit area, particpants will spend more time in the general exhibit area, and therefore more time visiting individual exhibits. The alternative is to stay on their feet, get tired, and leave the exhibit area for their rooms, the coffee shop, or some other place where they can sit down.

This discussion of age is a generalization. For each conference the DC must refer to the participant profile and predict who might be attending. This may indicate the type of facility most appropriate for the social area. Even younger participants would find a social area helpful, but might prefer to stand or move around within the area.

### From the Suppliers' Viewpoint

There are many suppliers involved in exhibits, but the exhibitor should not be considered a supplier. The exhibitor is part of the conference and sometimes is a participant as well as an exhibitor. Suppliers service all elements of the conference, including the exhibitors.

**Site Personnel Say—**

We welcome exhibits but they usually require much more coordination than that involved in providing bedrooms or meeting rooms. An accurate schedule for arrival and departure of exhibit materials is essential. With this, we can all work together to make the exhibit successful.

We should discuss our mutual needs openly. If there is an exhibitors' committee, and we suggest you have one, their representative should be in on our discussions. We can suggest locations for your exhibit as well as show how it can relate to other activities and facilities at our site.

After initial agreement, the Coordinator does not need to be involved in getting the exhibits organized and set up. Frequently, we have qualified personnel who can assist the exhibitors. If not, we can provide lists of those who can handle the packing, shipping, electrical, etc.

The exhibit opening is important. We hope it will be congruent with our site and not be offensive or irritating to any other guests. If necessary, we are prepared to help with the PR.

**Equipment Personnel Say—**

Many of us have a great deal of experience in providing for the support services exhibitors need. Some of us specialize in conference work and can handle everything from the arrival of your exhibit to its departure.

If you have your own exhibit, we can help set it up and then handle the knockdown. If you need an exhibit, we can make it. Some of us belong to associations whose members specialize in making exhibits. Of course, to make an exhibit takes much longer than to just set up and knock down, so give us sufficient time to do the quality job you want.

The site can also give you a list of those of us who are prepared to come in on an emergency basis when some part of your exhibit goes wrong. On unpacking, you may find parts missing, which have to be fabricated on the spot. Or, after you arrive you may want to make significant changes. We can work with you, but of course, the more notice we have the more likely that we can meet your needs exactly.

**Local Convention and Visitors' Bureau Personnel Say—**

We welcome exhibitors at conferences. Of course, we are fully aware that some of you will be in direct competition with our local people. We are prepared to accept this because of the general revenue our area will receive from your conference.

We can help the Coordinator find local exhibitors. Sometimes, these will be local outlets for merchandise and services available nationwide. However, the local supplier/merchant might be interested in a tie-in, hoping to get some business out of the conference. There are also local merchants who are unique, and would welcome the opportunity of exhibiting at your conference. Contact us and we can help you try to identify additional local exhibitors.

The question of selling at an exhibit is delicate. The Internal Revenue Service has changed its mind several times on what is taxable in relation to trade shows and other exhibits where selling takes place. We can help you interpret these rulings as they might apply to your exhibit. In addition, we have local laws, and if there is to be selling at the exhibit, a likely possibility, we should discuss it so that there is no legal complication.

If exhibitors are offering prizes, there might be some local options that would be of interest to them, such as theater tickets and free dinners at some of our leading restaurants. We can help make these contacts.

Some exhibitors find it expensive to bring their personnel to service the booths. If nontechnical personnel are needed, we can identify those who could staff the booths and enhance the image of the exhibitor. Some exhibitors may bring some of their own personnel, but would want to supplement them with local people.

# 8.
# The Conference
# Program Book

All of the previously discussed decisions and activities that make a successful conference must be recorded in the conference program book, which for simplicity will be referred to as the "book." The production of this book signals the end of the design committee's work.

As we approach the stage of conducting the conference, a new group comes into focus—the steering committee (SC). Chapter 11 discusses the SC in much more detail, but in the present chapter we will begin to see some of the work that is expected of SC members.

The Coordinator is still active, though he is not necessarily the same person who worked with the DC in planning the conference. Occasionally, the Sponsor may use an internal person as the Coordinator at this stage and dispense with the services of the external person who had been involved previously.

The conference program book is sometimes referred to as the staging book, as it resembles the book a director might use in staging a pageant or a similar complicated activity. For an ES or PS conference with fewer participants and simpler logistics the book might only be a folder. Whatever its form or name, there is the need for one set of documents that set forth all the decisions and activities in a way that does not allow for any significant omissions and is clear for all to see.

The book will probably be changed during the course of the conference, so it is helpful if its form allows for this. A common practice is to use a loose-leaf binder with tabs to designate the sections. Different sections can be highlighted by using different colored pages; this prevents changed pages from being inserted into the wrong section.

The book should be produced in sufficient numbers so that all who use it can have their own copy. A suggested list of those who should have copies appears in Figure 8-1. This is a minimum list and it is quite likely that additional copies might be needed, so the secretariat should be instructed to have several copies in reserve.

| Sponsor Personnel | Expected Use |
|---|---|
| Coordinator | Use for control and information purposes |
| Steering committee (one copy for each member) | Have entire conference information readily available for advice and/or decision making |
| Secretariat (additional copies retained here) | Check on facilities, supplies, personnel, etc. |
| Exhibitor committee chairperson (or exhibit coordinator) | Relate exhibits to total conference |
| Public relations | Prepare releases and coordinate with media |

| Site Personnel | |
|---|---|
| Conference manager | Use for control and information purposes |
| Front desk manager | Provide information as well as for scheduling front desk personnel |
| Switchboard manager | Respond to questions as well as to identify persons to be contacted |
| Food service manager | Coordinate scheduled food service |
| Public relations | Prepare releases and coordinate with media |

**Figure 8-1.** This is a suggested list of those who should have copies of the conference program book.

In the interests of saving paper and reducing information overload, it might be decided to give some persons on the list only that section of the book which relates to them. However, as the conference is an integrated whole, it is probable that each person on the list could have use for more than just their own section of the book.

The book should contain at least the following information, with a separate section for each item:

- Floor and room diagrams
- Conference design
- Exhibit information
- Special events

(Continued on next page)

- Daily events (sessions and activities)
- Conference administrative personnel

If desired, other sections can be added, such as registration procedures, conference program, and a list of participants.

### Floor and Room Diagrams

When the conference is utilizing the full facilities of the site, the listing of the various rooms with floor diagrams is helpful, but perhaps not crucial. Decisions will already have been made regarding the use of space and the assignment of rooms for the various events. There may be some need to shift events from one room to another, but if the full facilities are available, there are probably many options.

When the site is also being used by another conference group, pressure can be expected from both groups in an attempt to obtain the best space. Changes become more difficult, as there are others also seeking to obtain the best space for their conference. Specific diagrams and floor plans to which all can refer become an essential part of the book.

For the ES or the PS conference, where the number of participants can be controlled or may not be as great as for an MS conference, the need for shifting room assignments or making other physical changes will most likely be minimal. However, even for ES and PS conferences, floor plans and room diagrams can be helpful.

For the MS conference this section is essential. Even where the DC has done an outstanding planning job, there may still be the need for some changes just before the conference and during the conference as well. At the site the SC will probably be called upon to consider changes in meeting room assignments. Therefore, the Coordinator and the SC must be fully aware of the range of alternatives open to them. They need constant and similar points of reference and the material in the book can provide that.

The book must be very specific and should not contain merely the generalized room and floor diagrams that are part of the site's promotional literature. Too often, these are not to scale, and there may have been some changes since the promotional brochure was printed. The book should represent the actual situation at the time of the conference. For example, if the conference is being held in an area where air conditioning is essential, then the data in the book should indicate which rooms are difficult to air-condition properly (perhaps because of the southern exposure or the lack of heat-retarding glass in the windows). There may be construction going on outside some of the rooms, and this should be marked on the diagrams.

A common problem relates to designations of rooms. Some facilities might refer to their rooms by *numbers,* but they may have a numbering system that almost defies decoding. The site personnel will be familiar with the numbering and may suggest that an event be moved from Room 105 to Room 106.

The Coordinator may think of this as merely going to the room next door. Actually, the odd numbered rooms may be on one wing of the building and the even numbered rooms in another wing! It is not that the site personnel are trying to take advantage of the Coordinator, but they assume that the Coordinator is familiar with the numbering system. A specific diagram can avoid this type of confusion.

There is another confusing possibility and this relates to the tendency of many sites to *name* their rooms. The names are familiar to the site personnel but can cause confusion for the uninformed. Particularly where the names represent local figures or events, people from out-of-town can experience difficulty, and there is the need for a clearly labeled floor plan.

Even more confusing is the tendency to use designations such as "East" and "West." This is customary in large rooms that can be divided. For example, the "Lincoln Room" may refer to the large room, but "East Lincoln" and "West Lincoln" refer to the same room, after it has been partitioned. Even this is not a general rule.

———— • ————

The site was quite large and had many rooms which could be partitioned. The site personnel would change the room signs, as needed so as to indicate "Jackson 1" and "Jackson 2." During the early planning stages the Coordinator sought to simplify the confusion of using numbers by suggesting they be designated as "Jackson East" and "Jackson West." The site personnel involved with the Coordinator agreed to this change, though reluctantly. Room assignments for the different sessions were made with these names and the printed program carried those designations. It was not until the conference began that the Coordinator discovered there was confusion. The housekeeping personnel, not having been part of the negotiations, interpreted the "East" and "West" as referring to different parts of the building. They thought there was a misprint and that "Jackson East" should have been "Johnson East" which would conform to how the building was normally used. They set the rooms and signs accordingly—to the confusion of all!

———— • ————

This incident reinforces the requirement that the Coordinator walk through the facility, with site personnel, and confirm room assignments and floor diagrams. It is likely that the Coordinator had walked through the site, during the selection phase, but that was for an entirely different purpose. Before putting the floor and room diagrams into the book, a walk-through for the Coordinator is strongly suggested.

Room names also change when partitions are removed. While divided up, the various rooms can each have different names. However, with the partitions removed, the site may now refer to this space as the "Ballroom." For the participants this can be confusing unless there is some clear indication of the name change. The Coordinator might make the same mistake and complicate it by not realizing that when "Ballroom" appears on the diagram, the meeting room space is lost.

## Conference Design

The overall design of the conference should be part of the book. The form should be diagrammatic rather than narrative. An example is shown in Figure 8-2.

Note that each event has a number, which is essential for control. It enables everybody to refer to a session or activity by the event number. Medical terminology or scientific session titles can be incomprehensible to some of the site personnel. By using event numbers, there is no need for the site personnel to cope with unfamiliar vocabulary.

The date when the design is settled should be clearly stated. This will probably be a date before the conference opens. This makes it mandatory that all personnel be constantly informed of any subsequent changes in any of the events. This can be done by issuing an administrative bulletin for the Sponsor and site personnel who have copies of the book. The bulletin would specify the event and the change, and how this is to be reflected in the book. It may mean that a page must be removed and a new page substituted. Or it may merely mean a change in some instruction on the page for that event.

The larger the attendance and the more sophisticated the design, the greater is the need for the book to be kept constantly up-to-date. The Coordinator can set a time of day when the daily bulletin will be issued, usually the evening before the day the changes are to be implemented. This allows time for any questions or concerns regarding design changes. It is inadvisable to indicate changes in the design more than once a day.

## Exhibit Information

This section of the book should include a time schedule as to when the exhibitors are expected to set up and knock down their exhibits. It should also contain a copy of some of the preconference materials that have gone to the exhibitors, including a listing of the various resources and services available to the exhibitors, see Figure 8-3. Note that in Figure 8-3 space is left for the name of the person to be contacted. If this is known, it should be filled in prior to insertion in the book. Also, the organization should be identified. Some of these resources are part of the Sponsor personnel, some are site personnel, and others are contract personnel. Most important is the phone number. Sometimes this list can also contain the room at the site where they are located. If off-site, this is not necessary. If there are any restrictions on time when this resource can be reached by phone, this too should be indicated.

**MONDAY**

| Event | Time | Activity | Room |
|---|---|---|---|
| 1 | 8:30-9:30 | Registration | Lobby |
| 2 | 10:00-12:00 | Opening session (keynote speaker) | Ballroom |
| 3 | 12:00-2:00 | Lunch (as part of conference) | Sunset Room |
| 4 | 2:00-4:00 | Concurrent sessions | |
| 4A | | A- | 203 |
| 4B | | B- | 204 |
| 4C | | C- | 205 |
| 4D | | D- | 206 |
| 5 | 5:00-6:00 | Social Hour | Far East Room |
| 6 | 6:00-8:00 | Dinner (with speaker) | Sunset Room |

**TUESDAY**

| Event | Time | Activity | Room |
|---|---|---|---|
| 7 | 9:00-11:00 | General session (speaker) | Ballroom |
| 8 | 11:00-12:00 | Concurrent sessions | |
| 8A | | A- | 203 |
| 8B | | B- | 204 |
| 8C | | C- | 205 |
| 8D | | D- | 206 |
| 9 | 12:00-2:00 | Lunch (on their own) | |
| 9 | 2:00-3:30 | General session (summary of concurrent sessions) | Ballroom |
| 10 | 3:00-3:30 | General session (conclusion) | Ballroom |

Figure 8-2. A diagrammatic description of the conference design should be included in the conference program book.

| Type | Name of Person | Organization | Phone |
|---|---|---|---|
| Administrative contact (secretariat) | | | |
| Art work | | | |
| Assembly | | | |
| Booth assignments | | | |
| Carpentry | | | |
| Cartage | | | |
| Common carrier(s) | | | |
| Drayman | | | |
| Electrician | | | |
| General maintenance | | | |
| Laborers | | | |
| Painting | | | |
| Reproduction | | | |
| Security | | | |
| | | | |
| | | | |

**Figure 8-3.** *All the exhibitors should receive a list of resources and services that are available to them.*

This section should also state when the exhibit area is to be open to participants.

There should also be a list of those events that are to take place in the exhibit area. This would include the opening ceremonies, drawings for prizes, refreshments, etc. The sheets detailing this should also indicate responsibility for each event. (A sheet similar to Figure 8-4 can be used.)

**Event title:** _____ **#** _____

**Day** _____ **Date** _____ **Time** _____

**Resource person(s):**

_____

_____

**Room** _____ **Setup begins** _____ **Doors open** _____

**Host (introducer)** _____

**Equipment requirements:**

_____

_____

**Literature requirements:**

_____

_____

**Floor Plan**

**Housekeeping:**

Setup for (persons) _____

Water                    _____

Ashtrays                 _____

Signs                    _____

**Remarks:**

**Event coordinator** _____

*Figure 8-4.* *The conference program book should include an event control sheet for each conference event.*

## Daily Events

This is probably the most crucial part of the book and is certainly the fullest section. In this section there will be at least one page for each event at the conference. Figure 8-4 indicates the essential information which such a sheet should contain. Some of this information comes from the form used to gather data from the resource people on their objectives, methodologies, etc. (Figure 4-2), but it also contains other information that is essential to the orderly conduct of the particular event. There should be nothing on the sheet which is not needed. The *event title* should be stated exactly as it appears in the conference program, and the number of the event should be exactly as stated on the master conference program (Figure 8-2).

It may be redundant to have both *day* and *date*. This serves, however, as a cross check. If they are not in agreement, obviously there is some breakdown in the information. The *time* should be exactly as stated in the conference program. The *resource person* should be listed, but only the name is needed. Any other information on the resource person, for purposes of introduction or identification, will have been obtained prior to this point and is best kept in another record.

The *room* should be checked against the conference program. If the room has been crossed out (not erased) it signifies a room change and puts all on notice to watch for this and to make sure that the participants have been notified. *Set-up begins* refers to the time when housekeeping will start setting up the room. If there have been earlier sessions in this room, it is important that there is sufficient time for housekeeping to do its work. A mistake here can upset an entire day and sequence of carefully planned sessions. The setup time may also be important for the resource person if time is needed to bring in and set up special equipment. *Doors open* should be a realistic time after setup. It also relates to the scheduled time listed earlier. If the session is to start at 10:00 a.m., and a large group is anticipated, it may require that the doors open no later than 9:45 a.m. If the door opening is delayed until 10:00 a.m., the session cannot possibly start on time.

The Coordinator for a smaller conference may think it unnecessary to go through all this detail. Perhaps, but the following incident took place at a two-day conference for seventy-five people.

––––– • –––––

The first day was mostly general sessions with some limited small group work. The second day was a workshop conducted by two resource people. They started on time and everything proceeded as planned. The general feeling was one of real success when they went to lunch. During the luncheon, with all eating together, the resource people received excellent feedback and a feeling of excitement. The participants had been working in small groups at tables and were at the point where they would now return to their tables for some intensive work in these small groups.

However, when they returned to the room they found that the tables had been removed and the room was now set up in theater style. The papers they had left on the tables were now piled around the room with no clue to which pile came from which table. It was not possible to reset the room as it had been. The whole design was now destroyed. The small groups could not be readily reconstituted. Valuable time was spent in sorting out the piled-up materials. The physical setup made it most difficult to continue. The resource people did some rapid redesign. Some small group work was possible, as the chairs were not bolted to the floor, but the momentum had been destroyed and the workshop atmosphere obliterated by the unexpected change.

Later the Coordinator (and the resource people) endeavored to identify what had gone wrong. They found that the site personnel were working from the original plan that had the conference concluding with lunch. A later redesign by the Coordinator had not been directly communicated. The Coordinator had sent the site personnel a copy of the final brochure indicating that the conference would go for the whole second day. This had been checked, by phone, with site personnel who were not available on the day of the conference. The Coordinator had neglected to verify any change in writing other than the brochure, which the site personnel did not take the time to study.

—— • ——

The Coordinator should not expect site personnel to study the brochure or printed program to identify changes. They should look through the book, even if it only contains two pages.

The *host (introducer)* serves many functions. In this case, the event control sheet will specify who has responsibility for the resource person. The host should also have direct contact with the Coordinator, should there be any slippage in the planning.

*Equipment requirements* will have been communicated much earlier, and this sheet serves as a checklist for all concerned. The specific pieces of equipment will be listed. Similarly for *literature requirements,* which in this case refers to handouts, etc. It may be that the resource person will have his own literature, and it is also likely that he will have sent a copy to the secretariat for reproduction. If so, this should be listed under literature requirements.

The *floor plan* is most important. Some sheets provide a checklist of items such as auditorium, theater style, and conference style. We have found that there is not full agreement about these terms. Therefore, the event coordinator should actually sketch the position of the resource person, seats, doors or windows, podium, if one is used, and relative location of the various pieces of equipment. This way, the resource person is faced with fewer surprises and the housekeeping staff does not have to wonder about the meaning of technical jargon.

*Housekeeping* may be obvious, but there are some crucial points to be made. *Setup for persons* is perhaps the easiest item to deal with. This is the anticipated attendance figure of the DC. *Water* raises the question as to whether a pitcher and glasses will be provided only for the resource person or for all in the room. There are times, particularly for short sessions in air-conditioned rooms, when having housekeeping provide water for each table can be time consuming. If water is asked for, but the floor plan does not show any tables, this may also indicate a deficiency in planning.

*Ash trays* raise an entirely different set of questions. If the Sponsor is a health organization that has taken a stand against smoking, then providing ash trays can be seen as contradictory. Alternatively, if the Sponsor is a tobacco company, the absence of ash trays could be a serious omission. The resource person may have some preference, because of allergies or just a distaste for smoking. This raises the question of the rights of the participants. A frequent compromise is to designate one half of the room for smokers, and the other half for nonsmokers. This means that the ash trays should be placed to represent this division.

Each event will require signs. These may merely give the event title or may be very descriptive. The copy for the signs should be determined far enough in advance to assure production. A common practice is to have the host pick up the sign from the secretariat just prior to the setup time. This allows for another checkpoint, to be sure that the host is covering the assignment.

*Remarks* allows for any other important items that may not be covered by the rest of the sheet. If some items are repeated under remarks on several sheets, this may indicate the need for revising the sheet to accommodate these items.

The *event coordinator* is usually a member of the secretariat or the Coordinator's staff. Each event coordinator may handle several events during the course of the conference. It should be a person known to the host, or at least provision should be made for a meeting prior to the time the host arrives for the setup phase. Just prior to and during the time of the session the event coordinator should be in a designated place and easily reached. An event coordinator may be servicing more than one event at a time, and this requires staff assistance as the possibility exists that two events may require assistance at the same time.

Each resource person should receive a copy of the event control sheet that describes his event, and the host should receive copies of all of the event control sheets. This allows for another check on arrangements and expectations.

Once the book is put together, no changes in the sheets should be made without specific authorization from the Coordinator. It is possible for the Coordinator to delegate some changes, such as equipment, literature and housekeeping, to a staff member. However, it is preferable to have all changes funneled through the Coordinator, as they may indicate much deeper problems.

———— • ————

The book had been set and the conference was only two weeks away. A resource person asked that provision be made for a slide projector and screen. The resource person would be bringing his own slides. This had not been previously requested, and now required more than just changing the sheet to include the request for the equipment. First, the Coordinator had to ascertain that the equipment would be available, as others had also requested slide projectors and screens. Then, the Coordinator discovered that the assigned room had no provision for darkening the windows sufficiently for slide viewing. Other problems surfaced, such as the need for a table for the slide projector and a total rearrangement of the seats. The resource person had originally requested the conference style seating and had put a limit on the number of people who could attend. All of this signaled to the Coordinator that the resource person had made significant changes in methodology, which now required direct contact between the Coordinator and the resource person. The subsequent telephone conversation disclosed a change in the focus of the session that made the program announcement incorrect. The total situation was finally resolved, but it required more than just providing a piece of equipment.

———— • ————

Once the conference has begun it is even more important that no changes be made without the specific authorization of the Coordinator. During the conference, events can move very rapidly, and if decisions are made by more than one person, the domino effect can take place.

### Special Events

The variety of special events depends upon the kind of planning done by the DC. Among the events are likely to be field trips, entertainment, and recreation. It is possible to use the event control sheet for special events unless they are so complicated as to require a different sheet. If so, it may be possible to design one form that will suit the needs of the conference as well as those who are involved in the special events. No matter what form is used, there should be a separate sheet for each event.

The same admonition should be repeated that no changes should be made without the specific authorization of the Coordinator. Unfortunately, too many Coordinators see themselves as concerned only with the "professional" side of the conference and tend to leave the special events to others.

———— • ————

It was a small ES conference with an extremely tight schedule. One special event was a field trip to one of the local plants of the Sponsor. The Coordinator placed this in the hands of another person, since it was not part of the regular sessions. To her dismay, the Coordinator found that the other person had scheduled buses to arrive at 3:00 p.m., even though the sessions were not scheduled to end until 3:30. The participants were due at the plant at 5:00 p.m. and the 3:00 p.m. departure was essential, but the Coordinator, not wanting to bother with details, had not checked this out. The lack of attention to coordinating the field trip with the sessions caused considerable confusion, and the site personnel had to be placated, because two buses took up a great deal of space in the parking lot just at the time that new arrivals were coming in. The Coordinator had to spend a good deal of time apologizing and appeasing, when a much smaller investment of time earlier (in reviewing and approving the plans for the field trip) would have avoided all the difficulty.

———— • ————

### Conference Administrative Personnel

There are two kinds of personnel who should be included in such a list, as can be seen in Figure 8-5. The first are those associated with the Sponsor. Note that the design committee is not listed, since by this time they will have been replaced by the steering committee.

The list of site personnel could be much longer than shown in Figure 8-5. Some sites do provide a list of their personnel and if available, it can be inserted into the book. Generally, the list is geared towards those who are guests at the site, not those who are conducting conferences. Therefore, some important names and functions may be omitted.

### From the Suppliers' Viewpoint

The book is one area of conference activity which does not involve many suppliers. The two most concerned are site and equipment.

### Site Personnel Say—

The conference program book is a great idea! Whether a small or large conference, we find this most helpful.

| Title | Name | Room | Phone | Arrival | Departure |
|---|---|---|---|---|---|
| **SPONSOR** | | | | | |
| Coordinator | | | | | |
| Steering committee | | | | | |
| Secretariat | | | | | |
| Registration | | | | | |
| Reproduction | | | | | |
| Supplies & equipment | | | | | |
| Event coordinators | | | | | |
| Exhibitor relations | | | | | |
| Public relations | | | | | |

| Title | Name | Room | Phone | Hours of Duty | |
|---|---|---|---|---|---|
| **SITE** | | | | | |
| Site manager | | | | | |
| Conference manager | | | | | |
| Front Desk manager | | | | | |
| Business office Manager | | | | | |
| Switchboard supervisor | | | | | |
| Housekeeping supervisor | | | | | |
| Food service manager | | | | | |
| Public relations | | | | | |
| Security | | | | | |

**Figure 8-5.** *The list of conference administrative personnel that is to be included in the conference program book can be broken into two groups; those associated with Sponsor and those associated with the site.*

It is best if we are involved in reviewing parts of the book before everything if firmed up. There are materials that we think could help make it more useful. We need the chance to make these materials available.

We have some internal systems that complement the book. We use forms and processes which should be coordinated with the various sheets. In some cases, the sheets we use might actually be used by the coordinator in developing the book.

## Equipment Personnel Say—

The book is extremely useful for it provides a checklist of just what equipment will be needed, where and when. It reduces the chance of error or misunderstanding. One problem we found is that changes are made in the original book, and we are not informed. If the Coordinator can double-check this, we can be sure that we are in compliance with the book.

There is a minor problem. The book lists suppliers in our category, and the question is, which organizations and individuals should be listed? In our competitive society we would all like a chance to negotiate for providing equipment. If some of us are not listed, we do not have the chance to compete. We realize that in some of our major cities, the listing could be quite lengthy. It's better to have the book a bit long than to cut out some of the small businessmen who look for conferences as part of their market.

# 9.
# Registration

The process of registration is an important conference activity. It is sometimes ignored, and may not even be listed as an activity on the conference program. Yet this is one of the primary points of confrontation—the time when the participants come together and work of the design committee is tested. If the registration activity is properly handled, it sets the climate for the remainder of the conference. A negative experience during registration can sour participants and it will be several days before the effect wears off. By that time, the conference is nearly concluded or has progressed so far that it is not possible to create a more positive climate. In this chapter we shall be discussing

- Preregistration
- On-site registration
- Personnel
- Registration packets

## Preregistration

Preregistration is not a necessary activity for all conferences. For some it can be extremely helpful, but for others it may merely be an additional administrative step. If there is no need or benefit in having preregistration, it should not be imposed artificially. When there is a need, it should be carefully planned and conducted with sufficient resources to meet the goals.

The ES conference usually conducts preregistration of the employees/participants, for they have to be identified beforehand and agreement has to be reached as to who will be attending. Somebody produces a list of participants, sends out reminders, or engages in some other activity to clarify who is to attend, and when and where they are expected to arrive. If the conference is using a site, such as a motel, preregistration may be accomplished by returning cards to reserve rooms. Generally, preregistration is informal.

Size is a factor, even for the ES conference. As the number of participants grows larger, there is a point at which some form of preregistration is required so that the Coordinator will not lose control of the situation, and can provide necessary logistical support.

For the PS conference preregistration is usually a necessity. When a fee is being charged, the Sponsor may require preregistration so the prospective participant is committed to attend. This can be reinforced by requiring a deposit. There will be a date set prior to the conference, until which time cancellations will be accepted without penalty. After that date the deposit may be forfeited if the prospective participant changes his mind. Some PSs use a different approach and give a discount for early preregistration. The practice is to have an announced fee for early preregistration, which goes up at some point prior to the conference.

The MS seeks to encourage preregistration, and like the PS, may offer a lower rate for early preregistration. The exact lead time for this will depend upon the need to make space and financial commitments to the site. Preregistration also provides the DC with the number and kinds of people who might attend the conference. This can influence the design, and particularly, the use of space.

A major benefit for all the sponsors is that the more preregistrations that are received, the easier it is to handle the participants at the time of registration. Name badges can be prepared, as well as bedroom assignments, small group assignments, and materials that are needed in quantity. One difficulty is that preregistration may give no indication of the number or type of participants who will actually attend. The preregistrants tend to be slightly unique; they usually have more control of their time and are more committed to the objectives of the conference or to the Sponsor. Data from preregistration can be helpful, but should be utilized very cautiously.

A real benefit of preregistration is the possibility of commitment by the preregistrant. Perhaps it is only that the person does not want to lose the fee, if one has been required, but even when there is no fee, there may be a psychological commitment.

The Coordinator should arrange to have each preregistration acknowledged. The minimum should be a form letter or a card. A personal letter communicates interest and opens a channel for further communication. When the number of preregistrants might discourage a personal letter, technology has given us various means to produce mass numbers of individual letters. If this cannot be done, a duplicated letter or form is still better than no response at all. Sponsors may be interested in encouraging preregistration for entirely different reasons than the Coordinator. For the Sponsor preregistration with full or part payment of the conference fee means help on the cash flow problem that plagues many conferences. There is a significant outflow of cash during the time the conference is being planned, and without preregistration fees, the Sponsor must make cash available to the Coordinator. There could be several months during which the cash flow problem might be eased by preregistration fees.

The process of preregistration allows for many other benefits. The design may require that participants read certain materials before the conference. Without preregistration the only time for reading is between arrival and the first sessions. With preregistration the materials can be sent to the participant while he is still home. This allows for more leisurely reading and the possibility that the participant will be better prepared than if the material is not available until much later.

For large conferences with the usual problem of concurrent sessions overflowing, the preregistration forms can collect data on the intent of the participants. When the conference includes field trips or recreational activities, the data from the preregistration forms can be helpful in planning for transportation and accommodation.

The DC can use the preregistration to obtain feedback from the participants on the objectives or the design. The participants are adults and appreciate being treated in this manner. They can make significant contributions, which can be valuable to the design process, but they must be asked. If there is no way for them to communicate with the DC, it is difficult, and perhaps impossible, for them to make suggestions. The preregistration process provides an excellent opportunity for this kind of communication.

Just asking for suggestions communicates something to the participants. It signifies to them that they can influence and that the DC is striving to produce a design which reflects the needs of the participants. This contributes to the kind of climate that most conferences require.

Preregistration can produce jurisdictional conflicts. Is this step part of the planning/design process or part of conducting the workshop? In this book it has been put under the conducting phase. It can be in either place, as long as all concerned reach agreement on its placement and the relative responsibilities.

———— ● ————

The DC did its work very well. They built in preregistration, but they insisted that this should be part of the conduct of the conference and that the DC would not bother with it. The forms for preregistration were developed by the Coordinator, and the information that came back went to the Coordinator. In light of this information the Coordinator made significant changes in the design. When the DC arrived at the conference, they found it much different from what they had planned. The Coordinator insisted that this was so because of the new information received during preregistration. The DC felt that they had been manipulated, and vowed never again to be involved with this Coordinator. Some of the DC members were also on the steering committee and used these meetings to achieve the original design. The SC was unable to function properly because of the verbal combat that resulted. The result was a poor conference and bitter feelings.

—— • ——

This kind of conflict need not have happened if the Coordinator had clarified how preregistration would influence either in the design committee or the steering committee. Obviously, the Coordinator kept it vague in order to insinuate his own design and paid for it in a poor conference and a damaged reputation.

### On-Site Registration

Even though the participants have preregistered, they may still have to report to the registration area. With careful planning it is possible for preregistration to trigger an intermediate step. When the preregistration forms and the full conference fee are received, the materials and registration packets can be sent to the participants by mail, and they are expected to bring them along to the conference. Of course, the Coordinator will have additonal packets for those who have not received the materials or have not brought them along.

If materials can be sent beforehand, then on-site registration can be facilitated for the preregistrants. They may not even have to go to the registration area of the conference, but can proceed directly to register for their sleeping accommodations. If it is a conference that does not require bedroom registration, then the paticipants can meet at the social activity, which will be part of the opening of the conference.

If materials are not sent out beforehand, then *all* participants will come to the registration area.

### Physical Placement

During the site selection, the Coordinator and the site personnel will have explored the most appropriate place for the registration area. There are several possibilities, depending upon the decisions that have been made about the site and housing.

When all the participants are to be housed in the same building or facility, the registration area is best placed as close to the front desk as possible. This allows participants to complete both registrations (conference and housing) without having to traverse long corridors before they have become familiar with the site. Signs can minimize the difficulty when the registration areas are far apart, but there is still the problem of participants being forced to wander about before they have been made comfortable.

If the two areas are apart, participants should be advised which registration desk should be approached first, the housing or the conference registration desk. Occasionally, the participants can register for both at the same desk. A group of rooms are assigned to the conference, and the necessary forms are filled out and the keys given at the conference registration area.

With larger conferences the sessions will probably be in a special conference building, while the participants will be housed at several local hotels/ motels. The registration procedures are definitely separate, and the Coordinator only plans and controls the conference registration.

It is of prime importance that the conference registration area be located in a place where people are free to move around. Too often, the registration area is in a confined area that may be easy to enter, but difficult to leave. There should be an orderly direction for traffic flow so that participants can leave when registration is completed without having to retrace their steps.

When the conference has only a few participants, and all are not expected to arrive at the same time, it is possible to use the secretariat/administration office, or some other convenient room. No matter what space is used, emphasis should be on minimizing the physical discomfort for the participants at this crucial time. The importance of registration for climate setting cannot be overemphasized.

If large numbers of participants are expected to arrive at the same time, it is necessary to have more than one registration desk. The participants can be divided into groups by using the first letter of their last name. Usually this is a simple process, but if the conference includes persons from outside the U.S., the Coordinator may have to proceed carefully. What is a "last name"? If the participants come from South America or Spain, the last name may be their mother's name and not the family name. If they are from some Moslem countries, the last name may actually be the father's name; there is no family name. In such cases, the Coordinator should turn to those who have handled these problems before, or ask the participant how the name is to appear on the roster and other conference indicators, such as name tags. It is better to ask the participant than to contribute to misunderstanding and embarrassment.

If there has been preregistration, the breakdown by alphabet works well. This device can also be a facilitating mechanism when the bulk of registration is at the conference. It cuts down the size of the lines. There may be those who feel that this is too cumbersome and may wish to put in roped areas where the participants form a line between the ropes, and the person at the head of the line goes to the first registrar available.

Most readers will be familiar with the *take-a-number* system used in some supermarkets or similar establishments, where the flow is uneven and the work force is of a constant size. Participants can be given numbers as they enter the registration area, and therefore need not wait in line, but can relax and talk to friends as they wait for their numbers to be called.

Both the roped area and the take-a-number systems can work well, but the Coordinator has to assess the administrative benefits against participant reaction. Are the participants likely to feel that they are being treated as merchandise or customers, rather than participants? For some participant groups these forms of control will not only be acceptable but commendable. For others, particularly where the participants view themselves as humanists, Coordinators can expect an extremely negative reaction to too much control.

Whatever decision is made about handling the flow problem at registration, it is desirable to have at least one special desk for problems and difficulties. The sign for this desk should be stated in a positive manner and may be called "Hospitality Desk," "Supervisor," "Help Station," "Ombudsman," or some other words that will communicate the function of this special desk. The desk must be staffed by an extremely competent individual. It is annoying for a participant to come to the desk for help only to be referred to another person at another place. There are many problems that the person at this desk can anticipate, the range of which is great, and need not be detailed here. One Coordinator for an MS conference found it helpful to have the personnel at the special desk keep a tally of the kinds of problems that came to the desk. For the next conference the Coordinator was able to anticipate some of the problems and to make the necessary arrangements to eliminate or minimize them. This allowed the special desk personnel to cope with new problems, but fewer of them. After registration this special desk will still be needed for problems that arise during the conduct of the conference, and if it is at all possible, it should be kept in the same location. If it must be moved, there should be a clear sign announcing its new location.

The entire registration area should clearly be marked by large, correctly positioned signs. A smaller conference may not need signs, and to use them to excess can be considered pretentious. Too many signs at a small conference suggests a great deal of control over the participants, and this may not be the climate appropriate to the conference. As the number of participants increases, or if large numbers of them will be arriving at the same time, signs become a necessity and will be seen as facilitating rather than controlling.

Registration requires filling out forms. The forms should be clear, simple, and explicit. The forms should be tested out beforehand to make sure that participants will be able to complete them without having to ask the staff for information or for special help. The form should not ask for information that is readily available from other sources or which might prove embarrassing. Under the latter heading we find such items as age (both male and female), religion, or income range. It might be nice to know this information, but unless there is some specific need, the participant should not be expected to provide it.

If forms are to be filled out, the participant will need the physical facility to do it.

——— ● ———

The participants lined up to register and were handed a registration form that was a page long and attached to carbon paper. In order to complete it participants needed time and a hard surface on which to write so that the impression would go through the carbon. The registration desk only had a narrow rail. The personnel at the desk gave the form to the participants and then directed them to tables in another part of the room where they could complete the form. Upon completion, the more aggressive participants returned directly to the desk to complete their registration. The more timid ones fumed silently as they lined up for a second time.

———— • ————

In this case, as in many others, the information on the form could have been provided at a later date. It was not needed for registration, but was being gathered to have a profile of the participants. If the form can be returned later, the Coordinator must build in an incentive for the participant to return the form.

———— • ————

Upon registration, participants were given two forms. The first, a very simple one, enabled them to complete registration immediately, pay their fees, and receive their materials. The other, a longer form, was for other purposes related to the conference. Participants were requested to complete this form by the end of the first day. If they brought their form to the secretariat office, they would receive a list of participants. The Coordinator reported a 90% return on the form and no confusion in the registration area.

———— • ————

Evaluation is important and some Coordinators develop a form for preconference input that the participant receives at registration. Here the gamble is, how many will complete this form early enough for the data to be meaningful. As in the example cited above, the Coordinator can identify an incentive. A small conference can actually build in an activity, early in the conference, when all participants are expected to complete the form. If such an activity is planned, the participants can receive this form in their materials packet or it can be distributed at the session. It should not be required as part of the registration procedure.

## Time of Operation

The registration area, particularly when it also serves as a service area, should have announced hours of operation. It must be open before the first session of the conference, so that registration can take place. A smaller conference may require that the registration area be open only an hour or so before the first session. For larger conferences or those of longer duration the lead time may be extended to a day or more.

What if the conference is located next to a theme park, where participants can be expected to arrive a day or so before the conference to avail themselves of the recreational opportunities? What if participants merely wish to register early so as to avoid the later rush and have time to review the program and conference materials? The Coordinator will have to balance the pros and cons of early registrations, particularly for a large conference. It can ease the pressure that might develop later, and can allow the Coordinator to test out the registration procedure and make any modifications that are indicated. On the other hand, it may increase costs to provide staff for this early registration and for using the space in advance of the conference opening.

After the conference has opened, the registration area is still needed. Even though everybody appears to have registered, there are always some peripheral people and situations that must be considered. There will probably be some late registrations, and these people have to be accommodated and given their materials. For conferences of more than one day's duration, it can be arranged that *walk-ins* register for only one day of the conference, if they so desire. This requires a permanent registration area to handle this additional registration.

The charge for field trips, recreational opportunities and banquets can be included in the conference fee, which simplifies the registration process. There are reasons for not having a combined conference fee and charging a basic fee to which participants can add special activities as desired. This requires provision for participants to purchase tickets for selected activities, after the initial registration has been accomplished.

Some participants may not want to wait to purchase tickets for special events in case there should be only a limited number available. This means that provision must be made during registration to sell tickets for the special events.

The registration area should be open at all reasonable times. To have it open only from 9-5, when the sessions are being held from 9-5, forces participants to absent themselves from some regular conference activity in order to handle problems and questions. The registration area should be open prior to the first activity of the day, and remain open into the early part of the evening. It may close just before the dinner hour without causing too much difficulty to the participants. Having the registration area open before and after sessions also communicates to the participants that those responsible for conducting the conference are considerate of participant needs—and this helps establish the desirable climate necessary for a successful conference.

## Cash Control

An ES conference probably has little problem with cash control, as there will be little or none used during the conduct of the conference. If expenses are involved, they are either billed to the employee's department or unit, or the employee pays the expenses and is reimbursed at a later time.

A PS may be conducting a conference under a contract from a government agency, a private foundation, or some other cosponsor who is providing the funding. In this case, there is no need for cash control at registration. If there is a flow of cash, it will be from the Sponsor to the participants.

For the PS charging a fee, and for the MS, cash control is a vital factor. The extent of cash control will vary, but the size of the conference is not the governing factor, though more participants mean more money, and therefore could be more tempting to those who might seek to misappropriate the funds.

There should be a clearly identified cashier. When more than one is required, one person is designated as the chief cashier. It is inviting financial disaster to have an open cash box and to rotate this desk assignment. The cashier(s) should be carefully selected and provided with some learning experiences, if needed. If it is anticipated that there will be a large amount of money collected, particularly in cash, the Coordinator should consider the possibility of bonding the cashiers. It is worth the fee and should not be seen as evidence of paranoia or discrimination on the part of the Coordinator. Bonding cashiers is a common practice.

There are four different kinds of receipts that can be anticipated. Most frequently, participants will pay by *check,* and these will usually be personal checks. If this presents any problems for the Coordinator, the participants should know about this before registration. Usually personal checks are acceptable, but there have been cases where the checks have been returned marked "insufficient funds," and then the Coordinator must decide whether to follow up or write it off as a loss. Also, people frequently forget to sign their checks, and if the cashier does not spot this at the time, it requires additional processing. In some rare cases, we have heard of situations where the participants were so vehemently opposed to the conference, after they got there, that they stopped payment on their checks. This has not happened very often, and so does not pose a significant problem. It is most important that there be some control on the checks, so that they are not misplaced or invalidated in any way.

Some participants, not many, will pay in *cash.* This is not the usual method of payment, though it does occur in a one-day drive-in conference, when the fee is small and the participants are paying without expecting reimbursement or any tax advantages. Participants may use cash when they have preregistered by check, and only wish to purchase tickets for some of the special events.

A third form of revenue may be a *company voucher.* This is common for government employees, and if it is anticipated that there will be such participants, the cashier should have a clearly defined process for handling the vouchers.

——— ● ———

The cashier was experienced in handling receipts, but had no previous experience with government vouchers and had not been briefed on this procedure. The participant completed all the other registration procedures and came to the cashier's desk. The participant submitted the voucher, which the cashier took several minutes to read. Meanwhile, a long line was forming. The following dialogue ensued:

Cashier:    This piece of paper just says you're coming to the conference. Where's the money?

Participant: What you have in your hand is a voucher, which works just like a check.

Cashier:    I have never seen a check that looks like this.

Participant: It's not a check, but serves the same purpose. This is how you bill my employer, the government agency.

Cashier:    Oh, I don't send out bills. My job is to take in money.

Participant: But I've done this before at many conferences...

Cashier:    Sorry, I can't help you, and there is a big line forming behind you. Why don't you come back later?

——— ● ———

Obviously, the participant has two choices. One is to go home immediately, but this may be difficult to explain to the boss. The other choice is to seek out the Coordinator, and by that time the participant is so irate that the whole situation has become an unnecessary crisis.

Vouchers, whether government or private, should be handled by the cashier at the time of registration. The Coordinator should make sure the process was carefully worked out previously with whoever is responsible for the later billing.

A newer form of payment is the *credit card*. Some organizations have taken to including credit card information on their preregistration forms. Others have found that credit cards at registration are very effective. Most participants will have at least one of the major cards, and it reduces the need for the cashier to control negotiable instruments, including cash. If credit cards are to be honored, the participants should know beforehand which are acceptable, and the cashier should know exactly how to handle a credit card transaction.

If the Coordinator anticipates a significant amount of cash, additional security may be required to supplement the bonding of the cashier, such as an armed security officer. The security agency should also be consulted as to the appropriate placement of the cashier's booth or desk. As payment is usually the last activity of the registration process, it is tempting to put the cashier's booth adjacent to an exit. This also encourages the quick-hit artist to grab the money and run.

Most sites that handle conferences have their own security staff. The Coordinator should check with them and benefit from their experience in similar situations. This does not reduce the responsibility of the Coordinator, but it does provide an experienced resource.

During the conduct of the conference, there may be times when there is the need for immediate cash outlays, such as for a supplier, for personnel who deliver things, for small purchases, or for tips. This might be handled by a revolving petty cash fund, though it will require provision for rapid replenishment. It is tempting to go to the cash box. It is a sad Coordinator who finds that a considerable amount of cash has rapidly gone out, in small amounts, but sufficient to drain the box. That cash box may contain checks, vouchers, credit cards, and many slips of paper indicating cash pay-outs, and the bookkeeping becomes a major task. It is more desirable to have the cashier act merely as a receiver of cash. The petty cash, or check book, should be in the hand of a responsible member of the secretariat.

In some PS and MS conferences, there is the practice of offering either full or partial *scholarships*. This is a way of offering either a reduced fee, or charging no fee at all to people who might otherwise not be able to attend the conference. This has become a common practice when there are minority groups that might be excluded because of the fee, and when their presence at the conference is desirable. Among those minority groups are the usual ethnic groups who have been the focus of these efforts, particularly since the middle 1960s. The practice is also extended to full-time students who would not be able to attend professional conferences if they had to pay the full fee. Some Sponsors advertise that reduced fees are available to identified groups, while others merely note the availability of scholarships. Other Sponsors prefer to handle this in a more discrete manner. No matter which position the Sponsor takes, the cashier should be fully informed of the policy and procedure for handling scholarships. To embarrass a scholarship recipient is to contradict the policy that authorizes them. Usually, those people who have been granted a full or partial scholarship are not further identified. They receive the same materials and treatment as any other participant.

There are other reasons for reduced fees or no-fee participants. Offering scholarships may be a form of marketing, to encourage people to attend who might bring in other participants for other conferences. Sometimes it's done to encourage attendance by influential people whom the Sponsor wants at the conference. There is also the Sponsor/Coordinator who offers scholarships in order to boost attendance (a questionable but common practice). No matter what the reason for the reduced fees or no-fee status, it can be negated by improper handling at the cashier's desk.

## Availability of Materials

The ES usually have an advantage over most other sponsors in that they can predict fairly closely how many participants will be attending the conference. This allows for preconference work, such as preparing appropriate participant packages. A PS may have some clues as to the number of participants expected, but the MS seldom has this kind of data. Therefore, the MS must prepare additional supplies of materials and must not be dismayed when some are left when the conference closes. This is preferable to having participants complaining about the lack of materials, which others have already received, but which are no longer available.

The quantity and type of materials distributed as part of registration will cover a wide range. Items which could be included in a participant packet are

- Registration form
- Name tag
- Meal tickets
- Special function tickets
- Conference program
- Pad, paper
- Workbook
- Pen or pencil
- Reports to be read
- Local facilities information
  street maps, shopping tips
  language guide (for international conferences)
- Travel assistance requests (for return travel)
- Public relations forms
- Evaluation form
- Participant form

Materials may be prepacked or placed on a table as pickup items. Prepackaging has advantages, for the Coordinator can be assured that every participant has been given the same basic materials. Packaged materials are easier to handle at registration, and where the number of participants exceeds twenty-five, prepacking simplifies the process. Some Coordinators will even prepackage materials for a conference with fewer participants, though this is sometimes considered overplanning. Yet, there are times when even a conference with few participants can benefit from a comprehensive participant packet. If the objectives are concerned with rules, regulations, or legislation, and each participant is to have a copy of these, the conference process is facilitated by distributing these in participant packets rather than taking conference time to distribute these bulky materials later. It also enhances the conduct of the conference, for taking time to distribute materials slows the process and uses valuable session time for an activity that is better handled in other ways.

Prepacking costs staff time, takes up space, and requires handling and control at registration. The Coordinator must weigh the relative advantages and disadvantages for each particular conference.

Good planning allows for variations. Although materials are prepackaged, it is possible that additional materials may arrive too late to be included in the package. This could be information on last minute replacement of resource people, handouts for particular sessions, and information sheets with revisions and new information. For these additional materials, it is easier to set up a table in the registration area, rather than to try to add them to existing packets. Caution should be exercised that the materials on the table are not so numerous as to be impossible to gather up quickly. Some of the materials that appear on tables in registration areas could just as easily be made available to the participants at a later time.

If a table is used, there should be a sign indicating exactly what these materials are. The participant should not have to wonder if these are duplicates of what is in the packet, or if this is additional material to be picked up at this time. If the situation is unclear, the participant is faced with a choice of either picking up the material and finding it duplicates what is already in the packet, or not picking it up, and possibly missing something important, and that makes for unnecessary doubt and confusion.

During the course of the conference, participants may misplace their material, so provision must be made for replacements. Loss of materials can be minimized by setting up the packet so that the participant's name can be clearly written on the outside. This is not always easy with the plastic envelope packet, but using a gummed sticker can take care of this problem.

There are ways to reduce costs related to packaging participant materials. The popular plastic envelope can be supplied by an exhibitor as part of their own conference cost. The Coordinator will probably have to permit the exhibitor to place his name on the outside of the plastic envelope. This may seem reasonable enough, but the Coordinator should question if this does not appear to favor one exhibitor over the others. This is one of those issues which is best handled through the exhibitors' committee. Also, the particular exhibitor who is given this privilege should be marketing a product or service that is totally acceptable to the Sponsor, and in no way repugnant to the participants.

A PS may see this message on the packet as a way to advertise their own organization and therefore the cost is allocated, internally, between conference expense and general advertising costs. After the conference the participants will be walking around advertising the PS. This is acceptable in our world today, and many people use these envelopes, carrying the message long after the conference is over.

An ES may likewise utilize plastic envelopes with the company name on them. The Coordinator may find that these are readily available from company stock, and at a more reasonable cost than if they had to be purchased for that particular conference. An external Coordinator should determine the status of the plastic envelope in relation to conferences. The culture in the company may strongly suggest that these plastic envelopes are appropriate at one level of the company, but not at another.

The MS has the same options as the ES and PS. The MS conference usually has more exhibitors and supporting groups than either of the other two, and therefore, more resources who might be interested in providing the outside covering for the participant package.

Another pattern for packaging is to use a loose-leaf book. This format limits the kinds of materials to only those which will fit in the binder. Supplementary items, such as tickets for special activities, general information sheets, and local tourist information can be packaged separately. It is not necessary for the participants to carry these supplementary items to all sessions, and when they are included in a packet, participants tend to remove them anyhow. The loose-leaf book has other advantages, depending upon the objectives of the conference and the purpose of the Sponsor. Some Sponsors have the loose-leaf book cover made up in the colors of the Sponsor or bearing the logo or trademark of the Sponsor, particularly in the case of the ES. This emphasizes that the conference is a company sponsored program. The spine of the loose-leaf book can also be imprinted so that, as it sits on the participant's bookshelf, either at home or in the office, it communicates a clear message to all who see it that the owner was a participant at the conference. In some organizations, this is important information for any visitor to the participant's office or home.

The PS makes good use of this device, for it serves as a constant reminder to the participants, and serves as advertising to those who come to the participant's office or home.

For both the ES and PS who are using a loose-leaf format, the material on the spine should be carefully planned. If the conference is an annual event, it may be important for the year to be displayed on the spine. The spine may also indicate the topic, location, or some other information that might distinguish a particular conference from a series of conferences.

The loose-leaf book is preferable if the participant intends to continue to use the conference materials in much the same order as distributed at the conference. There may be a flow from the simple to the more complex, or a series of exercises and experiences that should be reviewed in a particular order.

The plastic envelope, or a similar method for holding papers together in one place, is more appropriate if the participants are to integrate different papers and handouts into already existing files in their offices.

Assuming a choice on the part of the Coordinator, the decision should be based on how the materials are to be used during the conference as well as afterwards.

**Personnel**

We have referred to the secretariat as that group organized around the Coordinator, which facilitates the design and conduct of the conference by providing staff support. The size of the secretariat depends upon the size and complexity of the conference and upon the budget available to the Coordinator. It can range from two to fifteen people.

There is the need for a *supervisor*. This should not be the Coordinator, who must be more concerned with process than with administrative details. Depending on the size and the quality of other staff, this supervisor can be more of an administrative assistant. The supervisor should be directly responsible to the Coordinator, and this information should be communicated to all concerned, including site personnel. The following tasks appear to be the responsibility of different people, but in a small conference the supervisor will be doing all of them.

The supervisor will need *clerks* for packaging materials, assisting in registration, and doing some of the other clerical tasks that are required during the conference.

There is a certainty that there will be a need for *typists*. While the conference is in progress, there will be many times when typing services will be needed, such as for typing name tags at registration. If a daily bulletin is published, someone is needed to type it and perhaps operate the reproducing equipment as well. There will probably be additional handout material to be typed on the spot, participant rosters, press releases, and copies of reporters' notes from work group sessions. The typists must be able to work under the pressure one finds in the secretariat during a conference. A typist who is good at correspondence may not be the correct person for this assignment. There is usually little, if any, correspondence during the conference. The Coordinator needs to look ahead and make a guess as to whether the typist will have to work from printed copy or handwritten, and it is probably the latter.

We have already discussed the duties of the cashier, but the position is listed here to reinforce the fact that the cashier should be responsible to the supervisor.

There are four basic sources for secretariat personnel, and the first source, and probably the most desirable, is *regular employees of the Sponsor*. One advantage of this is that the Coordinator can obtain information about the capability of these employees beforehand, and can assign them most effectively. In addition, regular employees will be more familiar with the terminology and some of the participants. This enables them to render better service than personnel who are new to the situation. These employees must be released from their regular duties so they can work during the conference. Some of the employees will have to be available during the planning stages, and right through to the follow-up. If the Sponsor cannot release these employees from their regular duties, the Coordinator will find that it is better to seek other sources. It is not good to merely add secretariat duties to those already being performed by Sponsor personnel.

Another source is the *personnel on the Coordinator's staff*. This is not a prime source, for Coordinators usually do not have regular staff members who can be released easily for conference work. Some people, who are conference newcomers, do have a staff, but these are not the kind of Coordinators we have been discussing. Usually, Coordinators work alone or have a very small administrative staff in their offices. This keeps the overhead low and allows them to function as Coordinators, rather than as booking agents or brokers for suppliers. As conferences keep growing, it is very likely that more organizations will be formed, composed of professional coordinators, with regular administrative staff, who can provide a source of personnel for specific conferences.

A third source of personnel is from the variety of private companies that provide *temporary help*. Some of these companies are nationwide, while others operate only locally. They have the advantage of being able to supply, almost on demand, most kinds of personnel needed for a conference, except for the supervisor. These personnel can be hired on a daily basis, and there is no need for personnel records or payroll taxes, because it is handled by the temporary help firm. A major limitation is that the quality of temporary personnel cannot be ascertained until they have actually worked. When a conference is of only a few days duration, it may be a day or more before the incompetent help is spotted, and by that time considerable damage may have been done. If possible, the Coordinator should build sufficient funds into the budget to hire some of the temporary personnel before registration, to ascertain if learning experiences or replacement is needed. The cashier may also come from an organization supplying temporary help, but then bonding and security become even more important.

A fourth source of personnel is *volunteers*. The ES will probably never tap this source, nor will the profit PS. Some PS conferences (university, nonprofit) and almost all MS conferences use volunteers. One good reason for using them is that it keeps costs down. They are not paid, although the Sponsor may provide transportation and meals. On the other hand, how does one fire a volunteer? It can be done, but it can be quite uncomfortable.

Volunteers come from many places, and the most common way to identify and recruit volunteers is to approach the local chapter of the sponsoring organization. This puts pressure on the Coordinator who will have little control over who is selected and how they perform. When using volunteers, the Coordinator may not be able to be as demanding as when the other three sources are tapped. A housewife who has never been in the labor market, and doesn't intend to be, may have a great deal of enthusiasm, but little skill or experience in dealing with participants who have complaints. A man who is a retired engineer may not be able to handle the cash box or a typewriter. Unless the Coordinator has some voice in selection, he will staff more people than actually needed, in order to have a pool which might contain some of the skills required for registration and other administrative functions.

## Resource Persons and VIPs

The Coordinator must make an early decision as to whether or not resource persons and VIPs (very important persons) are required to register. For some conferences registration is necessary to provide for housing, meals, etc. If there is no specific need for registration, then this step can be skipped.

There are many different ways to handle registration of resource persons and VIPs. The process agreed upon should reflect the role and status of these individuals. One approach is to have a previously selected host who will meet, brief, and assume responsibility for seeing that the necessary forms and steps have been taken for registration of the guest. This includes providing all necessary materials, information, and tickets for meals and events. Usually, these forms do not require a signature, and therefore, can easily be completed by the host.

The ES will have little difficulty with this category of personnel, but should provide for those who do not arrive when the conference opens. There may be VIPs who will arrive specifically for the final banquet or some other closing function.

The Coordinator should plan beforehand what materials VIPs and resource people should receive. Some of these people will want everything that the participants have received. Some will want nothing, and still others will want just the highlights. The Coordinator should plan these packets, and have them clearly marked for each resource person and VIP. These packets should not be stored in the registration area, for they might be distributed to the wrong persons. They should be kept in the secretariat's office and made available to the hosts as they arrange to pick up their respective guests. This provides another check on the host meeting the resource person and VIP. If there is no formal procedure for meeting, then the resource person can come to the secretariat to check in for the materials and briefing. The VIP should not be expected to come to the secretariat, for VIPs are entitled to special considerations, or they are not considered VIPs.

## Spouses

Preregistration usually includes spouse registration, as the participant and spouse are preregistered at the same time. What about the regular registration period? Should the spouse accompany the participant to the registration area? That increases the number of people in the area who have to be processed. There are several ways to handle the spouse registration, but whatever pattern is selected, the Coordinator should be careful not to communicate to the spouses that they are less important than the participants. If the group is not too large, there are advantages in having spouses register along with the participants. It provides an opportunity for spouses to meet each other, to renew old friendships, and to make plans. A participant may wish to register for the spouse, and the registration procedure should accommodate this, unless the signature of the spouse is required for some legal or administrative purpose. When the participant registers for the spouse, the materials for both of them should be available at the same time, in the same place. The participant should not be expected to go to another part of the registration area to receive the material for the spouse. Each packet of materials should be clearly marked, unless the contents of the packet are identical.

There are reasons for having the spouses register at the same time but in different parts of the registration area. The program for the spouses might provide activities about which decisions must be made at registration so the secretariat can make appropriate plans for transportation, materials, etc.

The Coordinator must decide the kinds of materials the spouses need or want, particularly when these are different from those given to the participants. If the design allows the spouses to attend all the regular sessions, activities, and functions available to the participants, then it is contradictory not to give the spouses exactly the same materials as the participants. This sometimes results in a situation where the spouses get more materials than the participants—they get the regular participant materials plus those related to the alternative activities for spouses.

The whole process of registering spouses should be a clear reflection of the decisions that have been made regarding spouses at the conference. To encourage their attendance, and then to treat them as superfluous will influence the behavior of the participants as well as the spouses.

### From the Suppliers' Viewpoint

Although registration is essentially handled under the direction of the Coordinator, site personnel, security personnel, office suppliers, and local convention and visitor bureaus are also involved.

### Site Personnel Say—

We are eager to cooperate on preregistration. Particularly where bedrooms are involved, the earlier we can get a good reading on your exact needs the more likely we are to spot bedroom problems. We prefer not to overbook, and some of us will never admit to overbooking, yet it is a necessity. We know too well the problem of last minute cancellations. Preregistration, particularly with a room deposit, can reduce the problem areas. If this is not possible, we are certainly willing to negotiate other approaches.

When it comes to registration, rely on us for help. We know that this can be a hectic and confusing part of the conference. If we are a conference site, and yours is the only conference, registration is no problem. If there are other conferences, the problems can still be kept to a reasonable situation.

If you are using a hotel/motel, and yours is just one of many conferences, then you must expect some compromises. We try not to schedule two conference registrations at the same time, but this can happen. We will try to put you on different floors, or different parts of the building. If each of you insists on the main lobby for registration, then you must accept the confusion this will produce.

There are times when we can supply special furnishings for registration. This can be special booths, tables, or other appointments which make registration areas functional. Tell us what you will expect a participant to do, and in what order. If you haven't thought it out, perhaps we can do it together to make registration a positive rather than a negative experience for all concerned.

## Office Suppliers Say—

For those of us who have been working with Coordinators and conferences for many years, the biggest problem is lack of sharing. We do have catalogues indicating name tags or badges, plastic conference envelopes, special loose-leaf binders, and much more. If you wish, you can order from the catalogue, and in some cases we will even imprint at no additional cost.

If you have a special request, let us talk it over. Your unique item of today can become our stock item of tomorrow. If you have developed a special logo for your conference, or a special theme, perhaps we can provide materials which support this.

## Security Personnel Say—

Some of us work for the site, and have a good idea of how to maximize the security aspects for cash and materials during registration. There are others who work for some highly reputable private security organizations with a great deal of experience in providing security.

We are a specialized field and we have various kinds of experts. We do need some lead time. If you have set up your registration area, and then ask us to provide security, the response may be that given your setup, it is impossible. Or, we can do it, but the cost will be much greater than if you had included us in your planning for registration. We could have made suggestions that would improve your process and reduce your security risks as well as costs.

## Local Convention and Visitors' Bureau Personnel Say—

One of the functions we can perform for you is to identify sources of personnel. We usually have access to both temporary and volunteer help. Some of these people have worked many conferences and therefore are more experienced than you would expect. Of course, we will not guarantee performance, for we are not normally in the business of providing personnel. But we do have experience with conferences and people and can be a very valuable resource in this area.

If you are using preregistration, then see us about material which might be enclosed. This can range from local information to coordinating housing. Each of us is a bit different, with differing relationships with the various sites. If you have worked with a bureau on a previous conference, do not assume that a different bureau works the same way. Ask questions, and explore. There is much we can do to assist in preregistration or registration on site.

# 10.
# The Participant
# Program Book

The participant program book (PPB) can refer to something as simple as a one-page listing of the sessions or a fifty-page multicolored book. The differences and possibilities will be explored in this chapter, but to minimize confusion, the document will be referred to as the PPB no matter what the style, size, or content.

Why have a whole chapter on the PPB? Too frequently the value and benefit of a well-designed program are lost because the participants cannot find their way through the mass of details. The Coordinator and the design committee have lived through the development of the program from the time it was a single page with a statement of objectives, until it is in the hands of the participants. The participant receives the PPB, usually at registration, with many other documents, folders, and leaflets. The PPB is the most important piece of material the participant will receive at the time of registration, and also the most complicated. Confusion as to its use produces frustration and hostility, or the opposite, a kind of anomie. The participant makes several attempts to sort through the strange listings of titles, rooms, etc., with no way of organizing or personalizing the information, and finally resigns with a soliloquy like, "I can't figure this out, maybe it's my fault. I better not ask anybody, I'll just sound foolish. I'll just listen to what other people are going to do. Or, I'll find somebody here whom I respect, and find out what he is going to do. Maybe it's just that I'm tired now. I'll look at it later. Anyhow, the time of the golf tournament and the banquet are clear. There were big banners about those things at registration, so I'll build around those two activities."

Many a participant has given up in disgust and not taken full advantage of an excellent program.

If the PPB is not clearly organized, it will be underutilized. Participants will put off making decisions as to which sessions to attend until it is too late, or their decisions may be influenced by the proximity of the session.

— • —

When asked why they attended particular sessions, during a post-conference evaluation, some participants responded that the PPB was so confusing, they just followed the crowd. Or sometimes, they just went into rooms which happened to be closest to where they were when it was time for sessions to start. Others admitted that their confusion was expressed by choosing rooms for concurrent sessions that were a distance from the general sessions so they could get some exercise. Sometimes, they decided to just go along with friends who seemed to have spent more time studying the confusing PPB, relying on their friend's judgment rather than on their own.

— • —

The PPB is intended to help the participant make meaningful decisions about the best way to utilize time during the conference. This is an individual decision, and the PPB should be organized in a way which enables each participant to readily analyze comparative information, particularly when there are several sessions or activities scheduled for the same time.

If the conference is a one-day affair, then a single sheet may suffice. Even if the conference lasts several days, it may not be necessary to have a very involved PPB. At one extreme the design may not provide alternatives, and therefore the number of decisions to be made are minimal. At the other extreme is a conference designed mainly around process, which the participants influence as the conference progresses. In this case, it is not possible or desirable to develop an involved PPB. For most conferences, particularly MSs and occasionally PSs, the PPB is essential. It should be the result of careful planning and must consider

- Decisions about the PPB
- Form
- Organization
- Cost
- Planning sheets.

### Decisions about the PPB

The initial decisions that must be made will influence factors such as size, shape, and form of the PPB.

### Objectives of the Conference

Because the conference objectives have guided the DC's work, they should be referred to constantly and be part of the participant materials. The Coordinator and the DC have lived with these objectives a long time—they have discussed them, reworked them, and reworded them. The initial information concerning the conference, which was sent out to the participants, listed the objectives and presumably influenced their decision whether or not to attend the conference. It is hoped the final objectives will not be too dissimilar from the initial ones, so that the participants do not get the feeling they came to the wrong conference.

The PPB should clearly and concisely state the objectives on one of the first pages. In some cases the sessions that relate to each objective can also be stated. This is not necessary but this form might be chosen when the Coordinator and the DC want to emphasize an objectives-oriented conference. This also puts pressure on the Coordinator and DC to assure that every activity is related to an objective, and that every objective has one or more appropriate activities. The participants should not have to take part in a guessing game.

Once included in the PPB, however, the objectives can become more of a controlling force than anticipated.

—— • ——

The PS conference was offered in England, using an American resource person who was not familiar with English practice. The PPB reiterated the objectives that had appeared in the announcement of the conference. It was a three-day conference, utilizing only one resource person. During the second day, the resource person began receiving feedback that there was discontent among the participants. They felt he had deviated from the stated objectives. Some of the participants gave notice that they were withdrawing from the conference and requested a refund of the conference fee. As was the custom, fees were returned upon a statement from the participants that the objectives were not being met. The American resource person was shocked. He was process oriented rather than content oriented and saw nothing wrong with deviating from the objectives.

—— • ——

This may no longer be the custom in England today, and if not, we have all lost by it. Allowing participants to seek return of fees when objectives are obviously not being met could introduce more quality control into many conferences. Coordinators and DCs would have to be more specific in their objectives, and resource people would have to pay more attention to how they are meeting the stated objectives. It is not a straight-jacket, but a guideline. If the participants are informed that there will be a review of the objectives during the conference, and appropriate redesign, few would opt to have their money returned. They have been informed that redesign is part of the design. When it happens without their prior knowledge, and with little ability to influence the directions of change, they have a right to seek redress.

Printing the objectives in the PPB is risky, and the Coordinator must decide on the importance of the objectives and the resultant consequences if some of them are not reached. For some MS conferences a statement of objectives is not necessary and could communicate a more rigid climate than would be welcomed by most of the participants. If objectives are not stated in the PPB, it should be the result of a clear decision by the Coordinator, not an oversight.

### Utilization during the Conference

The PPB can contain information that is important to the participants' effectiveness during the conference, such as data about resource people, which would help eliminate some of the lengthy formal introductions. The PPB can also contain outlines of presentations that the participants might want to have while attending a session and various kinds of instructions that the participant could find useful during the conference.

The Coordinator must decide whether the PPB should be used during the conference and then explore how it could be used. The implications of these decisions are discussed later in this chapter.

### Utilization after the Conference

The PPB can be organized so that the participant will find uses for it after the conference has been completed. This decision by the Coordinator will influence the form as well as the content of the PPB. To date, it has not been common to organize the PPB for use after the conference. Coordinators have therefore lost a valuable follow-up mechanism. They have not realized how the PPB could be made useful to the participant after returning home. However, some Coordinators have recognized this possibility and developed the PPB accordingly. One example is the evaluation form to be completed after the participant returns home. The form can be included in the PPB with other take-home materials, and this will encourage the participant to consider utilizing the PPB back home.

### Recognition

The PPB can be used to acknowledge the design committee and everyone else who helped arrange the conference. The MS can use the PPB as a way of recognizing the efforts of those who have provided much assistance, usually without any remuneration. The PPB can provide psychic income.

Caution should be exercised to avoid having the PPB contain page after page of names of people receiving recognition. If the list is too long, it depreciates the value of this recognition.

Since the PPB is printed before the conference starts, it is not possible to use this device to acknowledge the steering committee. In some rare cases the steering committee might be identified before the conference begins, and then their names would be available. However, to include their names is to risk the embarrassment of having to announce changes after the PPB has been published. The steering committee is best selected and announced after the conference opens. They certainly deserve recognition, but the PPB is not the appropriate place to accomplish this. The steering committee should include only those present at the conference. Though a participant may expect to attend, there are many factors that might make it impossible.

When names are listed in the PPB, recognition can be reinforced by sending copies to specially selected individuals. When an ES design committee is listed in the PPB, copies might be sent to supervisors of personnel on the committee. The copies can be marked up, indicating the particular employee being recognized. Perhaps an accompanying letter can be sent, if that is the norm in that particular organization. The PPB can also be sent to other parts of the organization in order to recognize the efforts of the particular unit that was responsible for the conference.

The MS can utilize copies in a similar manner. When individuals have given considerable time and energy to design the conference or to work on any part of it, their employer should be informed of these efforts. Today, there are companies that make their personnel available to membership and community organizations as part of their sense of social responsibility. Top echelons of such organizations should get feedback. They should receive copies of the PPB listing their employees who are involved. It is vital that the Coordinator make sure the employing organization is correctly identified in the PPB.

## Reviewed by Others

The PPB is important, so the Coordinator should have it reviewed before it goes to press. This places an additional step between the development of the PPB and its publication, and may present a time problem. The Coordinator usually waits until the last minute to print the PPB in case there are any changes. Interposing the additional step of reviewing the draft slows down the process. The trade-off is whether to rush into print and risk program errors, or to build in more lead time to make sure of content and form.

Whenever possible, the PPB should be reviewed in draft by various resource people. They should be looking not only at the sessions related to themselves, but also at what is being written about other sessions.

——— ● ———

All the resource people completed the various preconference forms sent out by the Coordinator, requesting suggestions for session title and for a twenty- to thirty-word statement describing the content. Fortunately, there was enough lead time, and after receiving the forms the Coordinator compiled them and had them reviewed by the ten resource people who were on the conference program. One particular resource person discovered that the topic and content of the keynote speaker was exactly what he himself had planned to do during a concurrent session. Not only that, but the keynote speaker was also scheduled to conduct a concurrent session opposite the resource person, following the keynote presentation. The resource person reasoned that as the concurrent sessions would be competitive, the participants would probably attend the concurrent session conducted by the keynote speaker. The resource person told the Coordinator that he would either change his topic or withdraw as a resource person. Because the Coordinator wanted this particular resource person on the program, a new topic was negotiated to their mutual satisfaction.

—— • ——

The Coordinator will also find it useful to have the PPB reviewed by others who are not resource people, not DC members, nor in any other way involved in the development of the program. The most obvious people who should be involved in the review process are prospective participants, as the purpose of the PPB is to communicate with them. A carefully selected group of participants can be given the opportunity to review the PPB before it goes into final printing.

Allowing a review carries the same danger as any situation involving feedback. It starts with the willingness of the Coordinator to ask for feedback, and his willingness to respond to it. It can be anticipated that some of the feedback will be very helpful, some will be predictable but not helpful, and some of it of such a nature that little or nothing can or should be done with it. The Coordinator must be capable of handling the feedback or he should not ask for it.

After the feedback is received, it is quite possible that even good suggestions will not be acted upon, because of factors the giver of feedback was not aware of. The Coordinator must be prepared to cope with persons who have given good, but ignored, feedback. An explanation to such people, before the conference is almost obligatory. It is most desirable to ensure that no doubts are cast on the validity of the Coordinator's actions in similar situations in the future.

### Form

There are three possibilities for the PPB's physical form, and each is based upon a particular intent.

**Carried with the Participant**

If the PPB is to be carried by the participant during the conference, then it must be of an appropriate size. A pocket-size PPB is a popular form. This is defined as a size which will fit into a man's jacket pocket or a woman's handbag. A problem arises when the participants are wearing leisure clothing that does not have regular pockets or when the size of the pockets are different from the traditional jacket pocket. Assuming that the participants would be either wearing jackets or carrying handbags, the pocket-size PPB can be utilized. For most conferences the pocket-size PPB can contain all the necessary information, and it may even include a few blank pages for notes.

The shape must be related to the bulk. The PPB can be of the right size to fit into a pocket, but contain so many pages that it is too thick to remove without danger of ripping a seam. The remotest possibility of damage to the garment reduces the possibility that the PPB will be carried during the conference.

A variation is possible when the conference program is not too complicated and therefore needs only several pages. There are many kinds of name tags, and one of them is in two parts. The top contains the traditional name tag in plastic, while the bottom, also in clear plastic, has a pocket into which the participant can slip the program, or a condensed version of it. As long as the participant wears the name tag, he also has the PPB or a piece of it. Some tags have a pin on the back so that they can be pinned onto the shirt or blouse if the participant does not have a convenient pocket. As discussed in the previous chapter, the two major forms of participant materials are the plastic envelope and the loose-leaf book.

The one-day conference program will probably be carried, if for no other reason than that the participant does not have anyplace to leave it. Also, the nature of a one-day design would not produce a PPB so bulky that the participant will not want to carry it.

If the participants are expected to carry the PPBs during the conference, many options are available. The PPB can be either produced to fit the plastic envelope or hole-punched so as to be inserted into the loose-leaf book.

**Not Carried with the Participant**

The program may be of such a form that it is bulky and a burden to carry. Or, the program can be so simple that once the day starts there are so few alternatives that the participant need not carry the program. In either of these extremes the PPB can contain other material and be organized in any way that the Coordinator feels would be suitable, including the cost aspect.

If the Coordinator has planned the PPB so it can be left in the bedroom, this should be indicated, so the participants can take advantage of the PPB format that the Coordinator has planned. As each conference is different, the participant may not realize the most effective way to use the PPB until time has passed. Therefore, the participant may be carrying around a bulky PPB and feel it is an encumbrance, whereas the Coordinator had designed it so it could be left in the room. If it is to be left in the bedroom, the Coordinator should caution anyone making announcements that they should not refer to any material contained in the PPB as the participants are not expected to carry this with them during the sessions.

### Combination

It is possible to develop a PPB that allows for both possibilities described above, and it is good to have this alternative.

The PPB can be arranged so that the details of the conference need not be carried around, but by using daily planning sheets the participant can identify sessions and activities of interest. Later in this chapter there will be examples of different kinds of planning sheets which facilitate this approach. The Coordinator can supplement this by having an enlarged mock-up of the conference design, from the opening to the closing, placed at some obvious point, such as the administration area, the registration area, or outside the room where the general sessions are held. This allows the participants to quickly review the total program if they find that their daily plan has not been adequate.

Another variation is to build the PPB with tear sheets for each day. The participant plans the day beforehand as to the sessions he wishes to attend, marks the sheet, and then in the morning before leaving his room he tears the sheet out of the PPB and takes it along. The tear sheets should be perforated so the tear out process does not damage the material remaining in the PPB. Obviously, this has the disadvantage that it is not reusable, and therefore the participant will not have a complete record of the conference program unless provision has also been made to have permanent sheets in the PPB that contain the entire program. The detachable sheets can be of such a size that they fit into the name tag holder described earlier, can be hole-punched for a loose-leaf book, or can be put into the plastic envelope or clothing pocket as the participant wishes.

### Organization

As the purpose of the PPB is to help the participant to function during the conference, it should be organized to minimize confusion. The more complicated the conference design, the more likely that the PPB will become an almost useless compendium. To produce more than one PPB for a conference is costly and can contribute to the confusion, but one PPB that is organized according to one or more of the following aspects is much less susceptible to such confusion.

**By Day and Time**

This is the most common way to organize the PPB. It presents a chronological sequence that is important in a conference where sessions are usually not repeated. There are some sessions that may be repeated because of the small size of the room, or the great appeal of the topic or resource person. Presumably, the DC provides for this and the participant can plan accordingly. The repeat session can also arise during the conference, and the Coordinator and the steering committee try to schedule a second chance for those sessions or activities for which there was great demand. Generally, the participant will only have those opportunities already stated in the program.

Figure 10-1 illustrates one page from a PPB, utilizing the chronological approach. Note that it may prove confusing when the design offers many concurrent sessions. It is sometimes possible to make this listing more useful by using different typefaces to indicate different kinds of sessions. This requires that there be a key for the participant so that the significance of each typeface is clearly understood. Those who have read airline schedules and railroad timetables know that different typefaces do not always communicate as easily

## Tuesday

| Time | Session | Room |
|------|---------|------|
| 9:00 | General session | Ballroom |
| 10:00 | Concurrent sessions | |
| | #1—(title) | 201 |
| | #2—(title) | 203 |
| | #3—(title) | 205 |
| 12:00 | Lunch | Ballroom |
| 1:30 | Concurrent sessions | |
| | #1—(title) | 201 |
| | #2—(title) | 203 |
| | #3—(title) | 205 |
| 3:30 | General session | Ballroom |
| 4:30 | Individual time | |
| 5:30 | Social hour | 210-212 |
| 6:30 | Dinner | Ballroom |

*Figure 10-1.* The sessions in participant program book may be organized chronologically, as shown here.

as the schedule designers indicate. Although it is possible to utilize different typefaces, the Coordinator should not depend upon this as the sole form to communicate the differences in sessions.

To set the individual days apart, the PPB can be printed with each day on a different colored paper. This is usually more costly than just plain white, but is worth it for purposes of clarity when scheduling a long conference with many alternatives. Another variation is to use colored tabs to signify the different days.

When the day and time approach is used, there should be one place in which the entire program for the several days of the conference, is set forth. The centerfold can be used for this purpose, as it provides a convenient spread sheet not readily available anyplace else in the PPB.

## By Topic

The Coordinator can emphasize the topics in the PPB. The focus then is on the titles of sessions, and it is important that they are consistent. Too often, people who are concerned with developing copy for this kind of PPB format will seek "jazzy" titles that will get the participants excited and interested. Such titles sacrifice clarity for attention-getting. The result can be disappointing to the participant, though it makes great copy. Using appealing titles for topic sessions is usually unnecessary. The titles should be as clear as possible to enable the participant to anticipate what the session will deliver.

The conference that offers alternative sessions to the participant should have clear topic designations in the PPB. The Coordinator can facilitate this by setting up a form for titles and then following this format for all the sessions. It is difficult to find one format that would be appropriate for all types of conferences and participants. The Coordinator should determine the vocabulary that will best communicate with the participants.

Figure 10-2 shows the daily program of Figure 10-1, but reorganized to put emphasis on the topic rather than on the time. The reader may question why it is necessary to repeat the listing of concurrent sessions, or to repeat the general session topic. After all, they are "obvious"—but are they? When studied carefully in the context of this book, or during design committee sessions, it does seem like repetition. However, the page should be read in the context of a participant who has never seen it before, and is under pressure not only to read, but to make decisions. The clearer the program is, the better the chance the participant has to make the appropriate decision, and to find the program and the conference of help.

In order to minimize the confusion that merely a title can produce, the PPB may also contain a brief description of the content. The proscription of "brief" makes this more difficult than it first appears. It is easier to write a 250-word description than a 50-word one. In many PPBs the description must be fewer than 25 words if the document is not to become too bulky.

| Session | Time | Room |
|---|---|---|
| "The Effect of Inflation on the Economy" | 9:00 | Ballroom |
| —Opening remarks | | |
| Break | 10:00 | |
| Concurrent Sessions | 10:15 | |
| #1—"Productivity" | | 201 |
| #2—"Consumer Price Index" | | 203 |
| #3—"Accounting Practices" | | 205 |
| End concurrent sessions | 11:45 | |
| Lunch | 12:00 | Ballroom |
| Concurrent Sessions | 2:00 | |
| #1—"Productivity" | | 201 |
| #2—"Consumer Price Index" | | 203 |
| #3—"Accounting Practices" | | 205 |
| Break | 3:30 | |
| "The Effect of Inflation on the Economy" | 3:45 | Ballroom |
| —Summary | | |
| Individual time | 4:30 | |
| Social hour | 5:30 | 210-212 |
| Dinner | 6:30 | Ballroom |

**Figure 10-2.** *This is an example of how sessions can be topically organized in the participant program book.*

Here too, as with titles, it must be consistent, so the participant is not trapped in word games. One way of spelling out the description is to have the resource person state what the outcomes of the session will be. It may contain a statement such as, "By the end of this session, the participant will . . . ," or, "The presentation will cover these points . . ." The description should strive for clarity rather than literary style.

## Type of Session

For some conferences the process is equal to or more important than the content. The participants want to know what is expected of them as well as what is expected of the resource person. The information for this part of the PPB is readily available because, as described in an earlier chapter, the resource person is expected to provide this information to the Coordinator and the DC.

The type of session is indicated in terms that are understood by the participants. The program should not be studded with esoteric terms that may reflect the sophistication of the Coordinator, but are meaningless to the participants. Above all, the intent is always to communicate as effectively as possible with the participants and to make the PPB as useful a document as possible.

The type of session should not overshadow the content, unless the emphasis is on process or media. If the session is to show the use of media, then the process and content merge. More often, the methodology of the session is designed to supplement the content. Figure 10-3 shows a flow for a day when the type of session is listed. For purposes of this figure the content (title) of each session has not been included so the reader can focus on the use of the "type of session" column. In an actual situation the title would be listed.

Listing by type of session indicates some of the various methodologies that have been utilized. This may be helpful to participants who have different kinds of cognitive maps. We know that each of us learns in different ways. Unfortunately, not enough has been done yet to best identify which types of sessions are most beneficial to each of us.

The experienced conference participant knows himself and will select accordingly, if the information is available to enable him to make a choice. Some participants may choose to attend sessions that are more media-oriented, while others may prefer those in which they can get more personally involved.

If participative approaches are to be utilized by some resource people, this should be clearly indicated. Presented with a particular topic and a specific resource person, some participants might choose to attend a session billed as participative, while others might prefer to be in a more passive role. For the participant to make this decision the information should be available in the PPB. This does not guarantee that the resource person will present as planned, or that the projector will not break down in a media session. At least, the participant has the benefit of having planned for the more common eventuality, that the resource person will conduct as indicated and that the projector will have been pretested and will work.

Another distinction that is difficult to make is whether the session is geared for information or learning. Both of these goals are possible in any session, though some are designed to be either one or the other. It is legitimate for some sessions to have specific learning objectives while others have informational objectives. The participant is helped by knowing which objectives apply to a specific session, as the participant may only want general information about a topic and would not attend the session if it has any other objectives, and the reverse situation applies.

| Time | Session | Type of Session |
| --- | --- | --- |
| 9:00 | General session | Panel |
| 9:45 | Small Group sessions | Discussion |
| 10:30 | Break | |
| 10:45 | Group reports | Panel |
| 11:30 | Presentation—film | Media |
| 12:00 | Lunch—speaker | Lecture |
| 1:30 | Concurrent sessions | |
| | #1 | Simulation |
| | #2 | Discussion |
| | #3 | Media |
| 3:15 | Break | |
| 3:30 | General session | Skit |
| 4:15 | Individual time | |
| 6:00 | Social hour | |
| 7:00 | Dinner | Entertainment |

**Figure 10-3.** *Sessions in the participant program book may be organized by type for a conference that places great importance on process.*

Even a lunch or dinner should be identified by type of session. There are many options for designing these mass feeding functions, and the design objectives of the DC should be very apparent. If the participants are not expected to eat together, this should be noted on the program. A common notation for this is "on our own." If the meal is part of the conference design, there will be some kind of activity. It could be a lecture, a media presentation, an award presentation, or just entertainment. This information should appear under type of session.

For large conferences with heterogeneous participants there is the factor of *level.* The same topic can be handled at many different levels of presentation, detail, sophistication, and involvement of participants. The DC has its profile of potential participants. This should be communicated to the resource people if there is any doubt about their knowledge of the participant group. The resource people will design their sessions for different levels of participants.

Among the professional groups the identification of level can also be useful. If the professional MS has different degrees of membership, then this is easily handled. Usually, however, the distinction of level is not that clear.

Therefore, the Coordinator must rely on the self-selection of the participants. To do this, the participants need sufficient information to enable them to make a decision as to how to guide themselves on level. There are many ways to establish the level, depending upon the organization involved. One method is to use the number of years in the business, trade, or profession. We may find the old story that "the person does not have twenty years of experience, but one year repeated twenty times." There is little the Coordinator can do to accommodate to this except to indicate that when the topical description notes that a session is geared for "participants with five years of experience," it means five years of different, progressively more difficult experience. Each organization will have its own variations and they might include

- New/old
- Schooling level—high school/bachelor/master/doctor
- Junior/senior
- Basic/advanced
- Years of membership

The difficulty in self-selection is the self-image of the participants. An older person might not want to be seen as being new in the field, even though it is a second career. When using level it is generally acceptable to allow the participants to utilize self-selection, and then to cope with their choices. A great deal of work remains to be done, as we have done too little to indicate the levels at many of our conferences, and this is an area in which much can be done towards improving conferences.

## Resource People

Resource people can be selected for conferences based on their attraction for the participants. When the selection is made on this basis, it is because the name alone communicates to the participants. The topic or type of session can become secondary when participants choose to attend because of the appeal of a marquee name. (This comes from the projection over a theater entrance which lists the names of stars.) To be included in the marquee category, a resource person must have performed effectively often enough that just the name communicates the possibility of a successful session.

Conferences should not be built strictly on marquee names, but the Coordinator cannot be blind to our competitive society and to the attraction of marquee names.

———— • ————

The Coordinator was building a conference design that was concerned mostly with learning, but with some information. For several of the mass feeding activities there was also some light entertainment. While the Coordinator was still developing the design with the DC, some prospective participants requested the names of the "well known figures" who would be on the program. These prospective participants indicated that the only way they could sell their organization on funding their attendance would be if they could give their supervisors a list of outstanding resource people who would be presenting at the conference. The Coordinator shared this information with the DC and a heated discussion took place during one of their regular meetings. There was a split between those who wanted to emphasize the marquee-name approach as contrasted with those who were more concerned with the content of the presentations. A compromise was reached whereby some sessions were designed based on the marquee-name resource person, while others were designed based on content. This was a reasonable compromise, but it was not reflected in the PPB, and the feedback from participants during and after the conference reflected this confusion.

━━ ● ━━

Marquee names are important! If the focus is on resource people, then the PPB should contain additional information such as pictures. Most resource people who do any significant amount of conference work will have professional photographs readily available. If at all possible, the Coordinator should set the ground rule that the picture should be no more than three to five years old. Ego being what it is, some resource people submit professionally retouched photos, taken many years ago. When the resource person arrives at the conference, there is little resemblance to the "official" picture. They usually have more pounds and less hair than pictured. The pictures of the resource people are not for a beauty contest, but a dissonance between the picture and the person can, first of all, prove disruptive to the host who is meeting the person for the first time. The participants may be equally disturbed and wonder why the resource person persists in using an old photograph. The wonder can get in the way of the session. Better no photograph than one that raises questions.

If the emphasis is on resource people, then biographical information becomes important. Here, too, as previously noted, the Coordinator should provide an outline for the kind of biographical information needed so there is consistency. This information should be relevant and make clear why a person is appearing on the program at a particular conference for a designated session. The participants should be informed on the following items:

● Present position, particularly as it relates to the topic
● Previous positions or experiences related to the topic
● Publications, as relevant (avoid a meaningless list of titles)
● Awards and honors, particularly as related to the topic

There is no figure illustrating the program when the emphasis is on the resource person. The simplest approach is just a listing of the resource people and their respective topics, as follows:

Armstrong, Barry—"The Use of Media in Marketing"
Bellows, John—"The Relationship of Media and Objectives"
Cartwright, Shirley—"The Use of Sex in Media"
Donegan, Arthur—"Media in the Future"

From this it is possible to build in many directions. One addition could be the biographical information. For a strictly marquee appearance the topic might not be as important when the individual will be presenting it. When the resource person is less well known, the topic is more important. Whichever direction is chosen, it should be done the same way for all the resource people, at least in the listing. In other parts of the PPB other factors could be emphasized.

Some Coordinators prefer to present the information about the resource people in another document, separate from the PPB. This allows for last minute changes, additional information, and other resource people. It requires an extra printing and is another piece of material to be handled by the staff and the participant. A decision is needed as to whether a booklet detailing resource people is something the participant may want to retain for future reference or to throw away after the conference. Coordinators may choose not to use a separate document for resource people as the benefits may not be worth the trouble and the cost.

### Combination of the Above

It is possible to use more than one of the approaches discussed above. They can be coupled more closely to meet the needs of the participants. The precaution is to avoid using so many of them as to make the PPB too involved and overly detailed. Yet, to strip the PPB to its bare bones can make it useless and leave the participant with no way to understand the carefully designed program.

The crucial point is for the Coordinator to select the particular approach to the PPB that is congruent with the Sponsor image and the participants' needs. This can then be matched with the financial aspects.

### Cost

The PPB illustrations given so far in the various figures, have all been single page examples. For a conference of several days there will obviously be several pages. Even for a one-day conference, it is possible that the design, when set forth in more detail, will require more than one page.

The format, organization, and detail will need to be weighed against cost. There are various ways of dealing with the cost situation. First, let us explore a decision to have the Sponsor pay for the PPB with no expectation of recovering or offsetting any of the cost.

The amount the Sponsor may be willing to expend will be related to the expected use of the PPB. If it is to be used only during the conference, the Sponsor is inclined to keep the cost as low as possible. In addition to its utility, however, the PPB is also an image creating document. If it is poorly reproduced in an attempt to reduce cost, it may communicate to the participant that there should be little attention paid to the PPB.

If it is to be used only during the conference, and therefore is strictly conference oriented, then the material in it will be limited to that which is useful to the participant during the conference.

The PPB can also be a take-home document. As has been indicated, it could include an evaluation form and important information that the Sponsor is providing to be of use to the participant after he returns home. For some conferences this can include items such as bibliographies, lists of participants (if known before the conference begins), and information about the Sponsor. An MS might include their constitution and bylaws within the PPB as a way of getting it to their membership. A PS, concerned with political action, could include lists of congressional personnel related to the conference objectives. Once it has been decided to have a take-home document, there are many items, in addition to the program, that could be included by almost any Sponsor.

The PPB as a take-home document contributes to image building. The MS can produce a "souvenir" booklet that participants take home and share with others, and occasionally, even look at themselves. If the PPB is to serve this purpose, it must be of a higher quality than one that is to be used only at the conference and then discarded.

To improve the appearance of the PPB, it can be multicolored for emphasis, as well as decoration, but each color adds to the expense. The cost incurred by these factors must be weighed against the intent of the Sponsor.

There are ways to minimize costs. Among the least desirable ways is to charge for the PPB. This is rarely done, but it is possible. At some conferences a copy of the PPB is distributed at registration, but if the participant misplaces his copy, or wants additional copies, there is a charge. This practice is not recommended.

It is more common to offset the cost through inserting advertising in the PPB. There are several ways to do this, but above all, the use of advertising and the revenue it produces should be balanced against the image of the Sponsor and the effect on the participants. Advertising can create a commercial image, which for some Sponsors may not be desirable. There is the temptation to have as many ads as possible, as this will not only offset the cost, but can actually produce income. For some trade associations this is highly appropriate. For professional associations and some membership organizations this is questionable.

There are several sources for advertising, once the decision has been made to include advertising in the PPB. An immediate and obvious source are participants. For an MS conference participants may wish to demonstrate their support for the organization, as well as to help defray the cost of the conference by placing an ad in the PPB. For a trade conference members of the association who are not exhibitors might be persuaded to take advertising space in the PPB, particularly if it is a take-home document.

A major source of advertising are the exhibitors—for a conference that has exhibits, naturally. The Coordinator arranges this at the time that fees are set for exhibitors' space. There can be a small additional charge, on a voluntary basis, for those exhibitors who wish to place ads in the PPB in addition to the alphabetical list of exhibitors that is ordinarily included.

There should not be any charge for the listing of exhibitors by name and booth number. When there are many exhibits covering a large area, the PPB can also contain a diagram showing booth location and number to assist participants to find the booths they particularly want to visit. All of this should be provided without any extra charge.

There can be an additional charge for advertising in the PPB which ranges from a ½-inch box to full-page color ads. Exhibitors have a variety of reasons for purchasing ad space in the PPB. As the participant will be looking through the PPB several times, he will probably see the ad several times. Also, it can communicate to the participant that the exhibitor is supporting the organization by this additional expenditure.

Nonexhibitors are also a source of advertising. Not every conference includes exhibits, but there may be organizations that wish to get their message across to the participants. The PPB can be useful for this as well as a source of revenue for the Sponsor.

Even if exhibits are part of the conference, there will always be those companies who, for their own reasons, have not taken exhibition space. The nonexhibitor may feel that the cost is out of line with the return that could be anticipated, or he may be committed to another conference being conducted at the same time in some other place. The nonexhibitor may advertise to test out a potential market. There may also be nonexhibitors who are on the periphery—that is, they are not directly related to the participants but have products/services that might be of some minimal interest. For these reasons and more nonexhibitors might advertise. Too often, Coordinators overlook this potential source of revenue to offset the cost of the PPB.

Obviously, if the PPB is to be used to reduce costs, then it must be much more attractive than one that is designed strictly for use by the participants. Making the PPB attractive should not be done at the cost of reducing utility. The major purpose of the PPB is always to serve the participants, and if this is minimized, the PPB may pay for itself in revenue but at the cost of providing an unsatisfactory experience for the participants.

Up to this point, the ES may have difficulty identifying how they relate to PPB advertising. Advertising, as a way of reducing costs, is still useful but the content of the copy would be different from copy for a PS or MS. The ES could use well-designed and well-placed ads in the PPB to inform the participants of products and services of the ES with which they may not be too familiar, or to reinforce what they have heard at the conference. A company could charge part of the PPB off to its advertising budget or to the budget of those parts of the corporation that take ads in the PPB. The same advantages and cautions described earlier would apply here as well. There are tax implications of using the PPB for income and these should be explored before a final decision is made.

### Planning Sheets

Let us examine a use of the PPB that is far too rare. Many times we have heard participants complain that the design and the PPB were so complicated that it was almost impossible to utilize them effectively. All that was needed was some kind of instrument that would enable the participants to translate the PPB into a personal planning sheet.

The participant planning sheet has many advantages. It enables each of the participants to plan his own participation in the conferences. This is extremely important when there are many alternatives among sessions. The participant can plan for the best choices and not have to continually thumb through the PPB, and not readily find the choice made during an earlier search. When the conference has many activities going on at the same time (special events, recreation), the planning sheet can be helpful. It should be for individual planning, and therefore the participant is not committed. It is possible for the participant to deviate from his own plan at any time, but it does give him a basis to start with.

Using a planning sheet can assist the participant in avoiding or eliminating conflicts. When there are several alternatives, the participant may plan on going to two sessions, and not fully realize that they are in a time conflict until they are actually written down on a sheet. Too few participants do this. The tendency is to check or circle the session in the PPB. For a conference of several days the use of the planning sheet will enable the participant to follow a track, a particular thread throughout the conference, or to choose appropriate sessions that will provide the desired mix. If the participant sets all of this down on a planning sheet, at the opening of the conference, he can see the kind of program he is developing for himself. He can review the totality and see if this will meet his needs.

For some participants it also provides a record of the sessions they have attended. Of course, if they change from their original plan, it may require erasures or crossing out on the sheet, but after the conference is completed, it can serve as a source that will help the participant to review his own experiences. When the participant receives a postconference evaluation form and tries to recall which sessions were attended, he can check back to his **PPB** planning sheet. He can also utilize the planning sheet on his return home, to organize his experiences preparatory to sharing them with others.

Let us look at some of the kinds of planning sheets that could be used. By no means does this cover all the possibilities, but it does give some examples

| Time | Session | Resource Person | Room | Alternative |
|------|---------|-----------------|------|-------------|
| 9:00 | "The Effect of Inflation on the Economy"—opening remarks | Jones | Ballroom | |
| 10:15 | Concurrent Session | | | |
| 12:00 | Lunch | | Ballroom | |
| 2:00 | Concurrent Session | | | |
| 3:45 | "Effect of Inflation on the Economy"—closing remarks | Jones | Ballroom | |
| 4:30 | Individual time | | | |
| 5:30 | Social hour | | 210-212 | |
| 6:30 | Dinner | | Ballroom | |

**Figure 10-4.** *A planning sheet helps the participant in several ways, such as selecting the appropriate sessions, avoiding conflicting sessions, and providing a record of sessions attended.*

and indicates directions. The planning sheet must reflect the actual program design, and supplement it. It cannot be used in place of a program description sheet. The participant needs the full program information in order to develop his own planning sheet.

One further note of caution. The examples offered here are for one day of a conference. The design has been kept simple, so attention can be focused on the planning sheet. At some place in the PPB there should be a planning sheet for the entire conference or enough pages to plan for each individual day. This would be desirable when the conference design uses a track system or a series of related sessions occurring on several different days.

To provide a basis for comparison, the planning sheets illustrated and discussed are based on Figure 10-2.

One way of offering the planning sheet is by providing the participant with one that is partially filled in. Those sessions that every participant is expected to attend are set forth, and blank spaces are provided where the participant has some choice. This is shown in Figure 10-4. Note the use of the column on the extreme right, marked "alternative." Even though there are planned sessions, the participant may choose to do something else. Or, the participant may find himself part of a caucus or small group that must miss the general session in order to do some other conference related work. A host, as described earlier, may have to miss a session, so his alternative is to meet a resource person at the airport or the VIP room.

The type of planning sheet shown here is highly directive and is intended to communicate to the participant that he is expected to show up at each of the specified sessions.

Another variation is shown in Figure 10-5. This is a more open planning sheet, and should be used when the participant has many choices. Of course, the Coordinator and the DC may have planned for everybody to attend each general session. But they probably also understand that not every general session will be of interest to everybody, and that some participants may want to skip a session in order to take part in some form of recreation or some other type of self-renewal.

The sheet is empty, except that there are time blocks. This allows the participant to schedule other personal activities, but still fit them into the time slots for the day.

This type of planning sheet has a psychological advantage. Rather than giving the participant a printed page to read, the participant is now encouraged to recopy what is important to him, and in a way, that makes a psychological commitment to attend those sessions. There is no research on this, but the shared experiences of Coordinators who have used the blank planning sheet for this purpose indicate that this commitment does occur.

| Time | Session | Resource Person | Room | Alternative |
|------|---------|-----------------|------|-------------|
| 9:00 | | | | |
| 10:15 | | | | |
| 12:00 | | | | |
| 2:00 | | | | |
| 3:45 | | | | |
| 4:30 | | | | |
| 5:30 | | | | |
| 6:30 | | | | |

**Figure 10-5.** *This open-style planning sheet provides the participants with a great deal of flexibility.*

The two examples we have presented here are the most common. Beyond that, we have seen many kinds of planning sheets, but they were designed for use with a particular program design. There has been too little use made of planning sheets, and it is hoped that this brief description will encourage more innovation and development in using them. It will then be possible to present more experiences and examples.

There is another kind of planning sheet, but it relates more to what the participant will do after the conference, than during the conference. Often, a participant attends a conference and meets some interesting people, hears some exciting ideas, and generally finds the whole experience worthwhile. His intent is to follow up and do something about the people and ideas. If the conference lasts several days, it is all too easy for his recollection of people and ideas to be overwhelmed by the later experiences. The increased use of name cards has helped to remember people, but we do not have any similar device to retain ideas, except for the occasional handout that a resource person has designed for take-home purposes.

**People I met and I want to contact:**

(name and address)                                                              **Reason**

**Books and articles I want to read:**

(author, title, date)                                                              **Why**

**Things to do back home:**

**New ideas I have heard:**

**Figure 10-6.** *This type of planning sheet allows the participants to follow up on ideas and people that were encountered at the conference.*

Figure 10-6 presents a very simple planning sheet for the future. In actual practice a separate page might be provided for each of these items. Other items could be added as relevant ideas surface. Perhaps it can be set up so that there is a similar page for each day of the conference, and participants can be encouraged to start a fresh sheet each day. This will enforce the use of this particular planning sheet.

### From the Suppliers' Viewpoint

The PPB does not involve many suppliers, but those who are related to the PPB have some significant comments to make.

### Site Personnel Say—

Although we have received the conference program book, we still need to see the PPB. This gives us another check to be sure that we have allocated facilities and staff in accordance with your plan and design. Extra copies for housekeeping and maintenance are also helpful.

Usually, we take your material and transfer it on to our own control sheets. A copy of the PPB just gives us another way of verifying that we are all working from the same schedule.

Changes should have reached us through the conference program book, but if you have any changes in the PPB, let us know about them. Even if a small conference can be less than successful if there are changes without proper notification. We will read the PPB, but will still rely on the conference program book.

### Printers Say—

We realize that the most important printed piece you will have at the conference is the PPB. It can also be one of the most costly printed materials you will use. We can understand your caution and your need to get several estimates.

We can give you better estimates if you can share your thinking with us about how you want the PPB to be used by the participants. There are many variations. Of course, each of us has some different presses and processes so you may want to spend some time with us. If you just send us copy, and ask for an estimate, you are not making full use of our services.

There are many variations in type faces, layout, paper, and form of the PPB and it takes time to explore these with you. If the PPB is a throw-away item, you will want to spend less time developing it and keep the cost as low as possible. We realize this, but even for the throw-away there are many possibilities.

We also need the lead time to do a professional job of printing and delivery. Planning together we can produce the best participant program book for your conference needs.

# 11.
# Conducting
# the Conference

If the work done during the planning stages was effective, there is a good possibility that the conference will be successful. Despite all the careful planning, there will still be the need for adaptation and change. The mix of participants, site, weather, resource people, etc. is always so variable that it is impossible to anticipate the kinds of changes which will be required.

There are identifiable areas of concern that will arise during the conduct of the conference. In this chapter we will discuss

- Steering committee
- Opening the conference
- Messages and communications
- Secretariat
- Public relations
- Resource people
- Closing the conference

We hope the reader will forgive some necessary repetition of material introduced in earlier chapters, as we pick up some aspects and weave these into the conduct of the conference.

### Steering Committee

No matter how well planned and fully supported, there is always the need for some fine tuning and changing during the conference that must be done by the steering committee (SC).

**Purposes**

The SC essentially has three purposes:

- To be available to participants
- To make design changes
- To respond to logistical problems.

The SC provides a consistent and effective feedback channel from the participants to the Coordinator and to others responsible for the conduct of the conference. It is expected that the DC's work will have produced an effective design, but it is always possible that contingencies will arise during the conference that require alterations to the original design. If redesign is left to the Coordinator alone, it requires that this one individual be inordinately sensitive, constantly accessible, and prepared to respond to suggestions and demands from what could be a large group of participants. This places a staggering load on one individual and makes the conference the property of that one individual rather than the collaborative effort of all the participants.

Whether we are concerned with a conference of only ten people or of one thousand people, it is important to provide some mechanism for each participant to exert influence. This does not mean control, and not every participant will avail himself of the possibility to influence. Just because a participant makes a suggestion does not mean that it should be acted upon. But there must be provision for receiving suggestions from participants and reacting immediately while the conference is still being conducted. Evaluations conducted towards the end or after the conference may disclose problems and concerns that could have been handled effectively during the conference. If there is no mechanism for this (the SC), all that can be promised is that "the next conference will be better." We can do better now—the SC can react *now* to the *now* problems.

The major actions of the SC will result in design changes. It should be agreed by all concerned that the SC has the right to make any changes in the design that are agreed upon by the members of the SC. Those who wish to block changes may point out that the DC had authorized a particular design, or that the Sponsor of the conference "would not like that to happen." The DC is now a thing of the past. If it appears that the Sponsor may have some objections to proposed actions of the SC, there are several courses of action available, one of which would be to invite a representative of the Sponsor to attend an SC meeting. Generally, this should not be necessary, as the Coordinator is representing the Sponsor. When the Coordinator is an external person, there may be a temporary need for an internal person representing the Sponsor to be consulted.

Some of the logistics problems that arise during the conduct of a conference can be handled by the Coordinator (or staff). There are times when the problem involves more than one individual or activity. This occurs when there is a question of reassigning space, or when, after the start of the conference, it becomes evident that some of the earlier decisions about site use are no longer appropriate. This happens when the conference is open to all who wish to register and the exact number of participants is not known until the day of registration. It can also be a factor when concurrent sessions are planned and the relative attendance at each is not known until the sessions start. Some of the logistics decisions can be handled quickly and easily by the Coordinator, while some may have to be referred to the SC.

## Organization

The Coordinator has the responsibility for organizing the SC. The membership should include the following:

* The Coordinator
* Representatives of the design committee
* Representatives of the participants
* Representative of the sponsor (optional).

The Coordinator must be a member of the SC, but he need not be its chairperson, though that is the tendency because it is sometimes appropriate.

Although the DC has been dissolved, it is expected that some or all of the members of the DC are participants at the conference. One or two members of the now dissolved DC can be selected for membership on the SC. The Coordinator may select these people, or the DC, in one of its last actions, may designate one or two of its members to be on the SC.

It is essential to have participants on the SC. If the SC does not contain participants it will be deprived of important input from those who are the core of the experience. Presumably, the conference is being conducted to meet the needs of the participants. The method of selecting participants to be on the SC should be a reflection of the design and objectives of the conference. For one conference the Coordinator may preselect the members of the SC. This communicates a high degree of control by the Coordinator, but when there is a very large group of participants this may be the most meaningful way to make the selection. For a smaller conference the Coordinator may set up the mechanism very early in the conference for the participants to choose their own representatives to the SC. Not only does this communicate a more open situation, but it also provides for a more representative SC.

A conference may contain various kinds of subgroups. They can be ethnic, geographical, sex, or just people from different departments in the same company. If the SC consists of such group members it can be considered representative. Caution must be exercised in using this approach, for this may reinforce subgroupings. It may force people to see themselves as members of subgroups rather than as participants, and this could be disruptive to the conference process. Still, if the conference does contain clearly identified subgroups, and they have been encouraged to attend the conference as subgroup members, then it is only logical to have these various groups represented on the SC.

There are times when a representative of the Sponsor is a member of the SC. This may be the individual from the sponsoring organization who contracted with the Coordinator for the conference. During the conference, this person may choose to take a more active role and may even signify his intention to be the chairperson of the SC. If the Sponsor is an ES, this is quite proper. This person is responsible for assuring that the sponsoring organization has the kind of conference for which it has contracted. Being a member, and even chairperson, of the SC provides the necessary control.

It is very easy for the SC to become too large. Size of the SC is a relative matter. Experience and research have shown that it is preferable that a small group should not exceed eight members. An SC that is this size or smaller will probably be more effective than a larger SC. There must be a trade-off between broad representation and size. If the SC has more than eight persons, it could require an excessive amount of time to accomplish the purposes for which it has been organized.

## Operations

The SC should be readily accessible to all participants. Contact with the SC should not be limited to accidental meetings, or to those who have friends on that body. Every participant should have direct and easy access to the SC if it is to meet its stated purpose. The SC is organized to be available and receptive.

Methods of providing input to the SC are varied and should be considered by those who are designing the conference. Messages to the SC can be forwarded through the secretariat. This is easily done by placing a well-labeled box in the secretariat's office. Participants should be encouraged to drop notes into that box, which will be opened at least once a day by the SC chairperson in order to prepare the agenda for the daily meeting.

It is also possible to use technology to accomplish this goal of facilitating communication.

———— • ————

There were more than 1,000 people at the conference, and the SC wanted to encourage inputs from the participants. In addition to written notes, provision was made to have a tape recorder in the secretariat's office. There was a large sign over the tape recorder which said, "Comments for the Steering Committee." Participants were informed that they could come to the office at any time, and make comments and suggestions to the SC. An instruction card was placed on the recorder, suggesting that the participant might want to indicate name and room number in case the SC wanted additional information. This was not required, though, and the participant could remain anonymous. Prior to SC meetings, the chairperson listened to the taped comments of that day. Some of the material on the tape was not in the province of the SC but were matters best left to the secretariat. These were referred to the appropriate personnel, through the Coordinator. Other matters were placed on the agenda of the SC.

━━ ● ━━

The tape proved to have other values. There were some comments related to design and administration which nothing could be done about during this conference. The Coordinator also listened to the tape and with the agreement of the chairperson of the SC, the tape was transcribed and selected portions were placed in a folder for use by the Coordinator and DC responsible for the conference the following year.

It is a poor idea to encourage inputs for the SC during a general session. Participants may make inputs because there was a request for them, not because there was a need for them. Once these matters are brought up before the entire conference, they can result in lengthy discussions that take time from the conference, do not solve the problems, and slow down the process.

A conference that has process as an objective might have no need for an SC. If the objective is for the participants to develop skills in working with groups, building in an SC may deprive the participants of experience in resolving group conflicts. Examining process and redesign should be the objective for all the participants, not only the members of the SC. Even in this situation, a form of the SC may be necessary, if the conference attendance is large. Small groups, looking at process, usually should not exceed twenty people. If there are many more than that, the design could include several groups, ranging in size from ten to twenty people in each. They are all part of the same conference, but each group would set its own agenda. This requires an SC consisting of a representative from each group. They will meet in order to minimize conflicts over space and other facilities, as well as any general logistics that would affect all the groups.

There are times when both design and logistics present concerns that call for SC action. The following incident took place during a conference in the Philippines, but something like it could just as well have happened in the U.S.

━━ ● ━━

Recognizing cultural differences, the Coordinator (from the U.S.) worked with a DC composed entirely of Filipinos. Their meetings were productive, and the design that was produced was expected to fulfill the conference objectives. It was several months later that the conference was conducted. An SC was formed, which included the Coordinator, two members of the DC, and five participants, representing the thirty participants. The conference started Sunday evening, and on Monday evening, the first meeting of the SC was held. They reviewed the events of the day and the proposed design for Tuesday. There was general agreement by the SC that everything was going well and there was no need for any changes in the Tuesday schedule. They were just about to terminate the meeting when one member, a participant, asked what plans had been made for the social evening. There was complete silence. Several pairs of eyes focused on the Coordinator (a non-Filipino) who could do nothing but stare back. Finally, the Coordinator muttered, "What social evening?" A discussion followed, which rapidly made it clear that a conference in the Philippines should include one evening for a major social activity. This should have been built into the conference design, but somehow this had never been discussed during the DC meetings. Fortunately, because there were SC meetings, this oversight was raised early enough in the conference so that a social committee could be speedily organized. On Thursday night, the social was held, and it was a great success. Various participants came in native dress (from their particular part of the Philippines), and many had apparently come prepared with special clothing and material for the social evening. This change required only a minor adjustment in design and logistics, but if there had been no SC meeting, there would have been no social evening, and there would have been much hostility and a very unsuccessful conference.

———— ● ————

The SC should meet at least once a day. If there are any significant problems that need more immediate attention, it is always possible to call a special meeting. The daily meeting should be scheduled for the end of the day, even though the members of the SC may be tired. The evening meeting allows for a review of the events of the day and offers the possibility of making changes in the design for the next day. It allows time to make new assignments, additional preparation, and the development of a new agenda. If the SC meeting is held in the morning, there is insufficient time to make changes and prepare a different schedule for the day.

If all is going well, the SC meeting will merely be a confirmation of that fact. If the SC members feel that they are being less useful because they are not making changes, they should be helped to realize that the DC did extensive work previously, and therefore, changes may not be required. This does not lessen the need for the SC, and it may be difficult for the Coordinator (but something he must do) to convince the SC that they are performing an important and necessary task, even if they do not make changes.

There is generally no need for the deliberations of the SC to be shared with the participants. If the participants have confidence in their SC, and if the conference is moving along in a healthy and positive fashion, all the participants need to know is that the SC is meeting, and that the participants can influence the SC. When there is tension or when the conference is not meeting the needs of the participants, it is important for the SC to share the deliberations and decisions with the participants. This can be accomplished by issuing a bulletin, or by having the SC give a brief report each morning. Such daily reports should not be made unless they are necessary to reduce the level of anxiety, tension, and dissatisfaction of the participants. Reports of the SC can be time consuming and should be built into the design only if there is a real need, other than the ego needs of the SC members.

The participants who are on the SC have accepted an additional assignment in the conference. They deserve some form of recognition, other than their own satisfaction in helping to produce a successful conference. The particular form of the recognition should relate to the cultural norms of the participants and the conference. In one situation each day of the conference concluded with a cash bar for all the participants. The members of the SC, however, were invited to the suite of the head of the sponsoring organization and were provided with free drinks and hors d'oeuvres. The amount of money was not significant, but the fact that being a member of the SC meant being invited to status territory was significant. In every situation it is important for the Coordinator to identify the kinds of recognition that are appropriate.

## Opening the Conference

A conference should have a well-defined opening, other than the registration experience. There are times when the registration will be part of the opening, and this will be discussed more below in the category of informal openings. More important at this time is the recognition that there is a clear distinction between registration and the opening, which consists of several aspects.

### Informal Openings

There are various kinds of informal activities for opening a conference that are related to the formal opening session. For illustration let us take a conference that has its first regular session on Monday morning. It is anticipated that the participants will be arriving at the site on Sunday. An activity is designed for Sunday night that will allow the participants to get together and see old friends. It can also be a time to make last-minute arrangements and to ascertain exactly who has shown up for the conference. It is an opportunity to set the conference climate. There are many ways to organize this activity. The Coordinator should not just delegate this to the site personnel for whatever they consider a "social hour." The objective may be social, but it is part of the conference and as much attention should be paid to this activity as to any other. In the minds of the participants the conference will have begun upon their arrival at the site, not at the moment when the first session is called to order.

One model for the social hour is the cash bar. It is set up in a separate room from the regular liquor dispensing part of the site. A bartender and liquor are provided, but each participant pays his own tab. The Coordinator should clarify this during site selection, as there may be a minimum setup charge if too few participants patronize the cash bar. The bar should not provide only alcohol, but soft drinks as well. It is not the flow of alcohol that makes it a social hour, but rather, the opportunity for the participants to meet and talk. Although alcohol may be necessary, there is a growing tendency among many adults not to rely upon alcohol to "be social." Omitting soft drinks can defeat the purpose of the social hour, since those who do not drink liquor have only two alternatives—to stand around not drinking and having to continually explain why they are not, or to leave the room where the social hour is being conducted. In either case, some participants will have been needlessly pushed out of a conference activity.

Religion will be discussed later in this section, but a note is required here. There are citizens of the U.S., as well as those from other countries, whose religion forbids liquor. To have a cash bar with only liquor means that they will be excluded from taking an active part in the social hour. Providing just "cokes" or a like beverage will not suffice as one group, the Mormons, do not drink anything with caffeine. Fruit juice or fruit based drinks would find acceptance among almost any group or religion, any place in the world, as a supplement to the usual alcoholic beverages.

An alternative to the cash bar is to have the cost of the social activity built into the conference cost. When a fee is charged, it is possible to recover this by including the cost of the social in the fee. For an ES the cost of the social hour can be absorbed into the general budget for the conference.

During the social hour various kinds of nonliquid refreshments can be made available. These can be hot or cold hors d'oeuvres, cold cuts, peanuts, and pretzels. The kinds of refreshments should not be left to the discretion of the site personnel, as it relates to aspects of climate setting and are best decided by the Coordinator in relation to the objectives of the social hour, what is to follow, and the available budget.

The informal opening activity provides an opportunity for participants to search out clues as to appropriate behavior and attire. Until people feel comfortable with these elements, they may not be able to devote their full attention to the conference. Differences in groups, sites, localities within the U.S., etc. are all factors that influence behavior and attire. In recent years this has become of less concern, but is still important. Female participants now have a wide range of acceptable attire, and appropriate clothing has become less of a problem. The male still has to contend with some local customs (almost regulations) such as those decreeing that after 6:00 p.m., a jacket must be worn in public places, and some dining rooms still require a tie, as well. If this is the custom where the conference is being held, it is important that the participants have this information to avoid embarrassment or discomfort, which can be disruptive to the climate the Coordinator is endeavoring to establish.

There can be an opening dinner. Just the mass feeding does not make this activity either formal or informal. Rather, it depends on the objectives and how it is organized. Here we will discuss the informal mass feeding experience.

One approach is the buffet. This allows for more mobility among the participants and can set a relaxed informal climate. It is expected that there will not be a speaker, though there may be some entertainment.

A sit down dinner can still be informal, if it is organized in that manner. There may be some casual announcements, as required. There should not be a speaker in the formal sense, though there could be an entertaining presentation.

Sometimes a formal and an informal opening can be linked together. When a conference starts in the morning with a formal opening, the Coordinator should consider the participants' travel requirements. At such conferences the formal opening is scheduled for 10:00 a.m. with participants expected to arrive that morning. This is a design used when the participants are from the same local geographical area or from the same employing organization, and are going to the conference instead of to their worksite. The informal opening, beginning at 9:00 a.m. is usually listed as "registration." During this time the design provides for coffee and cake, or a continental breakfast (juice, rolls, beverage) as the informal activity just prior to the formal opening.

## Formal Opening

The Coordinator of a conference with a past history (an annual affair), must consider what the formal opening was in previous years. The participants may anticipate and look forward to something that is reminiscent of former formal openings. It may be the rapping of the gavel accompanied by a formal call to order. It may be the singing of the national anthem, or some other ritual that is expected in convening that conference. The president of the MS may be expected to make the formal opening remarks. It does not mean that nothing can be changed, but the anticipations of the participants should be considered.

A conference that does not have a past history does not present the same problem. A formal opening can be designed that will relate to the participants, the objectives, and the site. If this is to be the "first annual" con-ference, the designers should be aware that the formal opening they plan for today can become the tradition of tomorrow.

The formal opening can be a media presentation that will serve as a stimulus for the entire conference. It should not be designed primarily for entertainment, as that is not the function of the formal opening session.

For a conference with stated objectives it is best to use the formal opening to provide the participants with an opportunity to review the objectives. The following example comes from a session within a conference, but could be just as appropriate for the formal opening of a conference.

— ● —

The resource person was to conduct a session involving 250 people in one room. He started by having everybody receive a copy of a workbook prepared for that session. The first page of the workbook contained the objectives. The first statement made by the resource person was a request that all the people in the room should read the objectives. If anyone found that these objectives were not what he had come for, he was free to leave before the session started. After a brief pause, three people got up and left the room. The resource person viewed this as valid. Those three people read the objectives and decided to select some other alternative. It was better to have them leave sooner rather than later. — ● —

A large conference places great reliance on the keynote speaker. The selection of this vital person was a function of the design committee. As part of the conduct of the conference, the Coordinator should review the selection of the keynote speaker, even though it is unlikely that there will be any change in the invitation. He should ascertain that the keynote speaker is familiar with the conference objectives and the opening session. This will lessen the possibility that the participants will be forced to sit and listen to a keynote speaker whose remarks bear little or no relation to the objectives of the conference. The speaker may be doing "his thing," which in some situations can be tolerated. For a conference, it is self-defeating. A dissonance will have been introduced into the opening climate, which the Coordinator and SC will have to cope with at some future time.

The dinner as an informal opening experience has been discussed earlier. The dinner can also be a formal opening, if it is so planned. It then becomes a much more controlled and organized experience. It will include a head table and provision for a speaker. In this case the topic should definitely be related to the objectives of the conference. It is possible for the keynote speaker to make his presentation at a dinner, and the first session the next day can go on from there with small group sessions or a reaction panel.

## Religion

Americans may not consider themselves religious, but we are perceived in this fashion by people in many parts of the world. We may say that the Moslem is religious who ends many sentences with "Insh-Alla," which means "If Allah wills it." Yet, do we not say "good-bye," which is a contraction of "God be with you"? We are strong on our separation of Church and State (the First Amendment to the Constitution) but then, we open each session with an invocation by a person of the cloth. Our metal currency carries the message, "In God We Trust." Yet, we do not have an official state religion and we point with pride at people in high office who profess a variety of religious persuasions.

Almost every conference will open with some kind of a religious activity. There may be an ordained minister, priest, or rabbi invoking the name of the Almighty. Sometimes the invocation may be handled by a member of the organization who is not ordained. Whether a dinner is part of the informal or formal opening, it is almost axiomatic that there be the blessing or invocation before the participants start eating.

It is not possible to say whether or not there should be an invocation at each conference, or at each mass feeding. This is a matter that must be decided for each conference, but it must be decided. If the DC neglects to make this kind of decision, they may be surprised when the dinner starts and the chairperson for the activity calls upon a participant to lead the group in the blessing. The resulting invocation could very easily be detrimental to the conference, even though done in good faith. The person offering the invocation may attempt to be nondenominational, but this has too many possible interpretations to be accepted without prior discussion. For some persons, nondenominational means that no distinction will be made among the various Christian sects. They do not include other religious groups who are not Christians, so everybody is asked to join in a blessing or a grace which invokes "the name of the Father, the Son, and the Holy Ghost." Imagine how non-Christians feel about this! It is like asking Christians to thank Allah for their food. It automatically puts some participants in a minority status.

For an international conference it is even more likely that a spontaneous or a less than carefully thought out invocation will alienate some of the participants. It is not being suggested that an invocation be deleted, but rather more attention be paid as to who will deliver the invocation and what form it will take.

Liberal persons of the cloth have many ways of coping with this problem. They can invoke the guidance and blessing of the Supreme Being without excluding any individual or group. The issue can be handled by providing for silent prayer, unless the participants are of the same religious persuasion and might resent the omission of a clear statement during the invocation.

Let's discuss another aspect of religion and conferences. Given the way we divide up our time, we generally start conferences on Monday when they are three or more days in length.

The informal time on Sunday is for registration, socializing, recreation, and other preconference activities. For many Americans Sunday morning is the time for church. If the conference is scheduled to start with a luncheon on Sunday, this may conflict with church attendance. It may be preferable to delay the opening to a later time on Sunday.

When the Sponsor is a religious organization (and this can be an ES, MS, or PS), the Coordinator should be sensitive to the rituals and proscriptions that must apply.

The following incident describes not only the opening, but also some design elements where the Sponsor was a religious organization and the DC had to consider various religious practices while designing.

———— ● ————

The organization was B'nai B'rith, a Jewish organization that observes the various traditional practices including during a conference. The particular conference was designed to enable the participants to conduct living room learning sessions. The conference was scheduled for a weekend so as to minimize problems of participants having to take time from their jobs or businesses.

The informal opening was on Friday evening with the traditional Sabbath meal. This was followed by the usual religious observance welcoming in the Sabbath. This was all still part of the opening, though now it became more formal as the religious service required. The service was conducted by one of the participants—a Rabbi is not necessary to conduct services. The sermon, delivered by a resource person, was on the role of the layman in Jewish adult education. After the service, there was a continuing discussion of the sermon, which was the first small group activity at the conference.

———— ● ————

The role and placement of religion in the conference should be a matter of open discussion.

### Messages and Communications

During the conference there is the need for both internal and external communications. *External* refers to those communications that originate from outside the conference. Participants do not want to be isolated from their families and employers. The absence of a communication process produces anxiety and discomfort that mitigates against full participation in the conference.

If there is no provision for external communications, the participants will lose valuable conference time trying to ascertain if there have been messages. They might even take to spending.conference time on the telephone to determine if there is anything going on back home about which they have not been notified.

To avoid disrupting the flow of the conference, the most common device is the message board, where incoming messages are posted as received. The participants can easily scan the board during coffee breaks and in the course of their other movements through the area where the message board is located. This can be supplemented (and the participants so informed) by a process that delivers an emergency message to the participants wherever they may be. Emergency situations may never arise, but the participants need to know that they can be reached in a hurry, if needed. It is helpful to notify everybody before the conference starts of this emergency message service with the strong injunction to instruct back home people not to label a message as urgent unless an *immediate* response is *absolutely* required.

For conferences of a long duration (usually more than three days) there may be the need to arrange for mail deliveries. There are a variety of ways to do this, depending upon the site and the volume of mail arriving for participants. If mail delivery is to be arranged, it is important to consult with those who have experience in this activity to avoid compromising the mails. In addition to making these provisions, be sure that the participants are aware of what has been done so they can devote full attention to the conference.

There are other less personal forms of external communications, depending upon the design of the conference. There are times when the "cultural island" design will be used, and external communications of all kinds are purposely discouraged. This can include radio, television, and newspapers. Unless it is counter to the design, these sources of external communications should be provided. If the site is a conference center, there may not be ready access to newspapers, particularly those dailies which contain international news. It may be necessary to make special provision for delivering these papers. Many hotels in the Far East have a pleasant custom of slipping the local paper under your door early in the morning. This custom might be adopted by some of our conference sites and motels/hotels in the U.S.

The availability of radio and TV will depend upon the site. It is rare today to find a hotel or motel that does not have in-room TV and radio. A conference center may purposely not have these amenities. If they are desired, the Coordinator should ascertain what other arrangements can be made.

Provision should also be made for *internal* communications. During a large conference there will be the need for communication among participants. The message board, as discussed earlier, can serve this purpose also. Most readers who have conducted conferences, or participated in them, are familiar with message boards. Nothing is more frustrating than not being able to find a pencil to write with, a piece of paper to write on, or something with which to mount a message (when you finally get it written) on the board. If the message board has alphabetical slots, that can be helpful. Usually the boards are of pressed wood, which are great for thumb tacks if there are any around.

Even in small conferences a well-placed and adequately provisioned message board can facilitate the various kinds of communications that are generated in an active and successful conference.

The placement of the message board (or message center, for a larger conference) should be carefully planned. To be effective it should be in some readily accessible area where the participants are most likely to pass during the normal conduct of the conference. Favorite places are outside the dining area, in preselected lounge areas where participants are expected to gather, and near the secretariat's office.

An alternative to replace or supplement the message board, usually a supplement, is the daily bulletin. This can be a one-page duplicated sheet that participants receive every morning. It may be slipped under their bedroom doors or be available on a table just outside the breakfast room. The method of distribution will be influenced by the site and the number of conferences being conducted at the same time at the site.

The bulletin should list any design changes (made by the SC) and any other information that will be helpful to the participants during that conference day. If possible, frivolous material should not be included, though there are times when such material can tell a great deal about the progress of the conference.

———— ● ————

It was a conference of thirty-five participants. The SC was using a daily bulletin to keep everybody informed of changes and general information during the two-week duration. The conference was not proceeding too well, as the Coordinator had essentially taken over and was directing everything, with little possibility for anybody to exert any influence. The most that could be done was through the daily bulletin, which was being edited by a participant.

During one session the bulletin editor noticed a participant very busily engaged in making an elaborate "doodle." These were her notes in reaction to one of the usual deadly lecture sessions. At the end of the session the participant left the room leaving her doodles behind on the table. They were retrieved by the bulletin editor. The next day the doodles were reproduced in the bulletin exactly as drawn with the notation, "These are the notes of one participant at yesterday's session, and they make more sense than the session did." That evening, at the meeting of the SC, various members of the SC tried to use this as a way to get the Coordinator to make necessary design changes. In the face of the bulletin and the discussion, the Coordinator agreed to make changes suggested by the SC.

——— • ———

It would be wonderful if the story had a happy ending, but the next day the Coordinator went right ahead with what he had already planned and did not implement a single change proposed by the SC. Needless to say, it was an extremely poor conference and never did reach most of the objectives. The bulletin helped surface the issues through internal communication, but the SC was not strong enough to override the Coordinator.

When there will be a bulletin issued each day during the many days of the conference, it is helpful to use a different colored sheet each day so that there is no question as to which is the bulletin for that day. Using white sheets, with successive numbers or dates does not communicate as well. Using colored sheets is also helpful if they are to be supplemented by announcements at general sessions, for the speaker can refer to the "green sheet" or the "blue sheet" and have a better chance of being understood.

Technology also gives us other alternatives for internal communication, if the bedroom facilities allow. Many hotels/motels and some special conference centers have closed circuit TV. A common mode is to have one channel of the regular TV set up so that broadcasts can originate from within the facility. The closed circuit channel is usually used to give the guests information about the facility, weather reports, etc. If the conference is using the entire facility or a major portion of it, arrangements can be made to utilize this closed circuit TV. Participants should be informed of the time and channel when announcements for the day will be made. The programming should be scheduled so that the maximum number of participants can be expected to be in their rooms. There should be alternative methods for getting the information to those who rise early and those who sleep late.

### Secretariat

The secretariat has been referred to many times in previous chapters. It is during the conduct of the conference that the need for this resource becomes most evident. For a conference with few participants the need for the secretariat may be minimal. In some cases the Coordinator may have to assume this function, though the Coordinator should not be expected to perform clerical functions. As the number of participants increases and/or the design becomes more sophisticated, the size of the secretariat can be expected to grow. Let us discuss some of the functions that have been discussed earlier.

A prime function of the secretariat is to act as a clearinghouse for all conference activities. Any areas of confusion, dissatisfied participants, or complaints from the site should be funneled through the secretariat. The personnel in the secretariat should either have answers for all the possible questions and complaints, or know where they can go to get them.

The secretariat office can also be the meeting place for the various staff members. It serves as the communications nerve center for all staff by taking messages and seeing that they are delivered as rapidly as required. A bulletin board or "condition board" can be set up in this office. It should contain a copy of the program for the day, with space for special comments and last-minute changes, with which all staff should be familiar. Another part of the board should contain general information of a current nature for all staff. One person should be in charge of the board and keep it clear of old messages and other material no longer needed. The Coordinator may use a portion of the board to post information for all members of the secretariat.

Most of the staff of the secretariat will be working in the same room. Some may temporarily be in the registration area, at a mass feeding activity, or some other place where staff support is required for limited periods of time. Then, they will return to this nerve center of the conference. For a large conference the normal secretariat staff can be supplemented by carefully selected and prepared individuals, who monitor the on-going activities and report back to the secretariat. These roving floorpersons can use two-way communication devices, or periodically, can physically check into the secretariat. In some of the large conference centers it is possible to equip the floorpersons with paging devices. These are the same as those used by physicians, engineers, and similar people on call. It is a small device that fits into a pocket or hooks on a belt. When triggered from a central point, in this case the secretariat, it notifies the wearer by an electronic signal that contact should be made. By picking up a nearby phone or walking to the secretariat, contact is made.

It is a rare conference that does not require reproduction of materials by any of the means currently available. The secretariat is responsible for the reproduction, as well as for their storage. This requires space and adequate controls so that materials are reproduced and available when required.

## Public Relations

During the planning stage reference was made to public relations, but not all conferences require an elaborate setup for public relations. Some may purposely decide to minimize or eliminate any public relations activities. The decision about public relations is not related to the size of the conference. A small conference may benefit from a carefully planned public relations activity, whereas a larger conference may find it detrimental.

Although planning for public relations should have taken place during the design stage, there will be new situations during the conference that may require changes in basic decisions or a modification of the public relations plan.

If there are VIPs on the conference program, it is better to notify the media than to have them rushing in with their equipment and disturbing the orderly flow of the conference. For an ES conference public relations may consist of information placed in the house organ, or a memorandum sent around to various parts of the organization so that everyone is aware of the conference. If a top-level company official gives a speech, copies can be made available to other company officers. This allows them to have first-hand knowledge of what their colleague has said in a public presentation, rather than having to read it in the press or hear about it elsewhere. There are ESs who have their own public relations units, and plans should be discussed with them. During the conference there might even be a company PR man on the secretariat.

———— ● ————

The Coordinator had discussed the conference with the company PR unit, but they had evinced little interest. The conference was concerned with the changes and opportunities of the work force. As the conference was in the same city as the company headquarters, the unit sent a person to attend some of the sessions as an observer. She arrived, checked in, and then went to one of the two concurrent sessions. She heard a resource person make a stimulating presentation, and some good discussion by company executives. She rushed out and called her contacts at the local TV station. Fortunately, she was able to arrange for a taping that evening with a talk show host who agreed to have the resource person and one company executive on the program. It was taped for showing a few days later at the regularly scheduled time. The resource person reluctantly agreed to the taping session, as it was an extra chore that encroached on his very limited time. The result, however, was an exciting show that enhanced the company image in the surrounding community, and gratified the resource person.

———— ● ————

In this situation the Coordinator was fortunate in having an in-house PR person with the right contacts to make the necessary arrangement in a short period of time.

At most sites there will be somebody with PR responsibility. This could be one person doing PR as a part-time assignment or a sophisticated and professional staff. When the site has limited staff, and PR is helpful to the Sponsor and the conference, the Coordinator may build an item for PR into the budget.

Care should be taken that the PR people do not let their enthusiasm get in the way of the conference. The function of the resource people is to contribute to the conference's success, not the PR's success. Sometimes these two purposes are compatible.

— • —

The resource person arrived from a foreign country, and was met at the airport by the Coordinator and a PR man. Allowing the resource person a very few minutes to refresh himself, they rushed him off to a radio station where arrangements had been made to have him interviewed. In the taxi, on the way to the radio station, they told the resource person that this particular program was extremely popular in the country and would be reaching prospective participants. As the Sponsor wanted a large turnout for the conference, there were many PR efforts, of which this was only one. The resource person felt he could not back out and agreed to be interviewed. (Perhaps his ego got in the way of his decision making.) The topic of the conference was controversial and the interview was rather heated. It brought many phone calls, and other evidence that the program had evoked interest.

— • —

If the incident had stopped at that point, it could be considered a plus for public relations. Unfortunately, there was a sequel.

— • —

During the conference the resource person made his presentation, as planned. When the time came for questions, some participants asked questions based on his radio interview, rather than on his presentation, which was on a related but different topic. As not everybody has heard the radio interview, and the topic was not what he had presented at the conference, the resource person tried to turn the questions back to his presentation. Several of the participants insisted on discussing his radio interview. The question period was a disaster! — • —

It is easy to find horror stories about how PR efforts have upset conference operations. It is unfortunate, for it communicates the wrong image of PR, and PR can be very helpful in supplementing a conference. The fault lies in not involving the PR people early enough in the planning to make their effort part of the total conference. There are many benefits to be derived from a well-planned and professionally executed PR operation.

The U.S. has many local newspapers throughout the country. Some are dailies, but many more are weeklies. These papers are eager to print news concerning people who live in the area they cover. Participants can be supplied with forms developed by the PR people that require only personal data. These forms will then be sent to the participant's local paper. This gives recognition to the participant and publicity to the Sponsor. Special forms can be prepared for resource people, and for some activities (notice of who won the golf tournament). It is hoped Coordinators and PR people will look upon each other as resources rather than adversaries.

### Resource People

There are many ways to design conferences, but most designs utilize external resource people. They may be external to the Sponsor, or part of the sponsoring organization, but not part of the unit that is sponsoring the particular conference. The identification and selection of resource people is the work of the DC.

During the conference, the Coordinator has a further role in relation to resource people. Despite the careful selection, it sometimes becomes apparent that somewhere during the process there has been a breakdown in communications. A resource person shows up with material different from that which the DC thought was being prepared. Or, resource people have made preparations based on the original intention, but as the conference progresses, needs arise that are different from those that seemed apparent during the design phase. These and similar situations highlight the need for further contact between the Coordinator and resource people after the conference has begun.

Given the pressures of time and distance, it is unlikely that the Coordinator can be in contact with the resource people between the time the conference begins and their arrival on the scene. It is possible, but usually impractical. Therefore, various forms of briefings are designed to link the arriving resource people into the conference being conducted. The Coordinator can designate a host, as described earlier, to meet the resource person at the airport and start the integration and briefing in the taxi ride to the site. The hospitality room has been discussed as another way of providing the necessary briefing and linkage.

The briefings tend to be one-on-one, with a designated host or the Coordinator meeting with a resource person. Another way to accomplish this is through the technique known as the fishbowl.

——— • ———

The conference was scheduled for five days, and the design called for a particular resource person to arrive and make a presentation on the last day. The resource person had been carefully selected as being a leader in the field, but the intent was that the resource person would react to some of what had happened during the conference, rather than to present new material. The plan was for the resource person to speak late on Friday morning, as the last activity. Arrangements were made for the resource person to arrive on Thursday afternoon and to be available after the close of the sessions that day.

The resource person arrived and met with the SC. Using the fishbowl technique, four of the ten-person SC sat in the midle of the room, with the remaining six members and the resource person in a circle around them. The four people sitting in the inside circle began discussing what they perceived to have happened since the conference began. They emphasized the highlights and surfaced the problems and concerns that had not been adequately dealt with. The ground rule was that after the first few minutes, anyone of the people in the outside circle could tap any of the four people out, and take his place in the fishbowl. The resource person could also tap in for a question, but then could immediately walk out of the fishbowl leaving an empty seat for whoever wished to move into it.

This process continued for an hour, at which time the Coordinator stopped the process and asked the resource person if he now had sufficient background on which to make the closing presentation. The resource person expressed tremendous satisfaction with what had occurred during the previous hour and said he felt very comfortable about making a suitable final presentation. The participants' evaluation of this particular resource person's presentation confirmed the fact that this form of briefing had been successful.

———— • ————

The Coordinator must also make provision for the "no-show" resource person. When resource people are selected, it is usually because they are prominent and desirable individuals. Most of them honor their commitments and participate as agreed (or they would not be called on so often). Despite all efforts at careful selection, there are reasons, most of them good ones, why a particular resource person becomes a no-show. Experienced Coordinators have many tales to tell of being caught without a resource person for a well-attended session.

Resource people are only people. They can have a personal crisis at the last minute, forcing them to cancel. A common cause is the weather. The resource person may have confirmed reservations, but finds the airport fogged or snowed in, or the flight cancelled for reasons beyond his control. Less frequent is the possible double-booking by the resource person. If they are busy and in demand, they may inadvertently have booked themselves into two conferences at the same time. This happens rarely, as most good resource people protect their reputations by avoiding this kind of error, but it can happen.

A resource person can arrive at a conference, be briefed, and then become ill. The list of possible crisis situations can be very long, yet these catastrophies do not occur too frequently. When one does occur during the conference, it can destroy even a well-planned one. The Coordinator is faced with the reality of the no-show and must take action

If the missing resource person is the keynote speaker or the presenter at a general session, finding alternatives may be difficult. If possible, the Coordinator should have a back-up position ready. He should have identified some alternatives prior to the opening of the conference, and the DC should have made some tentative plans. (We will discuss several of these a bit later.) When the missing resource person was to conduct a concurrent session, there are also alternatives. It is most imporant not to combine the session without a presenter with one where the resource person is present. Presumably each session has different objectives, and to mix them produces a situation where neither participant group will have their objectives met.

What can be done? If it is a major crisis, such as the keynote speaker, the Coordinator should honestly announce this to the participants. The Coordinator must resist the temptation to vent his frustration on the reputation of the no-show resource person. An honest and simple statement is all that is required. Most important are the alternative courses of action, not taking time to blame the no-show.

The most obvious decision is to cancel the session. This is not the best decision in most cases, but should be considered as a possibility. If cancellation is decided upon, are there other activities that will make that conference time valuable? It is difficult to replace a keynote speaker with another activity, for the conference has not yet developed the necessary momentum. If there are exhibits, the participants might be encouraged to visit that area until the Coordinator and the SC can redesign. In a small conference with no exhibits the Coordinator can explore some of the other alternatives described below. If the missing resource person situation occurs after the keynote and the opening, there will be more alternatives possible. Participants may be able to use the "free time" for individual work or for informal sessions. A swap shop (described in a previous chapter) is a viable alternative.

The Coordinator is also an alternative. Frequently, the Coordinator has skills in presenting as well as organizing. The Coordinator will have been in on the development of the sessions during the work of the DC and knows the objectives, as well as what had been planned. Caution should be exercised so that the Coordinator is not swept into replacing several resource people, or into making presentations where he lacks the expertise. Being the Coordinator should not prevent him from being a resource person when needed, but he should not be seen as being available and capable of replacing every resource person who might become a no-show.

Another alternative lies with the participants themselves. If it is a large conference it is very likely there are some participants who could handle a session and step in for the no-show. It is difficult, because the participant-resource person would not have adequate time to prepare and may not have the desired materials. Despite all these limitations, there are examples of participant-resource people who performed successfully.

If time permits, another resource person might be obtained. This is possible when the conference is held in or near a large city where many resource people reside. The Coordinator may even want to draw up a list of possible replacements in the event of a no-show, and informally contact some replacements to ascertain their availability should the need arise.

Where there is a no-show, the Coordinator has two responsibilities. One is to inform the participants after an alternative has been provided. Second, is to relate to the SC, and this may not be easily done. If the no-show is known about beforehand, early in the day or the previous evening, the Coordinator can call the SC together for an emergency meeting. The SC can be presented with alternatives, but they should be the ones to make the decision. If not, they will question their role in the conference.

The greater emergency occurs when there is no prior notice, and the participants sit waiting in a room and the resource person just does not show up. Right there, on the spot, the Coordinator may have to exercise one of the alternatives he had planned for just such an emergency. Generally, the SC is pleased when the Coordinator is able to handle the emergency no-show.

The hospitality room relates to the no-show situation. For a conference using many resource people the hospitality room becomes the check point where the no-show surfaces quickly. The function of the room should not be limited, however, only to negative and crisis situations. This is a room where those who are on the program have an opportunity to relax before their presentations and a place to go afterwards. This is not designed to keep the resource people isolated from the participants, only to keep them from being exhausted by them. Particularly in a large conference, popular resource people can be surrounded by admirers and others, and bombarded with questions and comments. When the time comes to start the session, resource people are not warmed up, but worn out.

When a conference is designed around only one or two resource people, the use of a hospitality room is artificial. As the number of resource people increases, the hospitality room becomes desirable as a mechanism for linking. The room can be used for briefing resource people who do not arrive until after the conference has begun. It provides a place for various "faculty" to gather and share their insights and experiences.

The hospitality room is also the place where leaders from the sponsoring organization can meet and talk to the resource people. These leaders may be officers of a membership organization or employees of the ES. It is important to use the room for involving the resource people in the conference, rather than to isolate them from all that is going on.

Sometimes, resource people are chosen for their subject matter expertise, and lack process skills. If this is known early enough, the Coordinator can as-

sist, as the Coordinator should have these skills. There are times when the
need does not surface until after the conference has begun.

——— • ———

The PS conference concerned the legal aspects of medical practice. The resource person had a medical background and was also
a practicing attorney. She was scheduled to present on Thursday,
but on Monday sought out the Coordinator and asked for help.
Previously, she had presented before legal groups with no difficulty. But the participants at this conference were medical and
lay persons with no legal background. She had planned to present
pertinent cases but now had the feeling that this would be too dull.
The Coordinator became a consultant to the resource person on
presentation techniques. Working together, they evolved a series
of overhead transparencies which provided simple statements for
each case. In addition, they worked out some individual work and
small group activity. The result was that a highly technical session
was extremely successful.

——— • ———

## Closing the Conference

A good conference has a well-defined opening and an equally well-defined
closing. There should be a specific closing activity, and the challenge is to
keep as many of the participants as possible at the conference until the closing.

A final speaker is often used to signify the closing. To keep the participants
around for the final session, one practice is to choose a speaker with a
national or international reputation. This is frequently expensive, but may be
well worth the cost. It is another place where a marquee name can have
benefits for the conference. The selection of the closing speaker is almost
more crucial than the selection of the keynote speaker. If the opening speaker
does not make a successful presentation, there are still opportunities to save
the situation in the remaining days of the conference. Once a closing speaker
has presented, there are no remaining days. The DC should give much attention to this. The Coordinator must make sure that the closing is conducted in
an appropriate manner, including a proper introduction and thanking of the
speaker. The Coordinator should not lose control at this last and most vital
moment.

——— • ———

It was a good conference, and the closing speaker was excellent.
At that point, one of the officials of the sponsoring organization
sent a note to the Coordinator, asking to be allowed to make some
brief remarks. The Coordinator gave way to the implied pressure

from the official. After briefly thanking the closing speaker, he introduced the official, who rose, came to the podium, and proceeded to give a thirty-minute reaction to the closing speaker. During that time participants slowly drifted out of the hall. At the confusion of the official's remarks, all the Coordinator could do was declare the conference offically concluded, though the end had actually occurred some thirty minutes earlier.

—— • ——

Depending upon the Sponsor and the design, the last words are probably best said by somebody other than the Coordinator. To close the loop, the DC can plan to have the person who convened the conference on the opening day conclude it on the final day.

There are many ways to bring about closure. There may be a banquet, or a dinner on the evening prior to the last day. If there is to be a session on the day following this event, there must be careful planning so that the last day is not an anticlimax. If the dinner/banquet has dancing and/or entertainment, it is unlikely that the participants will be available for an early session on the next day. The last day, therefore, may start a bit later but should still have a carefully planned design leading to a positive closing.

When the participants are from the same employing organization, there are several possibilities. The closing can be directed towards having the participants hear from the top level company officer, or to have the top level officer hear from the participants. The objectives of the session will determine the form.

When the emphasis of the conference has been on the participants working and producing something (reports, etc.) the closing session can be devoted to sharing reports. Good participants may not make good presenters, and the Coordinator may arrange to have the report in the form of a panel or dialogue rather than prepared speeches.

Awarding certificates is another kind of closure activity. Those who hold academic degrees may regard another piece of paper as being meaningless. For many people, including some with academic degrees, the certificates can be distributed much as at a commencement exercise, with participants marching to the front of the room to get the certificate and a handshake.

Another pattern is possible, and it relates to the objectives of the conference. We often state that one objective is to enable us to learn from each other at a conference. If this is so, the following practice might be considered:

—— • ——

It was a conference of thirty participants. The emphasis had been on learning together and helping each other, under the guidance of a resource person. Certificates were prepared and signed by the Sponsor and the resource person. When the time came to present the certificates, the Sponsor called out one name, and the participant came to the front of the room and received the certificate and handshake from the Sponsor. The next participant was called up by the resource person, with the appropriate ceremony. Then, that participant called up the next one, and presented the certificate and the handshake. This receiving participant now became the presenting one for the next participant, and so on, until all the participants had received their certificates.

———— • ————

Since taking part in this ceremony (which occurred in a conference we did in Venezuela) we have used this technique often, usually having either the Sponsor or the resource person present the first certificate. This procedure emphasizes that mutual learning has taken place.

We have discussed how a social hour can be used for an informal opening. A similar experience can serve for an informal closing. It should not take the place of the necessary formal closing, but can supplement it. If the conference ends before lunch, there might be "coffee for the road." If the closing is later in the day, there might still be some refreshments, but caution should be exercised in offering alcoholic refreshments just prior to driving. The informal social hour provides an opportunity for the participants to say their farewells rather than regretting later that they didn't have a chance to do that. The Coordinator may receive some valuable feedback on the conference, as well as some good suggestions. During this social hour the secretariat should be included and have the opportunity of receiving thanks from those they have served. For an MS it can provide an opportunity for members to congratulate new officers and wish them well.

Do not force a social closing if none is needed. Do not overlook it if it can be beneficial to the Sponsor and helpful to the participant.

## From the Suppliers' Viewpoint

Most of what suppliers will provide will have been identified and arranged for during the earlier phases of design and site selection. There are still some components which will be directly involved during the conduct of the conference.

## Site Personnel Say—

If we have been directly involved in your planning up to this point, things should go smoothly. Yet, we know they don't, because of reasons beyond anyone's control. It is important, then, that we have constant and immediate communication. We will assign one of us to be the contact between your conference and the site. It is important for you to also assign one person. If we get too many messages and instructions from too many people from your conference staff, it lessens our effectiveness.

You might give consideration to having one of our site personnel sit in on the SC meetings. This way, if there are changes recommended in the use of rooms or other facilities we could possibly give you an immediate response. Also, if we know the changes you plan we can provide information as to how this might influence other conferences being conducted at the same time. Our representative would be an observer and resource rather than an active member of the SC.

### Public Relations People Say—

We have probably been involved earlier, if you are considering any kind of PR. Plans may have been made, forms prepared, and perhaps even press releases. During the conference additional opportunities can arise that enable us to help you.

If we are part of the site (either direct hire or contract), we are continually seeking good PR opportunities. You may have many in your conference that you are overlooking. There is a crucial time element and we need to be closely involved to make maximum use of the PR possibility. We may have to tie in a crucial speech to the 6:00 p.m. news. If it is a dinner speaker, and you do not let us plan early enough, the opportunity may be lost for that evening. A day-old speech is difficult to get placed on the news.

When we are part of the sponsoring organization, we will be looking for long range implications as well as image building for the Sponsor. As Coordinator for this particular conference, you may not readily see the kinds of PR we think the Sponsor wants. Let us talk it over, and remain flexible during the conference so we can both take advantage of opportunities that might arise.

### Local Telephone Personnel Say—

Do you realize that we are a resource for external communications? For a large conference you may want us to provide additional phone lines and related facilities.

In some cities we will set up and staff your message center. We have trained personnnel and there are many reasons why we would consider taking over this task.

Your design might call for a tele-lecture (lecture by a resource person in another city over a telephone line), and we have special equipment for this, if you give us sufficient notice.

Have you considered us as a resource for presenting sessions? We are always interested in helping our customers realize the additional services we have that they do not utilize. Telephones are communication, so let us help your conference communications.

# 12.
# Linkage, Evaluation, and Follow-Up

The conference is over, and the Coordinator and secretariat breathe a sigh of relief! Emotionally and physically they are exhausted and there is an understandable letdown. If they succumb to this feeling, they will not have completed their tasks. The secretariat should be busy seeing to it that all participants have departed safely, and that the exhibitors are packed up and on their way. A debriefing with site personnel can uncover some unfinished business, like bills that have not yet been paid.

The Coordinator's work for this time may have been specified earlier, during the conference, and it must now center upon

- Linkage
- Evaluation
- Follow-up

## Linkage

The purpose of linkage is to have the well-defined activities conducted during the conference be the basis for participant behavior back home after the conference. Activities should be included which provide direct and observable links between the conference and back-home behavior. The kind and depth of linkage depends upon the specific conference objectives. When there is a high expectation that attendance at the conference will effect back-home behavior, there is the need for more linkage during the conference. If it is anticipated that some of the participants might, as a matter of course, use the conference experience back home, then the linkage requirements will be less.

The DC will have considered linkage during its deliberations, as linkage activities are part of the initial design process. It is not easy to do this, for the DC must try to predict the impact of each session on the participants. Unless the conference is a highly controlled experience, the possible effects can only be guessed at. If the conference uses a behaviorist model (in the Skinner mode), then the DC can predict some of the behavioral outcomes. Usually, conference design models allow for more variations in individual behavior. Therefore, the desired outcomes are predictable but not absolutely guaranteed. Linkage should be considered before the conference begins, and appropriate experiences designed. The application of the design must be left to the Coordinator and the SC. They will also have to be flexible enough to create linkage mechanisms, as some of them may not be apparent during the course of the conference.

## Sessions

The DC can build in sessions as part of the initial design that are devoted to creating linkage. One possibility is the *homogeneous small group* session. It is based on the understanding that no single individual, merely as a result of attending a conference, can change an organization unless that individual has enormous power in the organization, or is prepared to engage in assassination. (It has been noted that more organizations have been changed by assassination than by conference attendance.) Usually, the participant returns home with new ideas and new insights and a sincere intent to apply them, only to be met with rejection of his attempts.

When organizational change is an objective of the conference, participants should attend as part of teams, rather than as single individuals. These teams form the basis of the homogeneous small groups. Conferences with organizational development (OD) objectives usually require that a team of at least two persons from the same organization attend. This provides for reinforcements back home, but the linkage should start during the conference.

——— • ———

The participants came from several hospitals in the same state. One of the objectives was to help them to function as teams. Each hospital had sent a lay administrator, a medical director, and a board member. In the morning sessions they mixed with others, attending sessions for their specialty (i.e. board members). In the afternoon each hospital team met as a homogeneous team. The purpose was to react to the material presented in the morning in terms of what they could do with this when they returned home. The linkage to the back-home situation was built into each afternoon. The time allowed was flexible, and no reports or other specific outcomes were required from the group.

——— • ———

It should be noted that many months after this conference, the Sponsor shared the information with the Coordinator that some of these groups were still meeting back at their hospitals, and had involved others in their team approach.

A mistake frequently made in designing a conference is to urge participants from the same organization to meet during the conference, without providing logistical support for such meetings. If the meetings are desirable participant behavior intended to provide for back-home linkage, then the DC should design for the time and facilities required. The design should not make attendance compulsory. Participants can be permitted to absent themselves from such meetings if they so desire without fear of punishment. It is hoped that every participant will take advantage of the possibility to meet with colleagues from back home during the conference, in order to assimilate the material and to plan for their back-home activities. Research on small groups has shown that peer pressure can be a powerful force to encourage participants to attend these meetings. The Coordinator should leave the choice to the participants, rather than to arbitrarily force attendance at those homogeneous small group meetings.

Participants have been known to become so enamored of and committed to their homogeneous small group meetings that they neglected to attend some of the other conference activities. The Coordinator should be alert to this possibility, and have complete communication with the leaders of these small groups and know about all scheduled meetings. The Coordinator should watch for those small groups that schedule their meetings for the same time as regular conference sessions, forcing their members to choose between the small group and the sessions with other participants.

The members of the homogeneous small group may decide to hold their meeting in lieu of participating in a nonsession activity such as recreation, entertainment, or a field trip. Here the Coordinator must exercise discretion. He should realize that most nonsession activities are designed for voluntary participation. When attendance at small group sessions keeps participants from the benefits of regular sessions, the Coordinator should explore the situation.

When the intent is to utilize the conference acquired behavior back home, provision should be made for the participants to practice the new behavior while they are still at the conference.

During the height of the laboratory (sensitivity, T-Group) era, the last morning was often designed for this purpose. Participants were assigned the task of planning what they would tell people back home about their laboratory experience. They were then given the opportunity of role playing with other participants. They role played/practiced what they would say and how they would say it, while getting feedback from fellow participants. Of course, in this case all of them had the same experiences and could not be expected to be very critical. What the participants would face when they returned home would be very different. Yet many participants by virtue of this linkage session, avoided a back-home confrontation that could have been devastating.

An organization that sends a participant to a conference should have some expectations of what will happen when he returns. Too few organizations build in this expectation, and therefore, the conference designs do not provide for this kind of linkage. The material describing the conference can suggest that organizations that send participants should arrange for some form of reporting by those participants when they return. This can either be oral or written. The linkage towards the end of the conference should be designed to prepare the participant for the appropriate form of reporting. If oral, participants can be provided with the opportunity to prepare their report, present it to other participants, and receive feedback. If written, the same process can be used with participants providing peer group assistance. Sessions should be designed to facilitate this process.

It is also possible to provide a physical linkage. The following took place during a conference of an organization that has many plants located throughout the U.S. Each plant had at least one human resource development (HRD) person reporting to the plant manager.

—— • ——

The resource person was to present a three-day program for the HRD people from all the plants. In this case the linkage was built in to preceed the conference with the HRD people. A week before that conference was to start, the plant managers were invited to a one-day conference that was a shortened version of the three-day conference their in-plant HRD people would be attending. In this one-day experience the plant managers learned something of what their in-plant people would be getting in three days, and what they could expect when their people returned home. The three-day conference was then held, with provision built in for the HRD people to try out what they would report to their plant managers who had attended the one-day conference. The result was very successful, with the plant manager and HRD people both familiar with the same vocabulary and both understanding the HRD process.

—— • ——

It is also possible to build in a variation of this at the end of the conference. The following is from a nation wide R & D (research and development) organization. They came from sixteen different locations. In this case the HRD people reported to a personnel director who know little about HRD except that in his organization it was under personnel.

—— • ——

The conference was to be of four days duration. The first three days were devoted specifically to the HRD people, who examined their own roles and functions in the organization. They knew from the design that their supervisors (the personnel directors) would be at the conference on the fourth day. The personnel directors arrived on the evening of the third day. There was a dinner and the corporate level personnel director made some remarks to begin the linkage process. On the fourth day the design provided the opportunity for the HRD people to share with the personnel directors what they had gained from the first three days. This was followed by questions from the personnel directors. The last activity paired each personnel director with his HRD person, and they met to plan how they would use this new insight in their back-home situation. This was done at the conference, without the telephones ringing or any other back-home disturbances. Each pair developed their own plan for new back-home behavior on both parts.

—— • ——

Although not originally planned, an additional linkage step occurred. In most cases the pairs flew home together in the same airplane and continued their linkage on an informal basis.

There can be sessions growing out to the conference that have not been previously planned, but still provide for linkage. Although the following incident took place in India, it could have happened in many other places.

—— • ——

There were thirty-five participants at the conference from many states in northern India. One of the conference objectives was to identify the content for literacy programs for adults. There were several resource people, one of whom was a health educator from one of the states represented. He showed slides illustrating various kinds of childhood diseases, most of which were reversible through adequate diet. His point was that if the literacy program contained sufficient material about diet, mothers would be able to take appropriate steps to have healthier children. As he came to the end of his presentation, he showed slides of blind beggars being led by children, themselves on the verge of blindness. He told the participants that there were one million children in India under the age of twelve who were going blind, needlessly. Their mothers were doing the best they knew how, given the limitations of being illiterate. They could not read material that would tell them how to alleviate or eliminate blindness in their children.

The mothers were growing produce in their home gardens to sell at the local market place. With the money they earned they bought apples from the Himalayas, which were both scarce and expensive. They had heard that the fruit contained the vitamin A so necessary to combat blindness in their children.

The paradox, as the health educator pointed out, was that one of the items they were growing in their gardens and selling, had

480 times the vitamin A the apples had. The participants were stunned, and questioned the resource person to be sure they had understood. He then went further, and pointed out that the vegetable grown in the home garden was bitter until cooked, and was a basic item used in making chutney, a dish eaten by middle-class Indians. This helped to reduce the possibility of blindness in middle-class Indian children.

The participants asked that the next session be delayed and they then be allowed to probe further into this and similar material from various resource people at the conference. Although the design called for this to happen several days later, the Coordinator agreed to the change, if the participants would agree to continue this same kind of activity after the conference. The participants concurred, and set up groups to meet after the conference, within each state, to identify similar material for inclusion in their own literacy programs.

—— ● ——

These groups are much more productive when they are spontaneous than when they are formed artificially. In the case cited, the Coordinator was wise to alter the schedule to allow for the development of the groups rather than to try to hold them to the original design.

### Exercises

There are various kinds of exercises that can be used to facilitate the linkage. One which we have found extremely useful is called "Memo to Myself." Figure 12-1 lists the instructions for conducting this exercise. There are many possible variations to this exercise. During the time that participants are asked to think (process step #1) and not to write, it is helpful to have some background music. We are so media-oriented, with TV or radio providing a constant background noise, that many of us can no longer tolerate silence. If the Coordinator does not provide for background music, some participants may find the silence unbearable and begin to talk to their neighbors. In Figure 12-1 the term "facilitator" is used to describe the person who conducts this exercise. It could be the Coordinator or some other carefully selected person. Participants are asked to write *"three specific things"* (process step #2), but the instruction could just as easily have been one or ten. Experience has shown that asking the participant to write just *one* item forces a decision that is not necessary. There are usually many possibilities and the choices should not be reduced too rapidly. To ask for too many items can reduce this exercise to a writing experience rather than one preparing for linkage. The choice of the number of items to be written down will also be affected by the literacy level of the participants, as well as the use to which the Coordinator will put the data collected by process step #3b.

——— • ———

## Memo to Myself

### Purpose
To provide linkage between the conference and back-home behavior.

### Group size
Can be used with any size group.

### Materials
1. Carbonized sheets providing an original and two copies. (Alternatives are to have regular lined paper with carbons inserted. Less desirable, but sometimes necessary, is to have participants recopy so as to provide three copies. Regular carbonized memo forms are available in most stationery stores.)
2. Envelopes for mailing.

### Process
1. Facilitator asks each participant to *think* about the highlights of the conference. At this time, nothing is to be written. The question can be asked, "What do you intend to do back home as a result of having attended this conference?"
2. After a few minutes of silent thought, the participants are asked to write down *three* specific things they will do back home. They are instructed to write these without signing them.
3. The facilitator then gives the following instructions:
   **a.** Page 1, the original, is to be placed with your other conference materials.
   **b.** Page 2 will be collected at this time.
   **c.** Take the envelope we have given you. Address it to yourself, to wherever you wish it to be sent.
   **d.** Page 3, the last copy, is to be put into the envelope and sealed. We will now collect the sealed envelopes.
4. After all the envelopes have been collected, the facilitator should indicate when they will be mailed to the participants.

*Figure 12-1. The authors have found this exercise to be extremely useful in facilitating linkage.*

——— • ———

An important step in linkage is sending the sealed envelope to the participants who appear to be highly influenced by receiving their own good intentions, in their own handwriting at a time after the conference has been concluded. The term "mailing" has been used to cover the various forms of distribution. If the Sponsor is an ES, the mailing might be through interoffice distribution, if that is how they addressed their envelopes. If they chose to receive it at home, then outside mailing is required. For an international conference the cost of this kind of mailing (assuming air mail) could be quite expensive and may require a specific budget item.

Linkage can also be strengthened by taking page 2 (see Figure 12-1), which the Coordinator has collected, and reproducing a list of those items with only minimal editing. The Coordinator might correct obvious grammatical errors that might lead to misunderstanding, and remove any words that could violate anonymity. The compiled list is sent to all participants. This can be done in conjunction with the follow-up activities, as described later in this chapter. The participants find such a list helpful, for it gives them a feel for the kinds of activities some of their fellow participants had planned. A participant can also find new ideas on the list that prove useful even after the conference.

Another type of exercise utilizes a worksheet similar to that shown in Figure 12-2. This type of worksheet is designed for conferences where the participants are professionals who function in work organizations. In the first block on the worksheet participants can identify what they will do in their own work situation, when they return home. These are the things over which they have control.

In the second block participants identify what they will try to do in relation to their organization. In most cases these will not be things over which they have control, but they probably have some influence. It would be meaningless for participants to list what others should do in their organization. The focus should be on what they can do, with others, in their organization as a result of having attended the conference. Underlying the personal/organizational axis is what the sociologists call the pressures on "locals and cosmopolitans." People who hold membership in a professional association (using the term professional very broadly), and are employed by an organization, can find that there are conflicting pressures. They have the pressure exerted internally (locally) by their organization regarding their performance and this must be balanced against the external (cosmopolitan) pressure from their professional affiliation. By including this as part of linkage, the participant is able to see what kinds of actions might be appropriate to implement the conference learning under the dual pressures. As with the former exercise, this too could be done with carbonized sheets.

The last item, professional, has proven very valuable when the Sponsor is an MS that is a professional association or society. Participants can be given another sheet of paper, and asked to recopy what they have put under this item, and then have it collected by the Coordinator. The information gathered through this item proves very helpful to the Sponsor for follow-up, as well as the identification of future activities desired by the participants.

There are other exercises, but these are two that have proven most useful to us and our clients over the past years. Many of the other exercises we have

**Personal**—When I return home I will do the following in my work situation:

---

**Organizational**—When I return home, I will do the following in my organization:

---

**Professional**—When I return home, I will do the following in my professional organization:

---

*Figure 12-2. This linkage exercise allows the participant to relate conference experiences to three areas of involvement.*

used are related to a specific client need at a specific conference, with less general applicability. As a matter of procedure, the forms suggested in the figures could be included in the PPB or held separately for use near the end of the conference.

A successful conference can spawn a group of alumni. These are participants who develop a warm feeling of colleagueship towards each other during the conference and want to retain contact afterwards. If this is a desirable outcome of the conference experience, the linkage for creating the alumni needs to take place while the participants are still together. It is much easier to organize at that time than to wait until the conference is over. If the conference is one of a series, there may already be an alumni to which they can relate. Building an alumni group is not normally an outgrowth of most conferences, but if the desire does arise during the conference, the Coordinator needs to be able to assist and provide the linkage for this development.

## Evaluation

Every conference should have some kind of evaluation. It can range from the very simple happiness quotient to the very sophisticated documentation of actual changes that resulted from the conference.

The happiness quotient is the term applied to the type of questionnaire that asks the participants:

- Did you like this conference?
- What did you like about this conference?

If the objective was to get the participants to like the conference, then these are valid questions, though the second one does present an obvious bias. Although it is desirable to have the participants like the conference, there are usually other objectives.

Too often evaluation benefits are either overlooked or not built into a conference design because they appear too complicated and costly. This is possible, but it is also possible to have simple, direct evaluation with many values for all concerned.

## Purpose

Evaluation should have a purpose. Although we started by emphasizing that every conference should be evaluated, the purpose for evaluating can be different for each conference. Two major purposes can be identified if we utilize a concept recently introduced. There are two basic purposes of evaluation, *formative* and *summative.*

Formative evaluation is conducted during the conference so that it has a direct influence on conference activities. Thus, it will influence the conduct of the conference. These data should be put in the hands of the Coordinator and the steering committee. The intent is to improve the conference while it is being conducted.

Summative evaluation is usually done after the conference has been completed. The intent is to collect data that assesses the total conference. The purpose is to use this data for an overall report and as part of the feedback aspect.

## Process of Evaluation

Figure 12-3 presents a model for evaluation, It starts with *objectives,* which were the work of the DC. Without objectives there is very little which can be evaluated. Based on the objectives, a design was developed and the conference was conducted.

*Data gathering* is the activity that collects, through various methods, the information that can provide the basis for us knowing what has happened. Data are usually gathered from the participants, though it is also possible to seek some data from resource people, and perhaps the secretariat.

One of the most common methods is the questionnaire. It is used more than any other method, yet too few people take the time necessary to construct a good questionnaire. Designing a good questionnaire takes time,

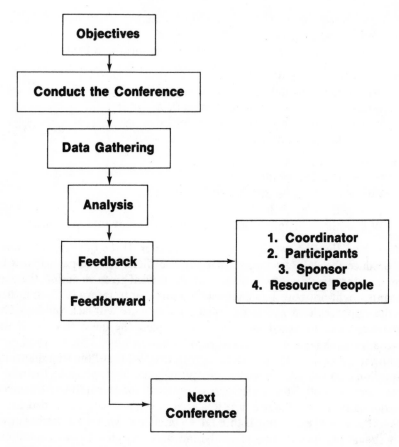

**Figure 12-3.** Shown here is a model that can be used for conference evaluation.

money, and people. If there is not sufficient time to develop a good questionnaire, it may be more desirable to not even try. A good questionnaire can be
designed if attention is paid to the following steps:

- Design the Questionnaire
  What do we want to know?
  What can we find out by asking a question?
  When will a "yes" or "no" suffice, and when do we need comments?
  When will a scale (1-5) give us the needed data?
  What length would be acceptable to the participants?
  Will the completed questionnaire be hand tallied or computerized?

- Test Out
  What test group is most like the participants?

Can a test group be found which can respond, or must some of the participants be used for the test?

How can the test group give feedback on form and content?

- Revise the Questionnaire
  Which questions did not produce any usable data?
  Which questions could be eliminated?
  Which questions need to be rewritten?
  If this data is typical, how can it be analyzed?

- Distribute the Revised Instrument
  When should it be distributed?
  Where should it be distributed?
  How will we get it back?
  Will we have to follow-up to assure a sufficient rate of return?

To bypass the first two steps is to risk disaster. If the questionnaire does not produce the data desired, or if it is too difficult for the participants to complete, the results will be less than satisfactory. If given an option, the participants might not bother to complete the form, or to return it. Even if they do, the responses to a poorly designed questionnaire will lack validity. The participants can be asked only once to complete the questionnaire. If the necessary data have not been gathered, it is almost impossible for the Coordinator to go back to the participants with the plea that "the first questionnaire didn't do the job, so would they please take the time to do the whole thing over again." This underscores the need for a carefully developed questionnaire, so that the one time it is used, it will produce the needed data.

Another way of evaluating is through an interview. This is not used as often as it should be since it is more costly and time consuming than a questionnaire. If there are many participants, the number of interviews may have to be curtailed, and reduced to only a sampling of the total participant group. This produces the kinds of problems faced when anyone uses a sample rather than the whole population. Even if the group is small enough to allow for interviewing all the participants, several interviewers may be needed. The interviewers should receive adequate preparation for this task, so as to eliminate the variables of interviewer style. With only one interviewer, however, the data can be influenced by the fatigue of the interviewer towards the end of each day, and certainly by the end of the task.

Despite all the limitations on interviewing, it is still helpful, if it can be accomplished. Particularly if a conference is to be repeated several times, using interviews after the first time can provide valuable data that can eliminate the possibility of repeating the same mistakes or shortcomings. An interview elicits much more information than a questionnaire, but the data can seldom be subjected to statistical analysis. To organize the narrative data takes time, but the data are a valuable resource to the Sponsor and Coordinator. Consideration must be given as to the best time to administer the questionnaire and/or interview. This will be discussed later.

After the data have been gathered, they must be analyzed. The form the analysis takes is related to questions, such as:

- Who will receive the evaluation report?
- What are they expected to do with it?
- In what form should the analysis be, so that those who receive it can make the best use of it?

These questions should not be asked at the end of the evaluation process, but at the very beginning. The answers to these questions indicate the type of analysis that will be most helpful, and the form that data should take. A good evaluator may use sophisticated data-gathering instruments and produce numerous tables with various statistical manipulations. This may indicate the competence of the evaluator, but if those who are to use the evaluation report do not have sufficient statistical background to use it, the effort is lost upon them.

*Feedback* depends upon intent. Who is to receive the feedback, and for what purpose. As Figure 12-3 indicates, the usual distribution of the evaluation report is to the Coordinator, Sponsor, participants, and resource people. Each will be looking for different elements in the report. This may require that four different reports be prepared, and that is not unusual.

*Feedforward* (a term borrowed from the systems people) indicates another use for the results of the evaluation. The evaluation report is valuable for the next conference, if there is to be a next one. This will be discussed later under follow-up.

### Timing of Data Gathering

The timing of the data-gathering step must be carefully planned. It should not disturb the conference process, but if certain data is not collected at specified times, the opportunity may never again be present.

Timing is also important in making an analysis of the data. Most question-naires ask the participant to provide a reaction, based on a comparison. The question is not worded that way, but when participants are asked to rate a session or a resource person, they will have to compare one with another similar experience. As the conference proceeds, the basis for comparison changes. Data gathered during the opening sessions of the conference should not be compared directly with that from later sessions.

———— ● ————

It was a large conference with many concurrent sessions. One resource person, who presented on the first day, received good ratings from those who attended his session. However, as the conference progressed, participants came up to him and said, "I rated your session quite well, but I wish I could rate it again now. My second rating would be much higher. As I have been attending other sessions, yours has gotten much better."

—— • ——

The time of collection has a significant effect on the data collected.

Conducting an evaluation after the conference has been completed might appear to be a waste of time. Quite the contrary, it can be an extremely helpful activity. In addition to gathering data from the participants about the conference, it can also encourage further action by the participants. There are times when just receiving the evaluation form can serve as a trigger to encourage further action by the participants.

It is hard to pinpoint the best time to evaluate once the conference is over. The Coordinator wants the participants to receive the form when they are in a position to respond—not so long after the conference that the experiences have faded, and not so soon afterwards that the participants are still involved with the back-home adjustment. If an evaluation questionnaire is to be sent out after the end of the conference, it is best to advise the participants of this before they leave, so that they can anticipate its receipt. They might even be encouraged to make notes so they can respond to the questionnaire when it arrives. If the evaluation is to be coupled with the "memo to myself" exercise described earlier, the participants should be aware of this so as to limit confusion.

## Follow-Up

Follow-up, as with evaluation, should be based upon the specified needs and objectives of the conference. It is not just something "nice to do," but a necessary part of the total conference package. If resources are to be committed to follow-up, then the reason for this activity should be clear to all.

### The Past Conference

A major reason for follow-up is the Sponsor's need to know what has happened as a result of the conference. If it is an ES, the follow-up can be conducted to determine what cost benefits resulted from the conference. This is one of the most difficult items about which to satisfy the Sponsor. If there has been no preconference measurement, it is almost impossible to assign a dollar figure to the postconference behavior. In recent years there have been PS conferences that built in some measures whereby the Sponsor could determine the financial return, related to conference participation. Some PSs advertise that there will be a certain amount of identifiable financial return to organizations that send participants to their conferences. This is admirable, and when a PS promises this kind of return, follow-up is essential, for without it the data cannot be gathered. This differs from evaluation in that there is no attempt to rate conference experiences, only the actual behavior back on the job.

Follow-up is related to the evaluation process in the area of feedback. As indicated, the evaluation report can go to a variety of people (see Figure 12-3). Unfortunately, unless somebody has responsibility for the follow-up, the evaluation report may be written, but nothing is done with it.

Some of the activities discussed under linkage (Figure 12-1) require that there be one person who is responsible for the follow-up phase of the conference. One difficulty occurs when the Coordinator is external to the Sponsor. His contract may call only for design and conduct of the conference, but not for follow-up. When the Coordinator is internal to the Sponsor, there is greater possibility that follow-up will occur.

Follow-up of a past conference takes money.

—— • ——

The conference had follow-up built into the design. The plan was to produce a manual of successful practices by the partici- pants, after the conference, as an aid to others in the field. This particular conference was concerned with helping the participants identify how they could improve the bridging between school and work. It was planned that six months after the conference, partici- pants would be contacted. A team of two participants and the Coordinator would visit those participants who reported that they had successful experiences as a result of the conference. From these reports a book would be developed detailing the successful experiences. The idea for the follow-up was excellent, the execu- tion was less than satisfactory. The follow-up required more budget than the Sponsor was willing to provide. The Coordinator had not received full agreement from the Sponsor, who indicated that the decision for follow-up would be made after the con- ference. When the conference ended, the Sponsor responded with enthusiasm, but no money. He greatly regretted the fact that funds would not be available to implement the follow-up.

—— • ——

Situations like this need not occur if the Coordinator raises the issue of follow-up early enough. If the sponsor cannot allocate resources for this ac- tivity, it is best not to raise the expectations of the participants. The difficulty is that too few Sponsors are aware of the benefits of a well planned follow-up of their conferences.

To tie off the conference, there are also some mundane, but necessary, ac- tivities that can come under the heading of follow-up. Although they are es- sentially the work of the secretariat, they are usually seen as the responsibility of the Coordinator. When a conference ends, there are bills to be paid. Site personnel and suppliers need a contact person with whom they can communicate about this. A creditor may find that communicating with the Sponsor is not entirely satisfactory, unless the Coordinator is internal, or unless the Sponsor has assigned somebody to this follow-up function. Too frequently a resource person waits many weeks and perhaps months and does not receive his honorarium and expense money, probably because of an oversight. Then comes the necessity to communicate with someone. Follow-up should include provision for handling the financial details as well as those related to the content of the conference.

A newsletter can be an effective follow-up mechanism. The Sponsor can develop a newsletter and send it periodically to all those who participated in the conference. There are various kinds of newsletters, so the purpose should be clarified. The newsletter can be a way of encouraging participants to apply what they learned at the conference. In that case the newsletter would contain examples of some things the participants have accomplished, as a result of having attended the conference.

A newsletter can also be a supplement. It could provide additional material related to conference content. The material for the newsletter could come from participants, resource people who were at the conference, and outside resources.

The PS can make very effective use of the newsletter, particularly when they offer their conferences for a fee. A one-year "subscription" to the newsletter can be built into the conference fee. If participants wish to subscribe for longer, they can do so upon payment of a regular nominal subscription price. During the year the participants will get additional material as a further benefit of having participated. The newsletter will also contain notices of other conferences offered by the PS.

## The Next Conference

If there is to be a next conference, follow-up is even more important. The follow-up of the last conference becomes invaluable since it is possible to learn from the past one and to improve the future one.

A follow-up of the past conference can identify additional needs of the participants who attended. The Sponsor may decide to have another conference with the same participants because of the additional needs which have been identified. If the Sponsor has absolutely no possibility of having another conference with the same participants, the follow-up should be designed so that this course of action does not surface.

Some sponsors offer the same conference periodically. This is true of most MSs, and the conferences are usually annual. An ES might have periodic conferences for certain employees, such as their sales people. The PS, which offers a conference for a fee, will prefer to conduct the same one many times to recover the original design costs, and to improve their profit picture on the conference. In each of these cases the experiences of the previous conferences are important. It is possible to avoid "rediscovering the wheel" if follow-up is built in, so that the experience of the previous conference is not lost. This is the essence of the "feed-forward" element of the evaluation process.

The material to be fed forward should be more than just the evaluation report. There may also be minutes of the DC, notes of the Coordinator, comments from the SC, and even informal feedback from participants, the site, and suppliers. All of this should be organized in some meaningful manner and deposited with the Sponsor. It then becomes the option of the Sponsor whether or not to use this material as the basis for the next conference, or to go in a completely different direction.

For the next conference the Sponsor may decide to use the same Coordinator. Even then, before initiating the planning for the next conference, the Coordinator and Sponsor should review the past conference. Each can learn from this, and it should be a mutual learning experience. If the Sponsor decided to use a new Coordinator, *they* should also review the material from the past conference, but the nature of this meeting will be different. The new Coordinator must carefully avoid the trip of being overly critical of the past Coordinator—that is simply a matter of ethics. Through a joint review of the past conference, the new Coordinator can get a feel for the expectations of the Sponsor.

For most "next conferences" it is undesirable to use exactly the same DC members again. It is not that they have not done a good job, but that it is too easy for them to be trapped into their own past self and mutual perceptions. They will tend to look backwards rather than forwards. To wipe out the past DC entirely, however, is to lose a valuable resource and a wealth of experience. The new DC should be composed of

- Coordinator (old or new)
- Some members of the past DC that the Sponsor wishes to retain
- Some new members (selected with attention to the material contained in Chapter 3)

The relative numbers of old and new DC members will have to be negotiated, with an eye toward the strengths and weaknesses of the old DC members, and the potential that the new members can bring to designing the next conference.

# 13.
# Some Other
# Interesting Books
# on Conferences

While writing this book we have relied mostly on our experience, supplemented by talking to others. Of course, we have been influenced by various books, but this influence goes back to before we sat down to write this book. We would like to share some books with you which we have found helpful.

The American Society of Association Executives, which has many members who conduct conferences, has put together a small book. Since it is only ninety-one pages, soft-covered, it might be dismissed as a pamphlet. But *Making Your Convention More Effective* (American Society of Association Executives, 1972) packs a great deal into these few pages. They cover items such as theme, promotion, registration, food, and convention income. As we have indicated earlier, the differences between conferences and conventions is usually one of semantics, and their material relates directly to what we have been discussing in this book.

The book also contains many kinds of worksheets that are useful. It concludes with a "Glossary of Hotel/Motel Terms" that can help Coordinators during site selection.

There are several magazines that Coordinators would find helpful. We have already referred to *Meetings and Conventions* (Ziff Davis Publishing, One Park Avenue, N.Y.). There is also *Sales Meetings* magazine (1212 Chestnut St., Philadelphia, Pa. 19107), which has been instrumental in issuing the *Convention Liaison Manual* (copies can be purchased from American Society of Association Executives, Washington, D.C.). This book is the work of a Convention Liaison Committee composed of eight different organizations involved in conference/convention work. Its value is in the numerous check lists and related forms it contains. It also contains a helpful glossary.

While we are on the subject of glossaries, the Exhibit Designers and Producers Association has produced a *Glossary of Exhibit Terminology* (ED & PA, New York, 1968). This thirty-one page pamphlet provides all the terms you could possibly need in order to understand what goes into exhibits. The secretariat should have at least one copy of this.

Higher education institutions do a great deal of conference work, and Kenneth E. Rindt has put together the *Handbook for Coordinators of Management and Other Adult Education Programs* (University of Wisconsin, 1968). It is geared mainly for Coordinators of university extension programs but could be used in many other conference settings. The Appendices contain many forms which can be helpful.

Many professional organizations conduct conferences, and to help them George A. M. Herous has written *Continuing Professional Education—How* (Illinois Institute for Continuing Legal Education, Springfield, Ill., 1975). It is written from the viewpoint of the Coordinator who is designing for a Sponsor that is a professional society. It contains material from "The Curriculum" to "Office and Personnel Management" for what we have called the secretariat. There are many check lists and a great deal of material on financial control.

On the process side there is *The Small Meeting Planner* by Leslie E. This (Gulf Publishing, Texas, 1972). Emphasis is on small group meetings with room layout designs. There are also check lists, and although designed for use with small groups, some of these can readily be adapted for use with large conference groups.

To get the viewpoints of several leading and experienced Coordinators, look at *Conference Planning* edited by W. Warner Burke and Richard Beckhard (NTL Institute for Applied Behavioral Sciences, 1970). They have brought together material from sixteen different people in the field. Some of the material appeared previously in other publications, but there is some new material. As in any book of readings, there is overlap but this proves helpful. It emphasizes that there is no one best way for the Coordinator to function. Rather, the Coordinator has to be aware of the wide variety of options available while planning and conducting conferences.

The book by Larry Nolan Davis and Earl McCallon, *Planning, Conducting and Evaluating Workshops* (Learning Concepts, Austin, Texas, 1974) is concerned with conferences. The authors focus rather heavily on those that are designed strictly for learning purposes, so they start their book with "Introduction: Working with Adult Learning." There are worksheets throughout the book which can be helpful.

A valuable resource for site information is the magazine *Meetings and Conventions* which is published monthly by Ziff-Davis Publishing Co., One Park Avenue, N.Y. 10016. In each issue they feature a different city, listing the sites and providing helpful information for a DC which might want to consider that city. They also publish an annual review of sites (Gavel) as well as other related information. Another source is the *Official Meeting Facilities Guide,* which is also published annually (P.O. Box 606, Neptune, New Jersey 07753). There are other guides available, some with general listings and some providing specialized listings. Also, ads from various sites are appearing more and more frequently in magazines read by Coordinators.

Coleman Finkel, of the National Conference Center in New Jersey, has written *How to Plan Meetings Like a Professional* (Sales Meetings, 1971), which is based on his columns in *Sales Meetings* magazine.

As we close this chapter, we should reemphasize that we have not attempted to produce an extensive bibliography. Rather, to share with you books we have found helpful and perhaps make the reader aware of a concern many of us share—to improve the effectiveness of conferences.

# Glossary

There are some common terms related to conferences, but, unfortunately, there is not complete agreement on all of them. To be helpful, we are presenting some of these terms which relate to materials, equipment, and design possibilities. By no means is this a complete list, but if all parties concerned can agree on these terms, it will certainly facilitate communication and reduce misunderstandings. Some of these terms may also be helpful to the Coordinator and design committee in suggesting alternative designs for general and regular sessions.

The comments under each term are purposely kept brief. It is possible to write pages for each item, but that is not the focus of this book. There are other sources for each of these items, but given the lack of agreement in the field, we are not making any specific suggestions. To select a description, by source, would necessitate an examination of advantages and limitations that goes beyond the scope of this book. With this caution, we present the following:

**Audience Reaction Team**—A group, composed of members of the audience, react to a presenter, to seek clarification of the material presented.

**Audio-tape**—Recording of a presentation or discussion, using tape. Possibilities are cassette or reel-to-reel. Can be reproduced for later sale, transcribed into printed matter, or stored in the files.

**Audio Visual (AV)**—Includes the wide range of devices to appeal to both sight and sound. Most audiovisuals are projected for either small or large group viewing and listening.

**Brainstorming**—A process for encouraging uninhibited generation of ideas. There are many approaches to accomplishing this, some of which require a highly qualified facilitator. The term is often used interchangeably with creative thinking and think tank.

**Buzz Group**—Small groups of six or fewer participants meeting as part of a much larger group. Usually, all groups are meeting in the same room (hence the buzzing sound that gives it its name) for a limited period of time. Helpful to react to a speaker, get questions, or stimulate thinking.

**Cable Television**—Delivery of a TV program over a controlled system to a specified audience. Similar to closed circuit TV (CCTV). Programs can be taped or live.

**Case Study**—A written account of an event or situation to which participants are to react. Emphasis is on decision making. A case study can be used to start a general session, or as part of a small group session.

**Chalkboard**—Surface which can be written on with chalk. This used to be known as a "blackboard" but it need no longer be black. Research has shown that green is a preferable color and should be coupled with yellow chalk. Can be used for messages to participants, as well as within a session for keeping notes or helping in communication.

**Clinic**—The clinic is based on all participants having experienced a similar situation, or at least being very familiar with it. The session concentrates on examining what happened and seeking ways of improving individuals and/or programs. Steering committee meetings are clinic sessions.

**Colloquy**—A discussion, usually in front of an audience, between two teams representing different points of view. Resembles a panel in that all members take an active part.

**Confrontation, Search, and Coping**—Described earlier in this book, but included here also. Based on a confrontation (need to know or learn something). This is followed by a search by the participant, with the Coordinator and design committee providing appropriate materials for the search. Coping is the opportunity for the participant to try out the results of the search to meet the confrontation.

**Contract**—A self-directed plan agreed upon by both participant and Sponsor. It has no legal force, but puts down in writing the plan the participant has for meeting his goals during the experience offered by the Sponsor. The participant planning sheet can be used as a form of contract.

**Critique**—An analysis of a past experience. This should *not* be used by the steering committee (see Clinic). It should be used by the Coordinator, secretariat, Sponsor, and perhaps a new design committee. Data for the critique can come from participant evaluation.

**Debate**—A formal and highly structured presentation by two teams having different points of view about an identified issue. Differs from the colloquy in that each presenter speaks in turn with no direct response or discussion. During a debate, the audience listens. (But see audience reaction team and forum.)

**Demonstration**—A presentation before a group which shows how to perform an act or use a procedure. See interactive modeling for an example of one kind of demonstration. Can be coupled with closed circuit television to allow large audiences to closely observe all elements of the demonstration. Participants can be involved by providing an opportunity for them to practice what has been observed during the demonstration.

**Dialogue**—A conversation between two individuals in front of a large group. Can be used for general sessions or large regular sessions. The presenters do not work from a prepared script (that would be a skit) but talk extemporaneously. Participants listen, but do not take part until after the dialogue is completed. In smaller groups, it is usually difficult to control participant behavior for if the dialogue is stimulating, participants will tend to interrupt, and it then becomes a discussion, led by two discussion leaders.

**Discussion**—An exchange of ideas among participants. There is usually an assigned leader or leaders, and a focus to the discussion. Usually, some kind of report or synthesis is required. (Contrast with buzz session.)

**Dyad**—A two-person group. Can be used in a general session by having each participant turn to a neighbor to discuss a presentation. Usually of short duration (not more than ten minutes) for the purpose of sharing some input they have both heard. Sometimes used to "warm up" a large group by having them meet other people through several dyads.

**Exercise**—A planned experience designed to allow participants to practice a new learning, to reinforce a previous learning, or to experience a problem. An exercise must be carefully planned so it reaches its objectives. There are many sources of exercises in addition to those which can be purchased. The exercise should be directly related to the objectives and the type of participants.

**Feedback Mechanisms**—Various kinds of response systems so the Coordinator can constantly determine if the participants are learning, pleased, participating, or getting ready to leave. For each feedback mechanism there should be a specific purpose and the possibility of doing something with the data gathered. Messages to the steering committee are a feedback mechanism. The use of a tape recorder as such a mechanism has been discussed in this book. In a general session, the use of colored cards to signal (red and green) are a feedback mechanism to a presenter.

**Field Trip**—A carefully organized group visit for first hand observation by participants. Can also be used for recreation and entertainment. (See Chapter 5.)

**Fishbowl**—Encouraging discussion by having some participants listen while others talk. (See Chapter 11-"Resource People.")

**Flannel Board**—Originally, a piece of flannel stretched in a vertical position. Items can be placed on it which have been prepared by being backed with sandpaper or a similar material. Such items can be rapidly placed and easily moved or removed. More sophisticated apparatus of this kind are now available, such as "hook and loop" boards or utilizing special adhesive materials allowing items to be easily rearranged or removed.

**Forum**—A period of open discussion by participants in the audience following a panel, debate, colloquy, or speech. Provision is made for direct verbal interaction between participants and presenters, under direction of a moderator.

**Handouts**—Written materials which supplement, explain, or amplify a presentation. Each participant receives the same material which can be distributed before or after the presentation. When there is reason to distribute during the presentation, the handout material should be directly related to the point being made, and the presenter should stop talking during distribution.

**Incident Process**—A variation of the case study. Instead of participants receiving all the material, they are told of an incident and then question the presenter in order to elicit the information. Can be used as stimulus for a general session, followed by work groups.

**Interactive Modeling**—Participants observe preferred or desirable performance and then attempt to emulate through their own tryout. The sequence is observation, tryout, receive feedback. The sequence is repeated as often as necessary.

**Interview**—A presentation conducted before an audience in which a resource person is questioned by an interviewer. There can be several interviewers for one resource person. (The reverse would essentially be a panel.) The interview can be followed by a forum or work groups.

**Lecture**—A well-prepared one-way presentation by an individual resource person. Can be coupled with forum, audience reaction team, etc.

**Listening Groups**—Used in general sessions. All participants are divided into groups, each listening for a different element in the presentation. (Could be lecture, multimedia, panel, etc.) This can be followed by work groups, breakout sessions, or questions to presenters.

**Magnetic Board**—A metal board on which material can be mounted, using magnets. Depending on purpose, magnets can be attached behind material, or on top of material to adhere to board. Useful for message center or for general notices. In small sessions, useful for presenting prepared material where movement of material indicates changing relationships.

**Model**—A representation of an idea or object. When the model represents an object, it can be much larger, and show working parts (then usually referred to as a mock-up). Useful for demonstrations.

**Newsprint**—Coupled with easel, markers, and masking tape, it comprises one of the most versatile and useful resources for small group work. Ideas can be written, diagrammed, and retained for future use. The paper, newsprint, is sometimes also referred to as butcher paper, wrapping paper, and artists' paper. Indeed, all are sometimes used in place of the commercially available "newsprint."

**Nonverbal Experiences**—Conducting sessions without discussion or other forms of verbal interaction. When cautiously used by experienced and capable individuals, adds a dimension to communication and understanding that is sometimes blocked by too much talk. Useful in small group situations.

**Opaque Projector**—A machine that projects written material directly on a screen. Does not require any processing or other paraphernalia. At present, a very heavy machine with a loud fan and limited distance for clarity. Despite these limitations, a useful projected visual device.

**Overhead Projector**—A machine that projects material on transparent sheets. The transparencies can utilize extensive art work including color, or be simple handwritten material. Useful in general sessions as well as small groups. Generally, the room need not be darkened for acceptable visibility. A versatile and useful device.

**Panel**—A group of two or more persons (usually not exceeding six) who have a discussion in front of a larger audience. It is *not* a series of speeches but a purposeful discussion usually utilizing a moderator. It can be followed by a forum or some other technique for audience involvement.

**Peer-Mediated-Learning**—A specialized type of small group session where the leader is one of the group. To be effective, the leader needs special preparation, specially prepared materials, and provision for feedback to the Coordinator. Useful with small groups with specified and limited learning objectives.

**Role Play**—A spontaneous situation, usually utilizing only two people, in which the general outlines of a situation are presented and the individuals interact. There are many forms such as multiple role playing (involving all in a general session) reverse role play (after the initial two person role play), and structured role play (where the situation is given in detail and each role player has a particular role other than what he would normally be).

**Seminar**—A discussion session involving several individuals, all of whom have something to offer. However, there is one seminar leader who also serves as a resource. Usually a small group of about fifteen persons, though multiple seminars can be conducted at the same time, each with its own leader. Not useful for introducing new material as each participant is expected to have something worthwhile to contribute to the session.

**Skit**—A rehearsed dramatic presentation where each player has designated lines (as different from a role play where no lines are given, only a situation). A popular form for general sessions is the "trial by jury."

**Slides**—Utilizes a projected material, usually commercially produced from 35-mm film. Requires a slide projector. Can be synchronized with an audio tape recorder for an audio visual presentation. Can also be used by a speaker to illustrate a talk.

**Symposium**—A series of related speeches by different people under the guidance of a moderator. (Note: this is much different from a panel. The symposium does not have interaction between the speakers.) Can then be followed with a panel, audience reaction team, forum, etc.

**Tele-con**—Telephone conference, or using a telephone to bring in outside resource people. Useful for a general session when an important and significant resource person is invited, wishes to attend, but cannot be present physically. Through a telephone hook-up, it is possible for the resource person to speak to a large group. Can be arranged to allow for two-way communication. Can also be coupled with slides or transparencies.

**Video-tape**—A device using a video tape recorder (VTR) and a monitor for playback. Capable of recording sessions and then playing back. Can also be used in conjunction with cable TV or CCTV. Requires special lighting in some situations to obtain an acceptable level of pictures (sometimes called the signal.) Useful for taping some sessions which can then be replayed for repeats when resource person is not available.

**Workbook**—A previously prepared written instrument. May contain many pages or only one or two. It is expected that participants will move through the book in a prescribed fashion, to achieve the objectives. Can be used by participants in general sessions, small group sessions, or for individual activities. Feedback can be built into the workbook for participant and Coordinator.

**Work Group**—A small group of individuals, usually fewer than fifteen, who have a common goal. Through discussion, exercises, and other approaches, it is expected that they will achieve a set goal. It may be to produce a report, to make suggestions, or to experience something, and to react. It is purposeful and though it most often uses verbalization, the objective is not discussion but the accomplishment of an assigned task.

This is by no means a comprehensive list, but, it is hoped, a useful one. The reader, who serves as a Coordinator, is urged to maintain a constant list of these terms and their meanings for him. They can be useful, not only in designing, but in communicating with Sponsors, exhibitors, and suppliers. Above all, this can facilitate communication with participants and contribute to a more useful conference.

# Index